*"**Unlock Behavior, Unleash Profits** is about 21st century leadership. The power of unlocking behavior in your organization starts with you, the leader. Dr. Braksick is herself a winner, and this book will be one and create many winners itself!"*

—*Brian McNeill, Executive Vice President, Danaher Corporation*

*"**Unlock Behavior, Unleash Profits** presents the missing link for success in business initiatives, performance concerns, and needed change—behavior. It still takes an above-average leader to make these models and concepts come to life, but there is no doubt about it—if you want to be a results-focused leader, here is the missing link to making it happen."*

—*Jay M. Duffy, Director, Executive Education and Leadership, Bayer Corporation*

"The influence of Dr. Braksick and her colleagues has dramatically impacted me and my leadership of one of the nation's fastest growing companies."

—*Michael G. DeGroote, Board Chairman and CEO, Century Business Services (CBIZ)*

"Dr. Braksick's articulate, proven prescriptions for analyzing, shaping, and measuring one's behavior and for coaching colleagues and family are vital elements for achieving stretch objectives in our meritocratic society."

—*Philip W. Heston, Retired VP, Citibank, N.A.*

"Using the approach and tools outlined in this book, we made dramatic improvements in the performance of our business. In addition, these tools make managing a much more satisfying and rewarding experience for managers themselves."

—*Peter McCrea, Vice President, Lubricants and Specialty Products, Chevron Products Company*

"Whether your goal is greater profits, greater productivity, or just a happier work environment, this book provides important new tools for success. If you are a leader or manager who doubts there is a science to behavior or that practical techniques can shape positive behaviors in the workplace, this book is for you."

—*Helene D. Gayle, MD, MPH; Director, National Center for HIV, STD, and TB Prevention, Centers for Disease Control and Prevention*

"A breakthrough in leadership capability that naturally motivates people to achieve and drives organizations to produce results . . . a key to building employee commitment toward excellence in business execution."

—*Rhonda Zygocki, Manager of Strategic Planning, Chevron Corporation*

"*Unlock Behavior, Unleash Profits* is written with the CEO and top organizational leaders in mind. Behavioral science is a technology they can use to change the performance of individuals, entire organizations, and the organizational culture. The appendices are great how-to summaries on effective coaching."

> —*Ward Sproat, Director of Strategic Programs, PECO Nuclear*

"The principles and tools of behavioral science that Dr. Braksick describes so clearly and comprehensively in this book have helped us improve behaviors—especially leadership behaviors—for better performance throughout the company."

> —*Jim Tighe, Former Manager, Corporate Quality, Chevron Corporation*

"Dr. Braksick's book does the nearly impossible! It explains behavior in a way that is technically and psychologically accurate, but also is useful and actionable."

> —*George Krock, Director, HR Planning and Development, PPG Industries, Inc.*

"Count me among those who hounded Dr. Braksick to write this book! It is clearly needed to unleash each company's potential by explicitly addressing behavioral issues. It is a thorough, practical guide on applying behavioral science to achieve important business results."

> —*Jack C. Beers, Managing Consultant, Chevron Chemical Co.*

"The skill-building guidelines in the art of giving feedback, integrated with behavioral science, increase my understanding of people. Dr. Braksick's book helps me make my personal and job worlds better places."

> —*David Tarnowski, Senior Electrical Engineer, Whirlpool Corporation*

"Dr. Braksick's book is hugely interesting and entertaining. I have read a lot of management books in the last few years, and this ranks with the best. I have 'met' all the people in her examples and would admit to some of the behaviors myself! I am recommending this book to my colleagues."

> —*Howard Lees, Bechtel Corporation, London*

"Dr. Braksick has advanced the business applications of social science a giant step in the right direction. She makes a convincing case for harnessing the power of human behavior to produce exceptional business results."

> —*Larry K. Durham, CEO, National Express Corporation*

"I've worked where behavioral management principles were widely applied, and I saw the results first-hand, including in my own management practices .... behavioral management had more impact than any other intervention ...."

> —*Jennifer Powell, HR Manager, Aetna U.S. Healthcare*

Unlock Behavior, Unleash Profits

How your leadership behavior
can unlock profitability
in your organization

LESLIE WILK BRAKSICK, PH.D.

McGraw-Hill, Inc.

New York   San Francisco   Washington, D.C.   Auckland   Bogotá
Caracas   Lisbon   London   Madrid   Mexico City   Milan
Montreal   New Delhi   San Juan   Singapore
Sidney   Tokyo   Toronto

Library of Congress Catalog Card Number: 99-76272

McGraw-Hill

A Division of The **McGraw·Hill** Companies

3 4 5 6 7 8 9 0   AGM/AGM   0 9 8 7 6 5 4 3 2 1 0

ISBN 0-07-135878-1

Text set in Garamond and Gill Sans by Lisa Berry and Paula Panagopoulos.
Printed and bound by Quebecor/Martinsburg.

McGraw-Hill books are available at special quantity discounts to use as
premiums and sales promotions, or for use in corporate training programs. For more information, please write to the Director of Special
Sales, McGraw-Hill, Two Penn Plaza, New York, NY 10121-2298. Or
contact your local bookstore.

Dr. Braksick's royalties from the sale of
this book are being donated to
The Heart Center at:

 Children's
Hospital of Pittsburgh

For more information:
(412) 692-5318 www.chp.edu

 This book is printed on recycled, acid-free paper containing a
minimum of 50% recycled, de-inked fiber.

Dedication

To MY PARENTS, Herb and Connie Wilk, who have loved me and encouraged me every day of my life . . .

To my husband Matthew, who is the wind beneath my wings that gives me flight . . .

To my children, Austin and Madeleine, in whose little faces I see my reflection, but whose wonderfulness I cannot take credit for . . .

And to Sydney Leigh, whose brief visit taught me the power of parental love and left me humbled, stronger, and changed forever.

Leslie Braksick

Contents

Foreword

IN THE PAST 25 years, I have served as a business school dean, a corporate consultant, and an executive coach, and I have worked in the areas of executive development, organizational effectiveness, and knowledge management. During this time, I have seen many a management fad come and go. As Dr. Braksick notes, America's top organizations have flirted with "flavors-of-the-month," each designed to be the next and best solution for improving the bottom line.

Many of theses fads have given lip service to the idea that people are the most vital and underutilized asset within any company. However, rarely has this resulted in capturing the true power of human assets. In *Unlock Behavior, Unleash Profits,* Dr. Braksick details an approach that explains the very real power of behavioral science as a tool to maximize corporate agility and bottom-line performance.

Recently, I had the opportunity to see Dr. Braksick's highly focused and dynamic approach take root within a mature and premier Fortune 50 company. The initiative came at a time of great uncertainty and anxiety. A high-profile merger had just been announced, and many questioned the timing and value of instituting a behavioral approach during such a major transition.

Employing the concepts in *Unlock Behavior, Unleash Profits,* Dr. Braksick and her team presented a behavioral approach that had the flexibility, clarity, and practical applicability to secure major breakthroughs and advantages during the transition. They were able to combine the essence of behavioral science (how and why people perform the way they do) with solid performance metrics. The result was significant and measurable impact to the bottom line.

Why does Dr. Braksick's approach work? There are three reasons. The first reason lies in understanding how executives truly develop. Over the years, I have asked hundreds of executives in all types of companies one very basic question: "As you look back, what has contributed most to your growth and development?" By far, the most frequent answer is "stretch assignments." These stretch assignments often are exceptionally challenging and difficult. Yet, once complete, executives recall them as periods of enormous growth in skill development and managerial perspective. Further, when asked, "What do you feel made the difference between success and failure during your stretch assignments?" executives usually credit coaching and mentoring that provided feedback on their performance and strategies. Unfortunately, many companies place leaders in challenging situations without the tools and support they need to learn and adapt. They rarely receive open, honest feedback—the very thing they need. The behavioral model presented in *Unlock Behavior, Unleash Profits* neutralizes this problem by creating a feedback-rich environment for leaders and by linking their development to business results.

The second reason that Dr. Braksick's approach is so successful is that it provides tools for managers at every level, tools that help them link critical business issues to the behaviors that will yield the strongest and most desired results. Moving beyond a practical explanation of behavioral science, this book provides clear examples of how to use these principles to affect change in the critical behaviors that link most directly to performance goals. One comes to realize that the ability to apply the principles of behavioral science consistently and day-to-day really is the hallmark of great leaders at every level of the organization.

The third reason for the success of Dr. Braksick's approach is its universal applicability. The application of behavioral science principles is powerful, whether applied in mature, traditional organizations or in newly evolving virtual organizations. The scientific laws that govern the behavior of people are always the same, regardless of context. From basic manufacturing to e-commerce, the approach laid out in *Unlock Behavior, Unleash Profits* exhibits great flexibility in leveraging the power of people as a virtually unlimited source for increasing performance.

Unlock Behavior, Unleash Profits helps us understand the power of behavior and the tools for linking behavior to the bottom line. In doing so, Dr. Braksick provides companies and their leaders with the keys to sustaining advantages as we enter the new millennium.

Winter Park, Florida   Richard C. Huseman, Ph.D.
September, 1999   Global Manager,
                                    Executive Knowledge and Education,
                                                        Mobil Corporation

Dr. Huseman is coauthor of Leading with Knowledge: The Nature of Competition in the 21st Century.

Preface

I'VE WATCHED many companies launch "silver bullet" training experiences, designed to transform their companies and their people, only to see them fail.

I've heard some of the brightest managers I've been fortunate to work with say that their superiors encouraged them to stay on a "technical track" versus a "managerial track" simply because they had "weak people skills."

I've met some awfully nice managers who were liked by everyone—but who couldn't get bottom-line results.

I've seen top-notch strategies falter over and over again because their implementation missed the mark.

What do all of these dismaying shortfalls have in common? *Behavior*—or rather the telltale signs of not attending to behavior.

These are all examples of how most companies approach "people issues"—the so-called "soft side" of business. But it is *not* the soft side; it's the hard side! "People issues" are the hardest of all. Fortunately, they can be understood and acted upon if we apply the power of a hard science: behavioral science. Behavioral science unlocks our understanding of human behavior and teaches us how to create an environment that motivates and sustains desired behaviors.

I wrote *Unlock Behavior, Unleash Profits* for leaders who are responsible for the performance of people or organizations. I wrote it for leaders who are interested in understanding why people do what they do, and who want to know how they can make the workplace a positive, productive, and profitable experience for everyone.

I wrote it for those of you who spend your careers trying to make a difference.

Finally, I wrote this book to set the record straight. We don't need culture change programs or personality analyses to see positive, supportive work cultures maintained by employees who achieve sustainable business results. There is a *science* to human behavior that leaders need to learn and apply consistently everywhere. Leaders need to evaluate *strategies, processes,* and *behaviors*—their own and those of their customers, their employees, and their work cultures—by using the science of human behavior. It's just that simple. And it's just that complicated.

Behavioral science is easy to master—as you'll see in this book—but challenging to apply consistently. *The ability to apply behavioral science consistently is a key distinguishing feature of great leaders.* Leaders who naturally do this, or who have paused long enough to learn how, see two effects: first, they see employees who routinely exhibit discretionary effort and high degrees of commitment to "do what it takes." Second, they have consistent, sustainable, bottom-line business results that reflect their approach to effective leadership.

Join the ranks of those leaders who have learned to unlock desired behaviors and unleash profitability throughout their organizations. And enjoy the book!

Acknowledgments

THERE ARE MANY, many people who have contributed to the writing of this book. I feel deep gratitude toward them all, on many different levels.

I am grateful to the behavioral scientists who have shaped my thinking and the direction of my career: Drs. B. F. Skinner, Tom Gilbert, Geary Rummler, Dale Brethower, Bill Redmon, Bill Hopkins, Paul Brown, Alyce Dickinson, and Aubrey Daniels. In particular, I recognize Bill Redmon, who has been my teacher, colleague, fellow trailblazer, and dear friend for as long as I can remember. I thank Bill Hopkins for his kindness and encouragement throughout my career, and Paul Brown for being a model behavior analyst from afar for many years—and thankfully, most recently, from up close as a colleague. Drs. Bill Redmon, Paul Brown, Tom Mawhinney, and Bill Hopkins provided valuable feedback on early drafts of the manuscript.

Many colleagues have impacted my work and my motivation. My cofounders of The Continuous Learning Group, Inc. (CLG)—Julie Smith and Larry Lemasters—shared a vision for what could be and helped make it happen. Colleagues and friends Steve Jacobs, Ned Morse, and Jim Hillgren were pioneers in their own right, traveling on different paths before joining CLG, but through similar landscapes. I have learned much from each of them and value their leadership within CLG and their presence in my life.

Several of my CLG team members provided invaluable feedback on early drafts of the manuscript and encouraged my writing the book. They are some of many at CLG who prove and reprove this science every day with their clients. For this and much, much more, I recognize and thank Galen Reese, Jim Joyce, Dick Sandrock, Denny Sullivan, Jonathan Freedman, Joe Laipple, Tom Wrenn, and Kathy Callahan. Additionally, there are those practitioners at CLG who have helped over the years to refine our approach and methodologies. With thanks I recognize David Uhl, Joe Wiley, and Frank Berardi.

Other reviewers represented the viewpoint of the audience. This contribution was most critical to the successful evolution of this book. These reviewers were Jack Beers, Steve Pendill, and Norm Braksick. Their own experiences in great corporations allowed them to evaluate the book for its usefulness in that setting.

I will always feel that one of my greatest fortunes has been the clients I've had the privilege to support. Darry Callahan, John Peppercorn, Jack Beers, Skip Culbertson, Ed Kura, Jim Lieto, Jane MacKenzie, and a multitude of their colleagues have left their handprints on CLG and on my vision. Stan Henderson, Pam Liberacki, Marsha Boggess, Edna Rothwell, Hugh Morton, Gary Pritchard, Bob Smith, Mark Kutner, Nancy Dreicer, Bonda Garrison, Ethel Batten, Brian Baker, John Simpson, Brian McNeill, Ralph Belrose, Bill Glantzburg, Andy Feldheim, Bill Mueller, Keith Busch, Frank Rab, and many, many others have provided me the opportunity to demonstrate the power of applying behavioral science within their organizations. Without this, I would not be where I am today.

Several CLG colleagues contributed wonderful content to the technical sections of the text. Consultants Tracy Thurkow, Karen Bush, Ravi Jariwala, Julie Oliver, Chuck Gibbs, John Dale, and George Greanias made the writing of this book possible through their personal time and talents, and through their encouragement to keep going.

My developmental editors Fred Schroyer and Jennifer Campbell are to be credited with the style and ultimate completion of this project. They modeled the principles taught in this book every step of the way, and they deserve enormous recognition for the publication of my—and my company's—first book.

I am also grateful to the thorough copy editors who carefully scoured the manuscripts for my rare (!) mistakes: Tom Miles, David Porter, Andy Schmidt, Lori Schwabenhausen, and Andrea Soccorsi. And I thank Donna Kullman for her quality-check of the final typeset material before it went to the printer.

The graphic artists of Envision Development Group, Inc. contributed their special touch to the graphics and layout of the book: Christina Gump, Ana Ilieva, Terri Kress, Daniel Leo, Andy Roberts, and Lisa Smith are all to be recognized for their skilled eyes and hands. And I give special recognition to Christina Gump, whose original design was selected for the cover and dust jacket.

The production side of a book lacks glamour and excitement, but I was blessed with production expertise second to none. Special thanks go to Lisa Berry, whose continuing ingenuity and software wizardry got the book to the printer in record time, and to Paula Panagopoulos for her expert composition. Christine Casasanta, Janet Jenkins, Sherry Perkins, Beckie Pestun, Amber Pollastrini, and Julie Terling also were skillful pinch hitters when the need arose.

A project like this does not get done without tremendous support and sacrifice from family. My husband Matt was always there with enthusiasm to attend to the other side of our life while I wrote and thought and revised. Special thanks to my young son, Austin, who was always there with a hug and words of excitement about how proud he was of his mama. My little daughter Madeleine was sweet and loving unconditionally, as always. My parents, Herb and Connie Wilk, and my parents-in-law, Norm and Carol Braksick, were the cheerleaders who encouraged and supported me every step of the way. My sisters and brothers-in-law shared their pride in me throughout and always inquired with encouragement about the project: Michele and Donald Haugh, Nicole and David Warhoftig, Karen and Jared Wells, Amy and Marv Baldwin, and Barry Braksick.

And finally, I recognize and thank Children's Hospital of Pittsburgh, which is the sole recipient of all my royalties from the sale of this book. The physicians and nurses at Children's perform miracles every single day. It is a very special place—a place you pray you never find yourself—and a place for which you give thanks when the events of life put you there. I will always be indebted for the skillful hands, brilliant minds, and warm hearts that comprise the team at Children's Hospital of Pittsburgh.

Great Execution Depends on Behavior

I remember the morning the Fortune *magazine arrived in my inbox. I went straight to the cover article, its title a menacing lure: "WHY CEOs FAIL." Mug shots of fallen CEOs were littered throughout the article, posted like warnings to the rest of us who might stumble unsuspectingly into the same traps. "They're smart people who worried deeply about a lot of things," the article read. "They just weren't worrying enough about the right things: execution, decisiveness, follow-through, delivering on commitments. Are you?" What really hit home was that I felt like I had a handle on things, but those CEOs probably did too. I wondered, "Could I be next? Would I even know if I were making the same fatal mistakes?" After all, these were all people just like me . . . they had each been successful in their respective businesses and had once achieved results in top companies. If they could fall, maybe I could, too. In my heart, I knew that formulation of strategy and planning had always been our strength, but that execution of strategy was our weak spot. Knowing this haunted me . . . and I knew that I needed to step up to the plate and head our company toward better execution.*

—Company President

EXECUTIVES ARE DISCOVERING that vision and strategy aren't enough to ensure the success of their organizations and the initiatives they want to implement. They're finding out that even the most compelling vision, and even the strategy that looks absolutely failure-proof on paper, do not always hold up to the test of implementation and execution. To compound the situation, the pace of work today has never been faster, and the pressure on leaders to perform and on organizations to deliver to shareholders has never been greater.

We all know that genuinely great ideas do not always see widespread implementation or increased profitability. We have all seen bright, truly motivated leaders who do not achieve the success they thought they could achieve. And we are all aware of how easily leaders and organizations can become paralyzed or misaligned with the numerous pressures they face.

Business leaders need help understanding how to manage more effectively and how to sustain existing high levels of performance. In the clamor to find a solution, "execution" has emerged as the missing variable. And with good reason: if you practice good execution, you not only have the "what," but also the "how" to back it up. If you can just follow through on your vision or your strategy, then it ought to work. It's a complete package.

All right, so you know that execution is the key. Now what do you *do* about it?

You are holding in your hands a book that can help you answer that question. I wrote it to share a science and my passion with you—achieving high performance by unlocking the hidden power that often lies untapped in organizations: behavior.

Behavior is the key to good execution and lasting results. That's what this book is about.

- This book is about the behavior of leaders in causing and sustaining profitable changes in organizations.
- This book is about the science of human behavior, called applied behavior analysis, which gives us the framework and tools to understand what got us where we are today and how we can do things better in the future. (I will refer to this science as behavioral science in this book.)

- The book is about the analytical tools of behavioral science, as you'll learn in Chapters 2 through 6. You will see how you can apply these tools to the complexities plaguing your business today—like supply-chain management, integrating mergers and acquisitions, cross-selling, Enterprise Resource Planning (ERP) implementation, etc. I help you to understand these behaviorally in Chapters 7 and 8.

This book is also full of stories and examples from some of the world's most highly respected companies and leaders with whom I've had the good fortune to work. Whether you lead a corporation or a Little League team, you need to read this book: it's about *why you and your associates behave as you do, and how to use this knowledge to improve.*

Behavioral Science: Built to Last

Why all of the focus on *behavior?* First, let's define it. *Behavior is anything a person says or does (good or bad).* It is also what a person does not say or do (sitting silently is still a behavior). The science that explains why people do what they do and say what they say is called **behavioral science**. It has the same properties as chemistry, biology, or any other natural science: careful observation, data collection, reliability of occurrence, replicability, measurability, etc.

Behavioral science (technically, applied behavior analysis) was first developed by Dr. B. F. Skinner. His experiments began in the 1920s, and the science has grown very sophisticated during the past 70 years of research. Behavioral science is younger than sciences like physics and chemistry, but it is every bit as powerful and enduring. And it is a science that American business *needs.* We need its reliable, replicable technology for managing behavior and implementing change.

Please recognize that the laws of behavior (that is, the laws of behavioral science) are always operating, like gravity, whether you are aware of them or not. You would never build a chemical plant without knowing thermodynamics and chemistry. You would never run a business without understanding the principles of economics and strategy. So, why is it that we try to lead people and manage people, but with no understanding about the science of why we do what we do? If you have no knowledge of the science of human behavior, then behavior will occur as a matter of chance, which most of us can ill afford. (It's like crossing your fingers and hoping that second-quarter profits will improve, or that your boss will always understand you, or that your employees will "come to life.")

By becoming aware of behavioral science, and understanding the laws that govern human behavior, you can positively influence the environment and behaviors all around you.

Just as behavioral science is powerful and durable, so is this book. What I tell you differs from other management and leadership books because I focus on the true root of profitability: ***how you and your people behave to create profitability, success, and improved performance that is sustained over time***.

So You'll Know Where I'm Coming from . . .

When I was a college student, I took a course called "The Psychology of Work." My classmates were older and included factory workers, managers, and tradespeople. I learned much more from listening to them grumble than I learned from the class material. *I learned that good people do not always work hard. High performers do not always get paid more. Angry people do not always quit their jobs and go elsewhere. Great places to work may not be profitable and may not survive. And no concept of "fairness" operates in the world of work.*

It was a crash course in the realities of the workplace, and I became fascinated with the crucial role that work plays in our lives.

It was the potential for positive action, and the potential for improving the lives of people and the success and profitability of organizations, that attracted me to the science of human behavior and consulting with organizations. I have never looked at things the same way since.

Most of us, including myself, spend our days and nights trying to make a difference—for our organizations, the marketplace, our communities, our children, and ourselves. Without my knowledge of behavioral science and attention to the role of behavior in all that I do, I'd be a lot less effective.

I find that the power of applying the principles of behavioral science to making a difference is especially great for people in leadership roles. Therefore, my advice in this book is targeted most toward leaders—not only leaders in a formal sense, such as managers and executives, but leaders in an informal sense, such as parents, clergy, and organization leaders—anyone who has influence over people's actions.

Four Major Themes to Remember

If "leader" describes you, and it almost certainly does in some way, I'd like you to consider four things that are absolutely crucial to your future success:

1. *Your behavior as a leader directly affects everyone within your organization.* (If you think it doesn't, try disappearing for two days without informing anyone of your intentions or whereabouts and see what happens!) Time and again, I watch executives underestimate the impact of what they *do* and *say* and the impact of what they *don't do* and *don't say.* People *watch* and *listen* to you very closely. I want you to understand the importance of *your behavior* to your personal success, the success of those around you, and the success of your organization.

2. *Everyone's behavior is a response to the environment in which it occurs. Organizations are perfectly designed to get what they get, for better or for worse.* In other words, what we reinforce or encourage, good or bad, is exactly what we get. As a leader, you directly influence critical parts of the work environment that in turn influence everyone's behaviors. *Work environment* includes policies, compensation, recognition systems, accountability, how meetings are run, etc. Collectively, this is called "corporate culture" (which I talk more about in Chapter 7). I want you to understand the importance of the *work environment,* which you largely influence, to your success.

3. *Your behavior directly influences your organization's profitability.* Most of your leadership efforts (your behaviors) are directed toward increasing profits and shareholder value. So, the better you understand the *effects* of your behavior, and the better you learn to analyze those effects separately from your *intentions,* the better you can really influence profitability. If the *effect* of your leadership behavior is to encourage people to feel good about themselves, their contributions, and their

potential to perform better, then *increased profits will follow* for your company and for the employees within your company. Changes in your leadership behavior can in turn produce changes in the key behaviors of others in your organization. So, you should understand how *your behavior* influences profits.

4. ***You have powerful tools for optimizing your leadership behavior and the performance of everyone around you.*** These "power tools" are neither idealistic nor hocus-pocus. They are *proven*, based on decades of scientific research and successful deployment in major corporations. What if I offered you a proven approach for retaining high-potential employees? How about a tool for improving manufacturing cycle time by 70 percent? How about a process for improving your ability to execute your strategy? Or behaviors that, if engaged in reliably, would reduce unplanned shutdowns by 40 percent? Or behaviors that, if demonstrated by you, would result in your being a more effective leader, parent, spouse, and friend? The tools, strategies, and processes to achieve these things are in this book. They all ultimately come down to behavior, and by using them, *you will become an even better leader and performer*, at work, at home, and in professional and social organizations—everywhere.

Behavior Is the Key to Success

Behavior is the key, not only to individual success, but to the overall success of organizations. Consider executing strategies, for example. My colleagues and I specify four major things that are required to successfully implement sustained change in organizations:

1. The right *strategic goals* of the business,
2. The right *processes* to make the business work,
3. The right *behaviors* for making strategy and process work, and
4. The right *consequences* to support the behaviors that drive all key outcomes.

This book is not about developing strategic business goals. There are already excellent publications out there on strategy. This book is not about reengineering your work processes. There are fine publications on that as well. Instead, this book is unique in teaching you about behavioral science and the role of behavior—especially leadership behavior—in implementing change and sustaining performance within an organization.

I present behavioral science against the backdrop of today's workplace challenges and pace—*so you can begin thinking about how to use your new behavioral tools right away*. I also will teach you the importance of consequences: how to identify them, how to analyze them, and most importantly, how to align them with the strategic outcomes you desire.

Behavior is the key that too many organizations are missing.

- Behavior is the secret to how your good strategies are *executed.*
- Behavior is the key to how your good processes get *implemented.*
- Behavior explains how your organization's cultures can be *integrated.*
- In fact, aside from market conditions, competition, and other factors you cannot control, the success of your organization depends on *your behavior and the behavior of your people.*

Don't get me wrong: having the right strategy is essential. Ensuring that your processes are efficient and reliable is essential. Having a scorecard by which you measure how you are doing on performances that matter (and whether you are winning or losing) is essential. *But behavior is the enabler that makes strategy and process work.* Behavior is what drives the numbers on your scorecard. Without the right behaviors from those who must execute your strategy and implement your processes, your organization will never sustain higher profits or greater shareholder return.

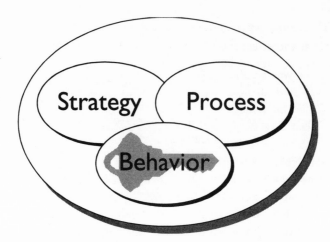

Behavior is the enabler that makes strategy and process work.

If behavior is the enabler, does that make it more important than strategy and process? Absolutely not. The three team together for success. Take away strategy, and your business wanders. Take away processes, and your productivity plummets. Take away the right behaviors, and nothing gets done properly and performance suffers. For example, your wonderful new accounting system, superior computer system, or takeover of a competitor will only trudge (or even fail) *unless your people's behaviors change to align with the changed objectives.*

In other words, *effective organizational change* requires *effective behavior change.* And changing behavior requires two things: behavioral science and the enlightened leadership to use it right. The science provides the tools for understanding behavior, and leaders align and reinforce behaviors necessary to enable the overarching business strategy and process.

Your Intention Versus Your Effect

One of the more eye-opening concepts for leaders who learn to apply behavioral science within their organizations is the difference between *intention* and *effect. Intention* is what you *intend* or *mean* to do—it's *why* you do what you do. It's the motive behind your actions. But *effect* is the actual impact upon others of your behavior or actions. In other words, *intentions* are in your mind, but *effect* is what is left after you act on your intentions.

This true story (names changed) dramatizes the difference between the intent and effect . . .

James was so pleased with the efforts of his leadership team! They had all been working hard for several months, driving against incredible stretch objectives to make the quarterly financial targets. James wanted to recognize his team's efforts. He decided to fly the group to Palm Springs for Thursday's leadership team meeting, where they would have a day-long meeting, a nice dinner, and a round of golf on Friday. Because his company office is on the East Coast, the group would stay an extra night for dinner after the golf game, and everyone was slated to fly back Saturday morning. A nice resort, golf, time away to bond as a team—all the very best of intentions.

But what was the *effect*? Eight of his ten leadership team members have children still living at home. Six of them have spouses who work outside the home. All had been working late most nights for the past three months and had worked at least one day each weekend as long as they'd been with the company. In addition, they were spending 40 to 60 percent of their time traveling. James just decided to increase their time away from homes and families for three additional days. Then there was the hassle of having to explain to their direct reports why, at a time of intense expense scrutiny, a golf trip to Palm Springs was acceptable. And while they were away, the voice mails and e-mails piled up . . . and, for that matter, how many of them even enjoyed golf?!

James' *intention* was clearly very positive. He wanted to recognize his team's outstanding effort. He wanted to show them how much he valued their hard work. He wanted them to relax. But the *effect* of his behavior (his actions) was very different. His team had *immediate negative consequences* to navigate with spouses, children, and themselves. They had to develop a plausible story for their direct reports about why it was acceptable to spend money on a junket . . .

So much for James' *intentions*! Can you feel the *effects*?

Remember: your effectiveness as a leader always comes from the *effect* of your actions, not your *intentions*. (Often, people don't even know your intentions.)

Behavioral science teaches us how to change our behaviors so that the effects of our behaviors closely match our intentions. To do this, we use tools called *pinpointing* and *ABC Analysis*. You'll learn more about these in the next chapters.

Let me share another true story, this one about how easily behavior can be misunderstood and improved . . .

In the early '90s I coached a senior executive in a high-growth energy company. (Let's call him "A.C. Power.") A.C. ran the trading unit. The unit bought and sold fossil fuel resources worldwide. He had been in this organization over 20 years, had risen fast, and was now seen as an outstanding performer by fellow executives and peers. He knew energy trading better than his peers and was widely recognized as one of the company's leading executives.

I visited his unit and saw about 100 people working at computer terminals on an open trading floor. A.C.'s office was one floor up. Despite this proximity, A.C. rarely went down to the trading floor: only twice in the past year. He seldom spent time with the traders. Folks in the organization viewed A.C. as aloof, unconcerned about employees, and interested only in results. Behind his back, they roundly criticized him for this. And this was tragic, given his knowledge of the business.

Further, his apparent lack of interest in the trading floor generated all kinds of speculation. I heard comments like, "Why doesn't he show up to support his people?" "Doesn't he care about our success or professional development?" "Is he more concerned with his own path upward than he is with supporting the folks within his organization?"

A.C. asked me to coach him to become a better leader and to teach him new behaviors for improving his performance. So, I asked why he never went down to the trading floor. You know what he told me? "Leslie, I'm an introvert. I walk down there, hands in my pockets, playing with the change. Everybody looks at me, and what the hell am I supposed to do? It's very awkward. If I don't have a specific purpose for going there, I feel like a jerk. These people are busy; they're always on the phone doing real work . . . . I walk in and everyone stares because I don't belong down there. My intention is to let them do what they do well without interruption."

Employees said that A.C. was conceited, or wouldn't lower himself to talk to the traders on the floor, or didn't care. Dead wrong! He simply didn't feel comfortable starting conversations with people. Since he felt so awkward, he chose to avoid the whole scene like the plague. Further, he didn't want to bother them when they were obviously busy.

I had A.C. pinpoint specific behaviors that he could work on. One behavior we targeted was "comfortable interaction with the traders on the trading floor." Clearly, we needed to increase his comfort to improve his performance. So A.C. started some new behaviors. He began phoning or e-mailing the leaders who oversaw people on the floor to ask them about important accomplishments. They gave him examples of breakthroughs or progress that some traders had achieved. This information fed A.C. some talking points that he could use during "casual" visits to the floor.

We also role-played conversation-starters, which rehearsed him in specific things to say when he felt uncomfortable. For example, he could go over to trader Kelly Watts and say, "Kelly, I heard you cut an awesome deal with the people at Electricoal. Tell me about it." And Kelly would brighten up and start talking about it. Of course, A.C. knew exactly what she was talking about since he was so knowledgeable. That broke the ice and led to good conversations and a better understanding between A.C. and the traders.

Once A.C. was comfortable enough to talk to the traders, he could say things like, "That was a tough trade, because . . . " thus demonstrating his deep appreciation for the deal's complexity and the individual trader's hard work. He also could offer praise, using specific knowledge like "that made us $500,000 yesterday. That will have a major positive effect on our numbers this month. Congratulations!"

Today, A.C. heads for the trading floor regularly. His visits look casual, but he is well-prepared. He walks in and says hello, shakes hands, and knows there are several people he can approach for a meaningful conversation—and he knows he can reinforce them for their accomplishments. *He now has a positive history of personal interaction with people in his organization and has received enormous praise for its effect on their behavior.*

A.C. discovered that reinforcing specific behaviors could encourage his traders to be more aggressive. In addition, A.C.'s own behavior gets reinforced because, as he told me, "You know, spending time with my people feels great"—now that he knows how to make it purposeful. Now Kelly Watts and the other traders receive praise from A.C. And this praise is absolutely genuine and feels natural. That's exactly what people wanted: for A.C. just to visit, to show that he cared, and to let them access his wealth of experience and insightful analyses. He had *always* cared, but his previous "avoidance behaviors" sent a very different, unintended signal.

Absolutely everybody won in this one! It's a good example of how behavioral science can be used to pinpoint behaviors that are critical to improving performance and providing good solutions. It shows the power of the right behaviors, of positive reinforcement, and of praise. It also cautions us about our powerful influence as leaders and the fact that we are evaluated on our effect on people and our effect on the organization—NOT on our intentions. Finally, it demonstrates how people can perform to their best potential if they know their work is truly valued, adds to the bottom-line success of the organization, and helps their personal future.

Throughout this book I will share true stories as a way to illustrate how we apply behavioral science in organizations today. I have chosen to use these stories because I hope that you will see yourself and others in them. It's also my way of honoring the models of greatness and learning I've seen in organizations.

A Short History: (Trying to) Improve the Organization

The learnings of behavioral science are applied in business and industry today—but not widely enough. Companies are beginning to recognize the need to use behavioral science to improve bottom-line performance of organizations, especially organizations in the throes of a merger, acquisition, implementing Enterprise Resource Planning (ERP), or other nerve-wrenching, large-scale organizational change.

If you have been around very long, you know all about Management by Objectives (MBO), Total Quality Management (TQM), Teams, and all those other flavor-of-the-month "innovations." (Sadly, they often have been failure-of-the-month!) Each method had its moment in our history of "How to Make an Organization Great." But their strategies faltered, and the results were usually disappointing relative to their expected impact. Were these methods bad or wrong?

No, they were just incomplete, because *none of them systemically addressed the behaviors needed to achieve and sustain the desired outcomes.* These approaches focused on strategy and process but did not consider the *behaviors* required for them to work. Those missing behaviors were the key enablers of success and sustainability.

Here is a quick scan of management history and of the reasons various approaches have worked to some degree, but not to their best . . . .

The 2x4 Club. In the beginning, there was The 2x4 Club. Managers who belonged to The 2x4 Club wielded a big stick. They said, "Do this because I said so, or I'll break out The 2x4." This method prevailed for centuries, working only because it brute-forced people's behavior.

Scientific Management. In the early 1890s, along came Frederick Taylor and his philosophy of Scientific Management. Taylor's best-remembered work is time-and-motion studies. He believed that if machines could be engineered, so could workers. Since engineers were the deities of the day, the workplace became engineered. And indeed, operations were managed with greater efficiency and reliability than ever before. The Scientific Management era sensitized us to the importance of measuring and examining the time and materials needed to increase efficiency.

Human Relations. Significant backlash to Taylor's mechanistic view of people contributed to the Human Relations Movement. This movement focused more heavily on the leadership of people than on the leadership of the task or business. (But it still did not focus on behavior.) The famous Hawthorne experiments, in which people performed better in a study simply because they felt singled out, demonstrated the powerful impact of supervision and attention to performance.

Management by Objectives (MBO). Attention then shifted to aligning employees' individual objectives with company strategy. This was called Management by Objectives, and suddenly there weren't enough MBAs to go around. MBO sensitized us to the importance of having a clear strategy and measurable goals and objectives. MBO promised that setting clear goals for employees so they knew exactly what was expected would make them maximize their efforts to attain the objectives. Sometimes it worked, but rarely for long.

With MBO, even when short-term improvements were achieved, progress eventually faltered. Companies quickly lost ground as employees resisted unrealistic goals and objectives imposed from above, because there were *no corresponding changes in the consequences for them, such as compensation or advancement.* Perhaps an even greater deterrent to success was the lack of employee involvement in setting the objectives.

Statistical Process Control (SPC). The need to monitor impact led to Statistical Process Control (SPC). SPC was developed by an American named Walter Shewart in 1931 and was made famous by Edward Deming in post–World War II Japan. SPC was practiced most faithfully in Japan in the 1950s, and then in the United States in the 1980s. The technique allowed companies to track variations in process and performance and to isolate the causes of the variations. They then could make process changes to reduce variability and inconsistencies.

Total Quality Management (TQM)/Reengineering. The learnings from all of these innovations were carried into the TQM/Re-engineering era in the late 1980s–early 1990s, along with the recognition that *simply telling people what you expected of them would not guarantee that the desired behavior would follow.*

Companies were getting better and better at changing and aligning key processes, but people didn't follow those processes consistently. In other words, even the very best strategies faltered because they weren't *implemented* correctly. The feeling grew that leaders needed to *involve employees more*—to have them participate in creating solutions.

Quality Circles and Teams. Thus, Quality Circles and Teams became the primary vehicles for implementing quality. Major processes were reengineered through employee participation in problem solving. Companies established steering committees, created employee-led teams, and launched TQM/Reengineering with the intent of involving employees much more than MBO had. This led to the infusion of employee involvement, professional facilitators, training in quality tools, etc.

Downsizing. To meet shareholder targets, companies have slashed layers of management, reduced headcount, eliminated entire businesses, and outsourced functions like Human Resources, Information Technology, Purchasing, Finance, and others felt to be peripheral to the core of their business. This outsourcing mania has fundamentally shifted how work is done within organizations and how transactions are handled electronically with outside vendors.

With all of these radical changes and implementations, companies still report disappointment with the return on their investment. Why?

The Obvious Answer: Behavior!

As I grew in my own application of behavioral science in the workplace, the answer became painfully obvious: *the necessary change of* **behaviors** *was being ignored*!

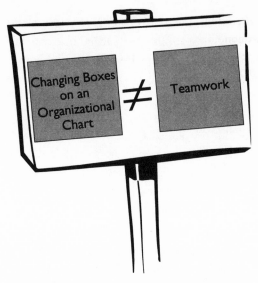

Tapping the Power: The Discretionary Effort Within Us All

Let's look at teams, for example. *Changing the boxes or titles on an organizational chart (as is often done with the implementation of teams) does not equal "teamwork."* Teamwork involves *behaviors* that may or may not occur as a result of many factors. Practitioners and leaders clearly understood this, because with any reference to teams, they included terms like "shared vision," "collaborative," or "interdependent." Further, the earliest reviews of unsuccessful team implementation included descriptors such as "individual interests prevailed over team goals," or "metrics for success were unclear," and so on. So, they were beginning to understand that individual behavior plays a powerful role. Fully understanding how to tap into that power was the missing piece.

I am reminded of a wonderful teamwork story told by one of my clients, Brian. He discovered the power of behavioral science within his large organization. I asked him how he became such a zealot of behavioral approaches to leadership and teamwork . . . .

I had an experience that changed my life a number of years ago. I was running a refinery in England. Times were tough, and the entire management team was trying to save the plant from closing. We were bailing the boat frantically.

It was the hundredth anniversary of our operations in England, and someone decided we should celebrate. The Board provided money for a celebration for a thousand people—£30 each, so we had £30,000 to spend on this celebration.

Frankly, I was more interested in whether there was going to be an organization next week than in having a celebration! So, I delegated the planning of the celebration to a small group of blue-collar workers. I gave them the £30,000 and said, "Organize something—have a good time." And I went back to bailing the ship.

So what did the celebration team do? They organized an event equivalent to a county fair in the United States! About 50,000 people came. It was beyond belief! They leveraged that £30,000 and probably got the value of about £1,000,000. Frankly, we would not have put this little team of people in charge of £2.50 in their daily work. Yet, here was this group, left to their own devices without any interference or direction from management, and they ran this magnificent event. I mean, it was just incredible!

So my management team and I went back and analyzed this experience to understand how these people had accomplished this tremendous task. It was obvious that they succeeded more than we thought possible because they were able to exercise their full capabilities. At work we had boxes and barriers all around them.

Ever since this experience, I've been trying to figure how I can tap into people's capabilities like that. Why was this team so successful? They succeeded because they owned the project, management let them run the project, and they had tremendous feedback from their peers, who would evaluate the success of their effort using criteria they all understood. (After all, you only get to celebrate a hundredth anniversary once, and their friends were going to be very rough on them if the celebration had been less than wonderful!)

This team had put forth great _discretionary effort_—the effort people want to contribute above and beyond what is normally required to keep their jobs.

So: if we always were to manage this way, would it encourage people's continuing discretionary effort? I believe the answer is unequivocally "yes." That's why I'm a leader committed to creating the conditions that encourage these behaviors! It's not always easy, because I have lots of old behaviors that I need to change myself. But I am committed to getting there—for the success of my organization, my people, and myself.

What we can take away from Brian's experience is . . . .

1. People often have capabilities that are "hidden" on the job.
2. The work environment is primarily defined by management and maintained by the consequences (positive and negative) that people experience.
3. When negative consequences are removed from the environment and replaced with positive ones, the desired behavior increases.
4. Leaders who identify the behaviors needed to be externally competitive and who create positive consequences when people perform those behaviors, will get more of the desired behaviors, ultimately leading to a more competitive organization.
5. Brian's instructions—"Organize something—have a good time"—were very weak in their effect relative to the employees' _known consequences_ of success or failure (expectations of their peers, family members, and community members, Brian's evaluation of their performance, etc.). This illustrates the power of consequences compared to less effective instructions.

As exemplified in Brian's story, you can create a winning scenario for employees at all levels by creating an environment that supports the right behaviors and removes barriers to discretionary effort!

Discretionary Effort

Discretionary effort can best be described as the extra level of performance people give when they want to do something as opposed to when they feel like they have to do something. People often refer to this as the difference between commitment (doing it because we want to) and compliance (doing it because we have to . . . or else!).

Behaviorally speaking, discretionary performance will occur only when behavior is positively reinforced. Positive reinforcement can come from sources internal to the person (we call this intrinsic motivation) as well as from the environment surrounding him or her. If people do only enough to avoid experiencing negative consequences, discretionary performance will not occur. (The behavioral term for this is "negative reinforcement," which we will address in detail in Chapter 4.)

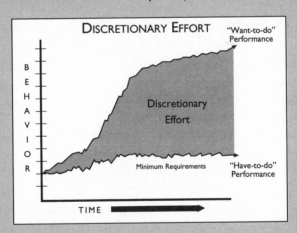

As leaders, we must ask ourselves, are we creating work environments where employees want to give extra effort? Are we positively reinforcing those behaviors when we see them? If the answer to those questions is "yes," there is a high probability that we are encouraging discretionary effort in the workplace.

If "keeping things under tight control so employees don't get too comfortable and slack off" is more descriptive of your leadership style or the leadership practices in your organization, you should pay close attention to the following chapters. You are likely preventing discretionary effort, probably unknowingly.

What Do I Mean by the Book's Title, *Unlock Behavior, Unleash Profits?*

I talked earlier about the difference between "intention" and "effect" . . . and how often the very best of intentions can create the opposite effect. The title *Unlock Behavior, Unleash Profits* gets at a similar issue. Time and again, I see desired, discretionary behaviors "locked" and "leashed" by the consequences in the organizations where people work. The company suffers, the individuals suffer, and profitability across many dimensions is diminished.

One company I worked with needed effective teamwork across functions and across business units in order for the customers' requests to be fulfilled. This organization paid people individually and force-ranked all employees when it came to distributing bonuses. As a result, there was constant competition between business units and finger-pointing among individuals. Were these people capable of behaving differently? Absolutely. Would the profitability of the people and of the company have improved if they worked in a more cooperative fashion? No doubt about it. Were the desirable behaviors needed for success made less probable by what got reinforced within the organization? Without question.

You can change that.

As a leader, you can create an *environment* that encourages desired behavior and discourages undesired behavior.

This is what behavioral science teaches us *how* to do.

We Are Not Changing People

Given that certain behaviors need to occur for us to be successful, shouldn't we then have license to change people to get them? *I believe not.* We have no right, as organizational leaders, or as citizens, to "change people." We have the right to create *environments* that foster and reinforce the behaviors we need to be successful as organizations, as communities, as families, and as productive citizens.

This is not about manipulating people or changing their personalities or beliefs. This is about creating a win-win situation where success comes for both the organization and its people. It's a "want to," not a "have to" approach to leading organizations and managing people.

The very role of a leader is to set strategy and to model and reinforce in others the *desired behaviors of the organization* toward achieving that strategy. This requires changing, encouraging, and discouraging *behaviors*, not people. It is within this framework that I write this book.

What Do I Mean by the Subtitle, "How your leadership behavior can unlock profitability in your organization"?

How is behavior related so intimately to profitability?

- The behavior of leaders unlocks and sustains profitability through encouraging employees to execute work processes as designed.
- The behavior of employees unlocks and sustains their "life profits" because employees can become more positive, predictable, and successful. In addition, they recognize how their work affects the success of their work group and of the entire organization. They see how they can make a difference, and they are encouraged to do so regularly. They feel better about themselves and about their ability to really make a difference. These positive thoughts and feelings have a direct impact on relationships at home and outside of the workplace.
- The behavior of leaders and employees together unlocks and sustains the entire company's performance and therefore improves shareholder value. Thus, behavior is directly related to shareholder benefit.
- Customers and suppliers also profit because needs and expectations are clearer and behaviors at all levels are better aligned to give them better service and product value.

Addressing behavior in an organization is crucial to everyone's success and profitability.

What's the Key to Managing Change?

In 1997, Price Waterhouse published *Coping with Chaos*, the results of their survey of global business leaders about change management. When asked about the biggest barriers to effective implementation of change, leaders consistently identified the following issues:

People Issues—e.g., employee opposition, middle management resistance, lack of senior management support, and culture changes

Project Management Issues—e.g., competing resource priorities and unrealistic change timetables

Communication/Perception Issues—e.g., inadequate employee communication and poor perception of the need to change

Integration Issues—e.g., working across boundaries (national as well as functional)

Although the survey did not directly connect these issues to behavior, it's clear that behavior is the key to all of them. To successfully address any change issue, an organization must address the behaviors that are the foundation of change implementation.

The study concluded that barriers within organizations are much more difficult to overcome than are national boundaries. Further, the study found that even though organizations have long known that involving people is crucial to successfully implementing change initiatives, most organizations still have difficulty involving people with lasting effectiveness. The study claims that two of the most significant barriers to successfully addressing this issue are managers' insufficient change management skills and their inconsistent prioritization of critical success factors.

If managers have these problems, it is because they do not know the importance and utility of behavioral analysis. Effective change happens when the behaviors of individuals are organized toward a specific goal. From this perspective, change management means something quite different than usual. It means that leaders must change their daily work behaviors and that management must align the tools, priorities, and reinforcers that make those changes possible.

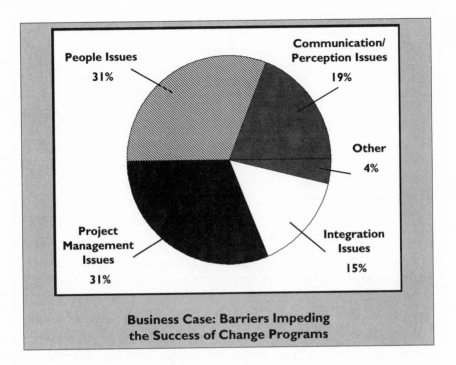

People Issues
31%

Communication/
Perception Issues
19%

Other
4%

Integration
Issues
15%

Project
Management
Issues
31%

**Business Case: Barriers Impeding
the Success of Change Programs**

Why Is Behavior the Solution to Today's Challenges?

The intensity and degree of change occurring daily is overwhelming. Inevitably, "Change Management" has surfaced as the magic bullet—but it will see only limited success *unless it follows a behavioral approach.*

Here are some of the common "change challenges" we are seeing . . .

Merger and Acquisition (M&A) Integrations. Former competitors are merging. They are expected to work collaboratively and support-ively, overnight! It's like saying, "We expect your decades of behaving to beat the competition, and behaving to show how your products and services are clearly superior to theirs, will go away overnight. Play nice and be friends." *I think we all know better than that!*

Corporate Creep (Sustaining a Culture). Prosperous startup or-ganizations begin to falter as the original leaders are exchanged with those from other parts of the company or from the outside. How can we sustain a positive culture? How do we keep it as great as it once was? How do we turn around a faltering culture? How do we prevent "corporate creep" from killing what we so successfully built from the ground up not long ago? *The answer, again, comes down to behavior.*

Enterprise Resource Planning (ERP) Implementation (Software Solutions for Managing Business). Companies are struggling through companywide software implementations such as SAP, Oracle, Peoplesoft, BAAN, and J.D. Edwards. These systems enable companies to coordinate and standardize information throughout the supply chain— from the customer's order, to the shipping dock, and beyond. But there are many impediments to achieving the desired results from these well-designed systems. Why? If you peel back many of the issues behind the difficulties in making corporatewide information systems work, once again, *it comes down to behavior.*

Cross-Selling Across Business Units. Traditionally, companies have been structured as separate and autonomous businesses. Now, in seeking greater control and influence, they want *cross-selling* among their own units and across product lines. They need geographic regions to work together. They need business units to collaborate and present a single company "face" to their customers. They need internal customers and suppliers to work hand-in-glove, with the needs and wishes of the customer always paramount. But if the goal really is cross-selling and collaboration, behavior also needs to follow, and the right behaviors must occur.

Supply Chain Management. Many companies have concluded that their success lies in their ability to manage the supply chain—the multiple handoffs of information, products, and services needed to make their product or service flow smoothly, cost-effectively, and accurately from product request to delivery. For the entire sequence to flow, these handoffs involve *behaviors that need to occur across multiple constituencies.* How do we establish and maintain the desired behaviors needed for all of this to occur?

Knowledge Management. Knowledge management (the system, processes, and behaviors needed to share best practices, reuse knowledge, and multiply learning) is critical to your company's future. It may be the fundamental differentiator of your company's ability to grow profitably and innovatively in the next millennium. Understanding the role of behavior in this is critical for successful design and implementation.

e-behavior for e-commerce. Companies are transitioning from human interfaces to electronic interfaces as a means of getting work done. Customers are talking less with a customer sales representative or salesperson to place an order. Now they interface with a Web site on the Internet. What aspects of the new sales or service interaction are needed for customers to *choose* to do business this way and to *feel better-served* than they did previously? And with their competitors trying to make e-strategy work for their companies, how can you make the interface with your site more reinforcing? For e-strategies to work, they need *completely new behaviors on the part of consumers of those products* as well as the service providers themselves.

The Answer . . .

The answer to each of these issues lies in our ability to understand *behavior* and *culture*, and to grasp the role of each in unlocking behaviors that lead to success and sustainable profitability.

In the chapters that follow, I will help you analyze each of the situations described above from a behavioral vantage point. I will de-mystify how things became the way they are and how you can change them by applying the principles of behavioral science to your leadership actions and decisions.

I'll begin by describing the basics of behavioral science. Then we'll walk together through the application of behavioral science to business challenges that confront us all today. You will then have a new framework from which to view your organization's challenges and successes.

Our Model for Applying Behavioral Science in Your Company

Throughout this book, I will share a model to help you navigate through your application of behavioral science. It's the CYBER Model (*Changing Yesterday's Behavior for Enhanced Results*). Just follow these steps to positively impact important business issues in your organization.

CYBER Model

1. Identify business opportunity

2. Target results and measures of success

3. Pinpoint and align behaviors that drive results

4. Understand the influences on behavior

5. Develop, implement, and adjust behavior change plan

6. CELEBRATE achievement of improved results!

1. Zero in on the business opportunity you face. Most current business opportunities involve executing defined business strategies to impact critical metrics for which you are accountable.

2. Target the specific results you will try to impact.

3. Pinpoint (identify) and align the target behaviors that most closely fit with, or drive, the target results.

4. Understand what most powerfully influences the pinpointed behavior. In particular, you should look for consequences that are immediate and certain to follow the behavior.

5. Develop a change plan of new triggers and consequences to help bring about and reinforce the new and desired behaviors.

6. After reviewing the results measures set up in Step 2, identify progress made and pause to celebrate, including liberal use of recognition and positive feedback.

Behavioral Science and You

Successful leaders I work with say, "So *this* is what I've been doing instinctively for most of my career!" If you are one of these people, congratulations! I hope that reading this book will serve to reinforce the positive behaviors you are already doing so well. Keep going with those behaviors; we need more leaders like you! This book will help you identify the specific behaviors you engage in and do so well—and facilitate your teaching and shaping of others to engage in similar behaviors.

For others, this book will offer a whole new way of looking at the world. It will challenge your approaches to leading and managing—and to parenting and personal relationships.

For everyone, you will be able to learn, as I have, from leaders with whom I've worked. The science will give you a framework and a set of tools. The stories will give you context and enjoyment. The analyses will give you insights into challenging business issues that companies currently face and will continue to face well into the next millennium. Altogether, this book will help you approach the issues in your world better, and with new confidence.

Let's begin our behavioral journey together . . .

Pinpointing and the CYBER Model

The Company needed badly to gain market share to stay competitive. Sales remained flat or showed a slightly decreasing trend in most territories while key competitors were growing by 20 percent a year. The Sales and Marketing VP chartered a team that spent 60 days studying the problem. They interviewed sales managers and field reps and identified possible improvement targets. In the end, the team identified the highest-performing sales reps and recommended that their "best practices" be included in the training for all sales reps.

All sales reps received five days of training in cutting-edge sales methods. But the results showed only minimal positive change in sales results! The frustrated VP set up a root-cause study to find out why. This team discovered that the best practices were indeed learned and used by most sales reps, as planned. However, the use of best practices didn't make any difference in sales results! Competitors continued to gain market share; sales at the company stayed flat, and yet another initiative was launched to improve performance.

THIS SAD—and common—example shows the importance of *selecting the "right" behaviors for change.* The VP and the first sales team assumed that they could identify the behaviors of higher-performing sales people and transfer these behaviors to others. They were successful in every respect but one—they selected the wrong behaviors, ones that did *not* lead to better sales. And the really serious damage was the loss of trust with the sales reps. The reps attended the special meetings, they listened and learned, and they implemented as instructed. But they lost ground and incentive pay. Next time, they won't be so willing to invest time and energy in the company's "silver bullet" sales program!

Too many companies have made mistakes like this. They have implemented initiatives that encourage behaviors that add little or no value to the bottom line of the business.

For example, with early TQM efforts, teams spent weeks identifying where to put the water cooler or created a process for awarding preferred parking spaces. While these efforts got more people "involved," they did nothing to help the overall success and profitability of the organization. This obviously ignored the business objectives to be supported by the teams.

What went wrong? Poor alignment of individual behaviors with important business objectives. Teams expended energy working on problems that produced little value for the business. In the end, people who became team experts and applied the team tools were not valued by management, and "teamwork" was unfairly relegated to second-class status as part of the dreaded "soft side" of the business.

CYBER to the Rescue

So how do you select the right behaviors to encourage? We use the CYBER Model: *Changing Yesterday's Behavior for Enhanced Results.*

The model shows us that behavior change starts with (Step 1) identifying the business opportunity or context. This comes from understanding the strategy, the needs of customers, and the marketplace. It is important to keep the larger strategy or business opportunity in the forefront as you prepare to drill down to the specifics of what is needed to improve.

Once we identify the opportunity, we (Step 2) select the specific target results and measures of success. Results are the outcomes that we and others use to gauge our performance effectiveness. These are often found on results scorecards or monthly and quarterly reports. Then, as Step 3 of the CYBER Model tells us, we must pinpoint and align the behaviors that drive these results.

Let's take a closer look at that step. For the moment, I'm going to focus on the first part, *pinpointing behaviors.* What does pinpointing mean? Pinpointing behaviors involves two essential steps:

CYBER Model

1. Identify business opportunity

2. Target results and measures of success

3. Pinpoint and align behaviors that drive results

4. Understand the influences on behavior

5. Develop, implement, and adjust behavior change plan

6. CELEBRATE achievement of improved results!

a. *Select a critical behavior* (or behaviors) from the many possible behaviors that could influence a business result.

b. *Describe that behavior* (or behaviors) in specific, clear terms so it can be communicated, observed, measured, and tracked.

Clearly, selection is the more fundamental of the two steps. If the behavior selected has no connection with business results, then you are wasting your time. *Pinpointing behaviors is the crucial link between behavioral science and business results.*

How Do You Select a Pinpoint?

My clients ask me, "Leslie, how can I choose the right behaviors to guarantee the results I want?" I cannot promise a sure-fire way to identify a behavior that will, beyond a doubt, have a positive impact on your business. That is something only you can do, because of your intimate knowledge of how your organization operates. However, I can offer you guidelines that my clients and I have used successfully for years. When I teach pinpointing, I start out by asking leaders questions that guide them through the CYBER Model. Let me share an example of a conversation I recently had with "Roy" to demonstrate what I mean . . .

CYBER Model

I. Identify
business
opportunity

My Conversation with Roy

Leslie: Roy, I understand that your unit is focusing on improving x for the next year because of y.

Roy: Absolutely. That's where the biggest potential lies for gaining a competitive advantage.

Leslie: Could you estimate the bottom-line value of that opportunity?

Roy: Yes I can. Based on x and y, I believe that it's worth z to us.

Key Points for CYBER Step I—

I ask leaders to review their strategy and identify the top goals for the year. Then, I ask them to estimate the bottom-line value for each opportunity. The area with the highest potential return is the best target. In some cases, opportunities that are worth less financially or have been tough to change over the years are a favored target, even if other opportunities are worth more in short-term dollars. Thus, the choice can be defined in nonfinancial terms if everyone agrees that the potential value is significant. *The business opportunity specified in Step I of the CYBER Model should align closely with goals included in written plans or strategy documents.*

> **2. Target results and measures of success**

Leslie: Great. To really move this forward, I think we need to agree on the results measures so you can align people around the goal and then track their progress.

Roy: Well, I'd like to use the existing structure we have established for tracking results.

Leslie: Your balanced scorecard for your unit?

Roy: Yes.

Leslie: I agree. Let's take a look at how to use the scorecard to (1) clearly identify a results target, (2) communicate that target to all affected employees, (3) monitor progress over time toward the target, and (4) organize recognition of the target.

Roy: Here's how the system currently works ....

Key Points for CYBER Step 2—

Many companies already use balanced scorecards. This makes it easy to measure change in business results. If they lack scorecards, I ask that measures for the selected opportunity be developed and agreed to by key leaders. At a minimum, I ask them to define current and desired performance to reveal the size of the gap to be closed. Then I request a regular reporting process to communicate the status on closing the gap (usually once per month). Regular reporting makes feedback on progress possible.

> **3. Pinpoint and align behaviors that drive results**

Leslie: Now I am going to guide us in the direction of pinpointing the critical behaviors that will contribute to your stated results target. There are two basic steps: selecting the right behaviors and defining the behaviors. We probably won't be able to finish this step ourselves, because we don't have the intimate knowledge of behavior that others on your staff have. But I'd like to talk it through with you, and then I'd like to talk with you about engaging others in the pinpointing process.

Roy: OK.

Leslie: Let's start by selecting the right behaviors. There are many behaviors that people perform every day that might or might not contribute to the results target. Could you brainstorm a list of the most critical behaviors that contribute to the target?

Roy: Sure. I would say [generates list].

Leslie: OK. As you can see, there's a lot happening. If we were to use that entire list, you and your staff would be consumed with trying to manage those behaviors. That's why I'd like you to narrow the list. Think about one behavior—or maybe two behaviors—that will have the biggest impact of all on the targeted result.

Roy: I can see why you need to include others in this process. They will probably be able to do this more effectively than I can. But for the purpose of our conversation, I think the most important behavior is *x*.

Leslie: Great! We've completed the first step: selecting the behavior. Now I'd like to walk through the second step: defining the behavior. The purpose of this step is to be very objective in our definition of the behavior so people will clearly understand what it is and how to recognize it. To do this, I think we should take a look at a tool called the NORMS of objectivity.

Roy: OK.

Key Points for CYBER Step 3—

Pinpoint—Selecting the Right Behaviors. The first step in selecting the right behaviors is to generate a list of the possible behaviors from which to choose. This isn't always as easy as it sounds. Where guesswork can be a problem, I ask people who know the business well (a good cross-section of managers) to list people whose performance directly influences the selected business opportunity. I then ask them to list all the relevant behaviors for each person. (The trick here is to avoid narrowing too quickly. Leaders will sometimes choose a favorite person or a couple of behaviors very early in the process and try to short-circuit the rest of the steps. I strongly discourage this.)

After I have a list of potential pinpoints, I guide the leaders in selecting the behaviors that have the most impact on results. Of all the behaviors across all the people who affect the business opportunity, leaders must choose one or two pinpoints that will have the greatest impact. I ask leaders who know the business to review the lists identified earlier, choose the person(s) whose behavior has the greatest effect, and identify one to three specific behaviors on the part of the performer that would make a difference.

The fewer the pinpoints, the better. Managing each pinpoint requires time and energy, a cost to consider carefully. I quality-check this step by asking, "If this behavior were changed, would you see a significant change in the business results?" If the answer is no, we go back to the drawing board.

Pinpoint—Describing the Behaviors. Once the pinpointed behaviors are chosen, I ask leaders to define them in objective, fact-based terms.

Defining behaviors clearly is best done with a tool called the NORMS of objectivity. This tool is described in detail in the next section.

Note that we have not yet talked about the second part of this step— align the behaviors that drive results. We will come back to that once you've had a chance to get more familiar with pinpointing.

A Quick Example of Selecting a Pinpoint

A good example of behavior selection comes from my work with leaders in an operating company that distributes industrial lubricants.

> **The Financial Manager of a key business unit was asked to cut expenses to improve profitability. Prices were already low. Competitors were cutting costs. New, smaller competitors**

were entering the market. Expense reduction meant survival. "Monthly expenses as a percentage of plan" was identified as the measure. A goal of 95 percent of planned expenses was set, and management checked measures monthly. A group of managers met with the financial manager to select pinpoints. Rather than identifying specific actions to be taken across the board, they identified a preferred behavior pattern for all managers. Here is how they worded the pinpoint:

Meet with direct reports monthly, review expenditures, and identify lines on the budget where reductions can be made. Obtain a commitment from an owner who will take accountability for each reduction. Describe steps necessary to achieve the reduction within a 30-day period.

In this case, the behaviors involved following a standardized process. The process was repeated each month but involved no specific budget category or action other than ongoing analysis and selection of budget targets. This approach avoided micro-management such as "identify and implement steps to decrease travel expenses by 10 percent across the board," or "negotiate with vendors for a 5 percent reduction in rates for contract services."

How Do You Describe a *Pinpointed Behavior?*

Earlier, I said that pinpointing involves two important parts: *selecting* a behavior and *describing* the behavior. We have seen how to select behaviors. Now let's look at how to describe those pinpointed behaviors as *objectively* as possible. We use the *NORMS of objectivity* as our test to ensure that we are focusing on *fact*, and not on opinions or hunches.

NORMS of Objectivity
N Not an Interpretation
O Observable
R Reliable
M Measurable
S Specific

For a pinpointed behavior to be described well, it must meet *all five* of the NORMS criteria. A behavior that meets the NORMS can be analyzed and managed more easily. We'll look at each of the NORMS criteria in more detail in just a minute. But first, here's a quick example of the importance of NORMS.

On one project, I worked with regional sales managers who supervised field reps. The reps were responsible for implementing the company's credit policy, which directly affected receivables and bad debts from nonpaying customers. When I asked the sales managers to pinpoint a critical behavior—a key behavior linked to business results—they selected "respect the credit policies."

Bad choice! This is very subjective. As stated, sales reps or anyone else would not easily understand it. "Respect" is open to interpretation and is hard to measure. Everyone would have a different idea of what "respect" means. Imagine if you were asked to "respect the credit policies." Would you know what to do? Would you do the same things as someone else? You might or you might not. That's the tricky part of describing a behavior objectively. It's important to minimize the possibility that people will interpret the behavior differently. In this case, I asked the sales managers to apply NORMS to make the requirements clearer.

Here is what they came up with:

- *Demonstrate understanding of the credit policy by passing an exam at 80 percent mastery.*
- *Inform each customer of the credit terms included in the policies and document this information in written form after the first meeting with the customer.*
- *Implement the credit policy by applying penalties for late payment and refusing to sell products to nonpaying customers.*

This conversion improved the pinpoint because it moved from a subjective description to one with observable actions and specific steps. As a result, reps would be more likely to know exactly what to do, and managers would be more likely to know whether the right things were being done.

Let's dig deeper into objectivity by examining each step of NORMS.

Norms—Not an Interpretation

We immediately get into trouble if we describe behaviors in a way that leaves them open to interpretation. *Interpretations are conclusions or assumptions based on facts, but they leave the facts unstated.* Therefore, interpretations are subjective, rather than objective. They are based on personal biases, opinions, hunches, or feelings, rather than clear-eyed, dispassionate observation.

In our sales example, the pinpoint initially proposed was "respect the credit policy." The word "respect" is subject to interpretation. Does it mean "carry a copy of the policy with you in your briefcase wherever you go so you can recite it upon need"? Or, "follow it unless there is a good reason to deviate"? Or, "document execution of all parts of the policy"? When interpretations like this occur, it usually means that the pinpointed behavior was not stated objectively.

Here are descriptions that are open to interpretation, with alternative, objective versions of each:

Open to Interpretation	Objective Pinpoints
Selling Products *(To what standard or level?)*	Achieving $5,000 sales/day Describing product features to customers Sending samples to prospects
Being a team player *(What does that mean?)*	Verbally supporting other team members with praise and suggestions Volunteering for team projects Completing assigned tasks on time and under budget
Taking unnecessary risks *(Such as?)*	Refusing to wear safety equipment Exceeding parking lot speed limit Spending twice the allotted budget on developing a new product line

NORMS—Observable

The second requirement of the NORMS of objectivity is that the behavior be observable. Observable behavior is just what it sounds like: something observed directly through your senses. Something is "observable" if you can see, hear, touch, taste, or smell it. Nonobservable behavior cannot be sensed directly, like a bad attitude, a value, or a belief. Here are examples:

Nonobservable Behavior	Observable Behavior
Being a micromanager *(What have you observed to prove this?)*	During our quarterly review meetings, asking for a root-cause analysis for each instance where performance fell short
Being a model employee *(What have you observed to prove this?)*	Offers to assist other coworkers without prompting Completes assigned tasks on time or before due date

Stick to behaviors you can directly *observe*. This is trickier than it sounds. Here is a way: think of yourself as a video camera. Whatever the camera lens sees or whatever the microphone records is true behavior. If you think your boss hates you, ask yourself: "Would a video camera record the hatred?" (Of course not. The video may show her frowning or pounding her fist, but that doesn't prove hatred.)

Try practicing your observation skills the next time you are in a restaurant. Observe people at other tables. Are they happy? Angry? Sad? Preoccupied? Hungry? You can't really tell, because none of that is observable. All you can observe objectively is that they are smiling, laughing, frowning, staring, etc.

Leaders who supervise employees can directly observe their behavior by sampling their performance. Direct sampling of performance establishes strong points for feedback and measurement. Observable behaviors are valuable in training too, for they can be communicated clearly to people as models for performing well. For example, it is far easier for a supervisor to show appreciation for "arriving at meetings on time" (observable) than for "showing commitment to the team" (vague).

NORMS—Reliable

Reliability means that *two or more people agree that they observed the same behavior*. This is a very good test of objectivity. If a pinpointed behavior is subjective, two different observers probably won't agree on what happened. Think back to the example about the regional sales managers. They defined a critical behavior as "respecting the credit policies." It's unlikely that two people could watch a sales rep and reliably identify when the rep had "respected the credit policy" and when she hadn't.

Here is a fine example of unreliability of observation . . .

A VP asked one of his marketing staff to improve her presentations to the marketing team. He called her past presentations "boring" and "too technical." The VP asked her to make the presentations more appropriate for her audience and more lively and interesting. Not knowing NORMS at that time, she accepted these false "pinpoints" and gave it a shot.

During the next meeting, the VP asked two marketing team members to provide feedback. The VP, presenter, and two observers met afterward to debrief her performance. One observer said, "You were better than the last time, and the stuff fit well with marketers. But I still feel you need to make some improvements to fit our culture." The other observer told her, "I thought you did a great job. This is a great improvement over your past presentations." At the end of the debrief, the presenter turned to the VP and said, "Now what?" Clearly there was a *lack of reliability* between the two observers' feedback.

The original behavior pinpoints were poorly defined and led to unreliable observations. The feedback was subjective and general. And the two team members disagreed. Effective behavior change is unlikely to emerge from this situation.

I suggested they first define what they wanted her to do in factual terms and then provide feedback on whether or not she showed the pinpointed behaviors. They agreed and settled on the following . . . .

"Open the presentation with a description of what you will cover." Spend no more than three minutes on this. Then, describe the new product being rolled out. Include the defining features, specs, and how it's different . . . Spend about ten minutes here. Smile and maintain eye contact with the audience. Close your presentation by restating how this new product will benefit the users, including naming the specific problems and complaints it will eliminate."

NORMS—Measurable

An objective description of behavior must include a way to *measure* it. Here are examples of measurable behaviors and ways of measuring them:

- Byron held face-to-face communication sessions *at all twelve locations within 48 hours* following the merger announcement.

- Francis completed *all six* of the required checks on the equipment.

We need statements that include measurement so we can assess the progress we are making (or lack of it). Here's an example of how specifying *measurable* behavior helps us stay objective:

Not Measurable	Measurable
Our market share in roll-aboard suitcases has really improved. *(This lack of specificity could lead unintentionally to a degradation in performance. By stating the number more specifically, individuals can monitor performance and make decisions accordingly.)*	Our market share in roll-abroad suitcases has gone from 32 percent to 56 percent for three quarters running because: • We've increased the frequency of new customer contacts from 15/month to 25/month. *(The behavior? Contacting new customers.)*

Not Measurable	Measurable
	• We've obtained new distributorships in five of eight strategically targeted states by offering long-term agreements. *(The behavior? Offering long-term agreements to distributors in strategically targeted states.)*
We are lousy at new product development. *(Without a numerical gauge, individuals have trouble shooting for an improvement in performance. When the behaviors are pinpointed in measurable terms, they can be monitored and managed more carefully and precisely.)*	• New patents filed decreased from 14 to 9 in the last quarter. *(The behavior? Filing patents.)* • Submission of new product ideas decreased from 8 to 2. *(The behavior? Submitting new product ideas.)*

NORM**S**—**S**pecific

Finally, the more specific a description is, the better it communicates. You need to describe your behavioral pinpoints as specifically as possible. In other words, you should include details such as who, what, when, where, how, and so on. For example:

General Behavior	Specific Behavior
Johnson meets deadlines. *(How can you tell?)*	Johnson submitted all required monthly reports prior to the deadline.
Vanessa supports her direct reports. *(How can you tell?)*	Vanessa meets with her direct reports twice a year to review performance and identify their succession plans.
Ogden does sloppy work. *(How can you tell?)*	Ogden's past three proposals had several numerical errors in the budget section.

The goal is not just to make pinpoints objective. *The goal is to establish a pinpoint that can be communicated to people so they understand exactly what to do and how to recognize when they do it.* Be as objective as necessary to accomplish this goal. In other words, be as NORMS-based as necessary to establish common understanding of the behavior. But don't go overboard in being specific. For example, it would be silly to tell a direct report, "I want you to contribute four comments, each between 30 and 90 seconds in length, in every meeting we have." Reasonable specificity would be, "I want you to make one or two constructive suggestions in our next meeting." The latter statement is enough to establish a common understanding of the desired behavior.

Quick Recap

Remember where we started: It is absolutely critical that you first understand your business opportunity and the results you wish to achieve. Then, think about the behaviors you need to meet the objective. Only after you have *selected clear pinpoints* and have *defined them objectively* is it worth your time to get deeper into the CYBER Model. The next steps in the CYBER Model help you apply behavioral science principles to actually influence those pinpointed behaviors. Those final steps will ensure that you achieve your desired results.

Getting the Pinpoint Right

I have talked about the importance of selecting a few key behaviors that will produce your desired business result. Let me show you an example of a company's attempt to increase sales that initially didn't work because they pinpointed the wrong behaviors . . .

> **GabCheap Telecom launched a major sales initiative to upsell services. Their customer service representatives made frequent contact with clients, so the company decided to take advantage of this and have the CSRs do upselling (selling enhanced services when customers called for help). The company spent a great deal of time and resources on training the CSRs to sell new packages to customers. They also provided strong incentives for selling.**

How well did the initiative work? Well, the CSRs had always seen themselves in a "helping" role. So, they were deeply offended by being asked to sell. In fact, the company had a near-rebellion on its hands, plus the threat of union grievances. Neither sales nor customer service ratings improved—nor did morale.

Then the company took a good look at the behaviors needed to achieve the business result of upselling . . . .

GabCheap refocused its efforts. Instead of pushing "selling," they promoted "needs-based solutions." CSRs were trained in uncovering customers' needs and creating the best match between a customer's needs and the company's services.

Training consisted of learning the services and developing good customer service skills: active listening, questioning, speaking, selecting opportunities, etc. Training also provided feedback, coaching, and recognition for performing the right behaviors.

In fact, to further strengthen their commitment to the sales system, the CSRs were actually encouraged to downsell if it better met the customer's needs! Because downselling had always been such a taboo, CSRs were leery of doing it. In fact, early in the program, the managers and coaches actually held daily end-of-shift events to celebrate downselling!

This time, the CSRs were delighted with their new role. After all, they were now meeting customers' needs—helping them— better than ever. And sales increased by 35 percent.

Of course sales increased! This time, the company pinpointed the right behaviors. Rather than focusing on selling strategies, the company focused on the behaviors that CSRs needed to better understand and meet the needs of customers.

Behavioral Pinpointing Must Remain Strategically Focused

Dr. Bill Redmon, a veteran consultant and colleague, offers one of my favorite examples of behavioral pinpointing. It demonstrates the need for a relentless pursuit of strategically important pinpointed behaviors . . . .

Bill was coaching a Vice President and his team of General Managers. Each GM was responsible for a strategic business unit, including profit and loss, new product development, technology, and marketing/sales. During pinpointing discussions, each GM agreed that *new product development* was the most challenging area. They felt they were already helping their immediate profits by managing spending, and they were affecting long-term success by hitting the milestones for ongoing development projects. But each of them found the product development process difficult to understand and manage. It was clear they felt this to be a significant opportunity.

Bill asked them how they wanted to *measure the success* of their new product development projects. All agreed that they did not want to get involved in the day-to-day details of product development or testing. However, they did want to track progress to manage the impact on the business. So, they decided (1) *to track expenditures as a percentage of budget* and (2) *to track percentage of project milestones achieved monthly and for the year-to-date.*

Bill had them identify people who affected these results and list their behaviors that were linked to the results. The GMs identified the project managers as the most influential people and listed the following behaviors on the first pass:

- Hold weekly team meetings to review expenditures and provide feedback
- Review only purchases above $5,000 to ensure that the most efficient purchasing procedures are used and provide feedback to purchasing agents
- Identify milestones at risk and take action early

- **Arrange for external quality reviews and follow up within 10 days on items identified as out of compliance**

Bill asked them to further narrow the list by picking *the one behavior that would make the most difference in staying within budget and on schedule.* They rank-ordered them and identified "Hold weekly team meetings to review expenditures and provide feedback" as the highest-leverage behavior. Some also gave high rankings to "Identify milestones at risk and take action early to avoid missing them." They elected to focus on these two primary pinpoints.

This completed the selection part of pinpointing. They knew *who the performers were and what behaviors they needed to manage.* They also selected behaviors that were powerful drivers for the results they needed.

Bill then had the team carefully define the pinpointed behavior so that all project teams would understand what they needed to do. This would also allow the GMs to measure progress easily. Here is their description:

Meet with the entire project team each Friday morning. Review the weekly reports of expenditures against budget for each major category. Review milestones achieved, at risk, and missed. For each item over budget or off schedule, develop a specific plan to correct the deviation. Identify an owner for the plan and a due date for each major step.

As a project team member, wouldn't you like to have that clear description of desired behavior? It truly clarifies what is expected of you. And it gives you a way to recognize when you are on target because it is NORMS-based.

And as a leader, wouldn't you like to have that description of desired project team behavior? It establishes your expectation of the project team and gives you a way to recognize when the team is on target. Further, when you see team members engaging in the pinpointed behavior, you have a clear opportunity to provide positive feedback. In other words, pinpointing the behaviors you want allows you to be a *proactive leader.* You can manage behavior—by providing both positive and constructive feedback—on a regular basis. You don't have to wait for the results to come in to know whether things are on track or whether you're missing the target and need to take corrective action. That's the true value of objectively pinpointing behavior. It gives you an edge as a leader: it helps you proactively create business results by managing the behaviors that contribute to those results.

Caution! (Just One or Two Behaviors, Please)

I need to offer a few words of caution. It is tempting to select many pinpointed behaviors, but this is a trap! Let's look at why. First, you only need to focus on one or two critical behaviors to make the biggest difference. Second, analyzing and managing behaviors takes time and energy. If too many behaviors are pinpointed, leaders can end up with far too much to do because they must consistently manage each behavior. This extra workload can dampen the enthusiasm of even the most dedicated leader. This is why I *emphasize* efficiency in pinpointing and advise leaders like yourself to choose the *smallest amount of behavior necessary* to produce a meaningful business result.

And your reward for being efficient? Investing a small amount of time for a large return makes you likely to continue to invest even after your initial enthusiasm has passed. Why? Because you get measurable business results. Efficiency is especially important when you are first learning how to use behavioral science tools. After a few months of success, the scope can grow with a lot less risk.

Aligning Pinpoints to Maximize Results

Now you understand how to pinpoint behavior. Let's go back to the CYBER Model for a moment. The third step of the model tells us to "pinpoint and align behaviors that drive results." We've already covered pinpointing, and now you have the tools for pinpointing behavior under your belt:

a. *Select the right behavior.* This involves identifying the many behaviors that contribute to results and then selecting the one or two top contributors.

b. *Describe the behavior.* This involves using the NORMS of objectivity to describe the desired behavior so that you establish a common understanding of the desired behavior.

Next, let's turn our attention to the second part of CYBER Step 3: align behaviors that drive results. It is important to organize multiple pinpoints to create a meaningful impact on business results. This is because business results occur when behavior is aligned across performers or work units. Leaders often mistakenly assume that if they make the strategy clear, everyone will know what to do. This is not true at all. Deliberate, focused, and organized attention to behaviors is needed.

Let's look at an example that clearly shows how behavioral pinpoints can be organized across multiple units to produce significant results in a short time.

CYBER Model

1. Identify business opportunity

2. Target results and measures of success

3. Pinpoint and align behaviors that drive results

4. Understand the influences on behavior

5. Develop, implement, and adjust behavior change plan

6. CELEBRATE achievement of improved results!

1. Identify Business Opportunity

At PCs by the Ton, a PC sales and distribution company, times were getting tough. Errors in computer orders, inaccurate invoicing, late deliveries, and damaged shipments brought a monsoon of customer complaints and a loss of market share in this fiercely competitive industry. PCs by the Ton recognized their biggest opportunity: improving end-to-end processing of customer orders.

2. Target Results and Measures of Success

Managers created the Exact Order Index (EOI) to track effectiveness in end-to-end order processing. The EOI included measures of effectiveness at all key points throughout the process. It generated a total score from 0 to 10, where 0 indicated that fewer than half of the necessary customer specifications were met and 10 reflected perfect performance. The average EOI at the beginning of the project was 6. The target was set at 9. Managers calculated that an average score of 9 would ensure that 98 percent of the customers were completely satisfied.

3. Pinpoint and Align Behaviors That Drive Results

Key jobs for the end-to-end process were identified in four work units: Order Input, Assembly and Testing, Invoicing, and Shipping. Behaviors related to target results were pinpointed for each key job in each work unit. Here is a sample of these pinpoints:

Work Unit	Pinpointed Behaviors
Order Input	• Respond to customer phone and fax orders by creating a complete customer order form within 4 hours of receipt
	• Input order information without error
	• Forward completed order to assembly and testing

Work Unit	Pinpointed Behaviors
Assembly and Testing	• Obtain units identified on the product order form
	• Insert components into appropriate box with packing materials and latest manual for each component
Invoicing	• Enter materials codes and unit prices
	• Calculate a total price and ensure that credit card transfer of appropriate payment is approved
	• Forward final invoice with equipment and manuals in sealed container with complete customer address to shipping
Shipping	• Complete all information on shipping label and arrange for pickup
	• Track package to final delivery and confirm receipt in perfect condition
	• Resolve shipping problems to the customer's satisfaction within 24 hours of detection

The end-to-end process required the coordinated behaviors of several people in key jobs. The pinpoints defined the behaviors needed for successful Exact Orders. All of the behaviors across the units needed to be organized and managed together. As a group with shared accountability for the entire process, the managers pinpointed behaviors and set up a plan for managing each behavior to create a high EOI score.

Any compromise at a key point in the process undermined the entire process and created customer dissatisfaction. So, pinpoints had to be organized across work groups, which required a cross-functional effort. To ensure this, all managers agreed to pinpoint and manage key behaviors during the same timeframe.

Measuring Behavior: Just Do It!

You probably are very good at measuring results. You know your operating margins, your sales figures, and so on. But I'll bet you don't track
behaviors in the same way. However, it's important to do so, because it
allows you to be more aware of what is happening at the individual and
work-group levels.

Good measurement helps you figure out how to change behaviors
when you do not get the results you expect. Measurement also helps
you identify successes to celebrate and problems to attack. Finally—
perhaps most valuably—good measurement helps you to observe and
track important pinpoints so you can learn more about behavior and
whether it is working for you or against you.

Measurement adds incredible power to your leadership tool set.
Determining *what to measure* and *how to measure*, and whether to measure
both behaviors *and* results or mainly one or the other, can get pretty
detailed. I have chosen to treat this information in detail in Appendix
A. That way, it's there if you need it, and it won't slow your reading if
you don't.

How Come We Don't Measure Very Often?

There are very real reasons why we are so weak at actually measuring
behaviors. First, it's hard to do—and it can take a lot of time. Behavioral pinpointing is hard work. Second, we all have experienced measures that produced too much data and not enough information. It is
important to remember that the purpose of the process is not to create
sophisticated measures. *The purpose is to collect data for use in evaluating success and guiding analysis and action.*

In my opinion, the simpler measures work best. A few checkmarks
in a notebook beats an automated spreadsheet if the measures in the
notebook are collected consistently for important behaviors that can be
altered to improve the business.

I, and many others, view behavior as only a cost until its value is
clearly defined and its return on investment can be determined. After
all, behavior spent on one initiative is, by definition, taken away from
another. Or, behavior spent in the classroom or coaching sessions is
behavior not invested in sales, manufacturing, shipping, or project
management. I suggest that we start to view behavior like we would a

stock purchase—an investment of known quantity (time and effort) made in an area that is very likely to deliver a profit (return on investment).

The Bottom Line on Pinpointing

At this point in our journey into applying behavioral science, we've covered some very important foundation pieces. Let's summarize the top five points I hope you take away from this chapter.

1. The CYBER Model helps you apply behavioral science to help create real business results. In this chapter, I showed you how the model guides you through the process of aligning behaviors with business results. In the next few chapters, I will show you how to use the model to proactively manage behaviors to create results.

2. Always start your efforts by understanding your business opportunity and by being concrete about your results targets. If you don't know where you're going, you might take any road to try to get there. But once you know where you're going, you can pinpoint behavior.

3. Results targets are always the foundation for behavioral targets (pinpoints). Developing a pinpoint involves these steps:

    •   *Select the right behavior.* This involves identifying the many behaviors that contribute to results and then selecting the one or two top contributors.

    •   *Describe the behavior.* This involves using the NORMS of objectivity to describe the desired behavior so you can establish a common understanding of the desired behavior.

4. The NORMS of objectivity is your tool for describing behavioral pinpoints objectively. NORMS means:

NORMS of Objectivity	
N	**N**ot an Interpretation
O	**O**bservable
R	**R**eliable
M	**M**easurable
S	**S**pecific

5. Last but not least, remember that pinpointing is not always enough to create success. You must also ensure that pinpoints are *aligned*. In other words, people who work in different departments or at different levels will influence results. Each of those people must have behavioral pinpoints that are aligned with one another. If one group of people does not have aligned behavioral pinpoints, you will be missing a piece of the puzzle. You will *never* be able to achieve all the results possible if a piece of the puzzle is missing!

What's Next?

You have seen how to pinpoint and align behavior. Our next step is to proactively manage behavior to create business results. In the next two chapters, I will give you the foundational pieces of behavioral science that pull it all together. Once you master these principles, you will understand what you need to do to manage behavior.

Know Your ABCs!

I spent over $6 million implementing this state-of-the-art sales automation system. It was supposed to improve our efficiency by 50– 75 percent. Everyone was trained on it—all of our directors, managers, supervisors, and salespeople. But fewer than half of our people are actually using it! And we have <u>not</u> seen the savings anticipated—in fact, our problems have increased, because we have some folks operating with outdated information derived from manual reports. Now we have inconsistency in product pricing information out there with our distributors and customers. It was never this bad before. <u>Implementation has been a total failure!</u> We were better off before this @!#$^$!!#*!! change.

—*Disgruntled Executive*

I CAN'T TELL YOU how often I hear some version of that story when I work with corporate leaders. Their problems often center around initiatives linked to technology (as in the example above) or to culture change, quality, or cross-selling. This is appalling, considering these leaders spend hundreds of millions every year on initiatives aimed at improving their business results.

Occasionally, the investment pays off. But more often, there is a big announcement, a flurry of activity, and a temporary improvement at best. Why?

It's because implementation efforts and plans rarely address <u>people's behavior</u>. Implementation maps processes and new interfaces, but fails to address that people must behave differently. Behavioral science has discovered the principles that govern all of our behavior (recall that "behavior" is anything we do or say). But most leaders do not apply behavioral knowledge when dealing with people. *This leaves implementation, planning, and behavior unaligned—and leaves them all to chance.*

Leaders invest a lot when they try to do all the right things. They "create the compelling vision." They "communicate the vision" so that it "links the strategy to the people." They "involve people" in planning the change. They "align processes with the vision." They "create champions and owners" at all levels of the organization.

This all *sounds* like it focuses on

> ### Behavior
> Anything a person does or says. Examples: writing an e-mail, smiling, praising a direct report, brushing teeth, making a decision, driving a car, planning the next day, saying thank you, promoting someone.

behavior, but it doesn't. It doesn't address what people really do and say. It's all designed to *inspire* change, but inspiration alone doesn't make change happen. Have I pounded this home enough? *It takes new behavior or different behavior to make change happen.*

> ### Behavior rate
> The number of times a behavior occurs divided by the time interval (hour, day, week, month) during which the behavior is counted. Behavior rates often correlate well with important results, like higher rates of sales calls resulting in higher rates of sales revenue.

So, how do you actually change what you do and how you do it? And how do you get your people to do the same? Behavioral science gives us the answer.

In Chapter 2 you learned about pinpointing—selecting the behaviors that will most impact the result you want. Once you have identified those behaviors, the next step is an ABC Analysis. This analysis lets you discover why critical behaviors aren't occurring and what is needed for them to occur consistently.

CYBER Model

1. Identify business opportunity

2. Target results and measures of success

3. Pinpoint and align behaviors that drive results

We are at this point in the CYBER Model. This step actually involves several parts, which I'll explain as we move through the chapter. For now, you need to know that understanding the influences on behavior begins by understanding the ABCs.

4. Understand the influences on behavior

5. Develop, implement, and adjust behavior change plan

6. CELEBRATE achievement of improved results!

Understanding the Influences on Behavior Starts with the ABCs

To implement any change, you need to know your ABCs: *antecedents*, *behaviors*, and *consequences*. These three things are powerfully related. We view it like this:

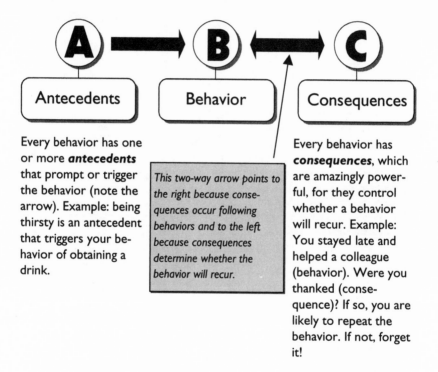

Every behavior has one or more **antecedents** that prompt or trigger the behavior (note the arrow). Example: being thirsty is an antecedent that triggers your behavior of obtaining a drink.

This two-way arrow points to the right because consequences occur following behaviors and to the left because consequences determine whether the behavior will recur.

Every behavior has **consequences**, which are amazingly powerful, for they control whether a behavior will recur. Example: You stayed late and helped a colleague (behavior). Were you thanked (consequence)? If so, you are likely to repeat the behavior. If not, forget it!

This concept of antecedents-behaviors-consequences gives us a consistent technique for analyzing behaviors—both current and desired. The following figure shows important characteristics of each element.

ABC Analysis

A snapshot of behavior and its surrounding environment. It is used for two reasons:

* To understand why certain behaviors occur or not
* To identify strategies for encouraging desired behaviors and discouraging undesired behaviors

Antecedents

- Are events that precede or prompt behavior
- Have short-term effects if not paired with consequences
- Have less impact on behavior than consequences
- Are overused compared to consequences

(Examples: training, job aids, equipment, individual abilities, behavior of others, past events, requests, goal statements, pep talks, cues in the environment like vision statements and safety posters)

Behavior

- What a person says or does
- Pinpointed behaviors correlate with business results

Consequences

- Are events that follow behavior
- Increase, maintain, or decrease behavior
- Have a great influence on whether behavior occurs again
- Positive consequences are the most desirable form of consequences

(Examples: feedback from supervisor, money, awards, mugs, T-shirts, completion of a task)

Let's look deeper at our opening story about the $6M sales automation system that so perplexed the disgruntled executive . . .

This large company, which we will call **SellMation**, had developed a really impressive technology solution for its salespeople. They created software that gave salespeople direct access to pricing information, inventory data, manufacturing schedules, etc.

The project team was empowered to handle all aspects of the system. The team helped select vendors, customize the system, and plan the implementation. Ultimately, they oversaw the rollout across the regions and divisions of the company.

The system's objectives were clear: improve data-entry efficiency, improve data accuracy, and cut order response time to both distributors and customers. When the team analyzed the workflow, it found that errors popped up and value-reducing delays occurred during the steps involving multiple handoffs in the process. So, the team had the salespeople interface directly with the data, which eliminated several handoffs.

Also, fewer keystrokes were required to process an order. Everyone seemed very pleased.

But there was one little oversight: the team never really looked at how using the new software would impact the salespeople's *behavior*. As our hapless executive said, "Implementation has been a total failure!"

Specifically, here is what the team missed: salespeople had always relied on customer service representatives (CSRs) for pricing information, order entry, and data gathering/tracking. Although the new system required fewer keystrokes, which sounds like a plus, the salespeople previously didn't key in *anything*. So, to them, the elimination of middlepeople was a huge increase in what they had to do—a real step backward!

Further, in the old system, a salesperson who needed information simply phoned a CSR. The salespeople made such calls very efficiently, using cell phones as they lunched or drove between customer visits. But now they had to lug their laptop computers along, find an analog line, dial up the system, and navigate it to find information.

The whole problem was that the new software required dramatic changes in behaviors. But in this implementation, those behaviors were ignored. *Behavior change was the cornerstone of this change implementation.*

And the salespeople revolted—as you probably would, too. They didn't want to use laptops to interface directly with the data, regardless of how well the software worked. They didn't want to invest the time or energy (or endure the headaches) of traveling with a laptop and a thick manual and having to log on after a long day. And they didn't look forward to the hassle of connecting directly from client sites, where analog lines might not be available for dialing outside the client's system.

The bottom line: **the time they spent fooling with computers and entering orders was time they lost with customers, when they could have generated more business, earned commissions, and helped achieve the company's stretch goals!**

(For those of you who relate personally to this example, I will share later in this chapter the approach we took to moderate the negative consequences of the new system.)

The problem here is clear: this new software system required several new behaviors from the salespeople. *But the consequences for their engaging in those behaviors were <u>always negative</u>.* The consequences virtually guaranteed an implementation failure!

Now, what could this executive (or the original implementation team) have done to get the new behaviors going? And what can *you* do to help the people in your organization go smoothly from their *present* behaviors to the *new* behaviors needed for change to happen?

In other words, how can you *really* implement the change and do it gracefully?

True to the science of human behavior, we must begin by understanding why people behave the way they do, even if it is not the way we wish. In other words, let's use the ABC Analysis to understand behavior.

Sample Behavior: Phoning a Customer Service Representative (CSR)

A key behavior in our example above is *phoning a CSR* (to place an order, check shipping information, or get current pricing information).

Why did salespeople, under the old system, call CSRs? First, they were taught to do so by other sales reps. In addition, their sales training manual said to call a CSR for help. Both reasons are *antecedents*—events that come before a behavior and prompt it to happen.

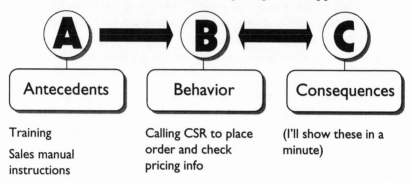

Antecedents

Training

Sales manual instructions

Behavior

Calling CSR to place order and check pricing info

Consequences

(I'll show these in a minute)

Remember that antecedents come before a behavior, set the occasion for the behavior to occur, get a behavior started, tell people how we want them to behave, and have about 20 percent influence over what we say or do.

So, **antecedents** triggered the *call-a-CSR* behavior from the salespeople. And why did the sales reps continue to call CSRs with orders, questions, and information needs? Because of **consequences**. They continued the behavior because they received a payoff—they got a question answered, they learned a shipping date, they got pricing information needed to close a sale, etc.

These are all **consequences**—events that follow a behavior and affect how often it occurs in the future. Consequences are directly linked to a behavior in a way that will either encourage it to happen again (*reinforce* it) or discourage it from happening again (*punish* or *extinguish* it). Here is the ABC Analysis again, with consequences added:

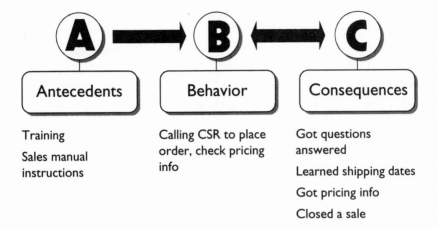

Consequences are greatly underused as a means of influencing behaviors, especially positive ones. An important goal of this book is to help you learn to effectively manage the consequences for behaviors you need in your organization.

Our Antecedent-Heavy Culture

Especially in corporate settings, we rely too much on antecedents to get new behaviors to occur. And then we provide even more antecedents when people do not behave as we wish: we issue memos, deliver pep talks, develop training manuals, and restate our expectations. The result? Wonderful initiatives are kicked off, ride high for a while, and then decline, sputter, or fizzle altogether.

Think about the training classes on "what it means to be a leader." These classes teach that leadership practices include being a good communicator and coach, for example. Our expectations of these traits, plus the leadership training we provide, are antecedents for desirable leadership behavior. *But remember, antecedents have only about 20 percent influence over what we say or do.*

What often occurs with newly trained leaders is that they emerge from a class excited to "be a great leader." Then they see very different leadership behaviors exhibited by people at higher levels. They also see people who exhibit totally different styles of leadership getting promoted, and these new leaders struggle to find more than the one or two senior-level people who do what the leadership class taught.

Such powerful consequences encourage leaders to behave *opposite of the way they were taught or told.*

So, the antecedents prompt the "talk," but the real consequences dictate the "walk." Leaders whose "talk" and "walk" don't match confuse the very people they are trying to develop as future leaders. Ultimately, consequences prevail—and unwanted behaviors prevail for longer than most would prefer.

INFLUENCE ON BEHAVIOR

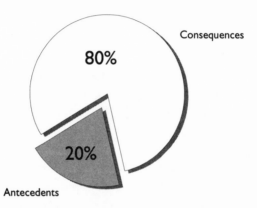

Consequences are much more powerful influencers on behavior than antecedents—and four times more effective!

Appendix B presents another interesting example involving purchasing agents at IF Corp.

Personal Note: Antecedents at Home

The ABCs really hit home when you think about your efforts to change the behaviors of your children. One frustrated executive with two teenage daughters confessed to me, "I've been using 500 pounds of antecedents and no consequences for most of my parenting lifetime. No wonder I've gone gray fast, I'm balding, and I *still* have teenage daughters who do as they please!" When I asked him to elaborate, he shared the following . . .

I realized that I've been spending most of our interactions demanding things of them to get them to do things I think are important. Those are all just antecedents. I need to spend a lot more time providing positive consequences for the things they are doing . . . I'm tired of my own voice repeatedly asking for the same things: "Why isn't your room clean?" "Have you finished your homework yet?" "You're not wearing that, are you?" "Set the table before you make your phone call." When I really stop and consider it, they are doing a lot of desirable behaviors I am not reinforcing. I'm missing opportunities that would make us all feel a lot better.

ABC . . . Where Do I Start?

At this point, I've given you a quick tour through the ABC Analysis. Let's revisit CYBER so you can see how the ABC Analysis fits into the larger picture. The figure shows the three steps of an ABC Analysis: identify antecedents, identify consequences, and conduct a "PIC/NIC analysis." (I'll explain this later.) I will now walk you through each step, starting with Step 1, "Identify antecedents for your pinpointed behavior."

CYBER Model

Conducting an ABC Analysis:

1. **Identify antecedents for your pinpointed behavior.**

2. Identify consequences for your pinpointed behavior.

3. Conduct a PIC/NIC analysis on those consequences.

1. Identify business opportunity

2. Target results and measures of success

3. Pinpoint and align behaviors that drive results

4. Understand the influences on behavior

5. Develop, implement, and adjust behavior change plan

6. CELEBRATE achievement of improved results!

The Role of Antecedents

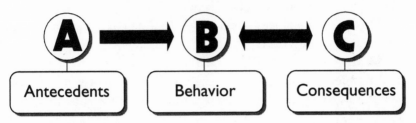

Now that you've seen an overview of the ABC Analysis, you know that the B part of ABC—the behavior—is the foundation of the analysis. Pinpointing the behavior is the first step. Identifying antecedents is the next step.

Antecedents are the events that come before a behavior and set the occasion for it to occur. Antecedents are prompts or triggers that give the signal, "It's now time for this behavior to occur." Note that antecedents set up the conditions that make behavior more *likely*, but they do not guarantee its occurrence. For example, a yellow light is an antecedent for your behavior of depressing the brake pedal in your car. Seeing a yellow light makes you more likely to stop—but it certainly doesn't guarantee that you will stop every time.

Most initiatives designed to inspire change in the workplace focus their energy on antecedents. In fact, whether intended as parts of change or not, a wide range of events can serve as antecedents to our behavior. Common antecedents for our behavior in the workplace include . . .

- Training
- Job aids
- Individual skills
- Behaviors of others
- Request to do something
- Vision statement

- Telling people what to do
- Equipment
- Performance objectives
- Time of day
- Posters, signs, or banners

Relating Antecedents to Behavior

Here are some additional **Ⓐ** antecedents that prompt our **Ⓑ** behavior, but which may be less apparent:

Ⓐ Someone's presence in a meeting might prompt you to Ⓑ share an idea you would otherwise have kept to yourself

Ⓐ Expressions of frustration or delight from colleagues might trigger you to Ⓑ share a relevant story

Ⓐ Message from the President that doesn't mention the positive results achieved in the past two quarters might prompt you to Ⓑ say how frustrated you feel that "you never hear about the good things we do"

Ⓐ Reading this book might lead you to Ⓑ conduct an ABC Analysis on a behavior that's been baffling you for a while

Ⓐ Only getting three hours of sleep last night might prompt you to Ⓑ go to bed early

Ⓐ Hearing your coworker remind you about what occurred in your last job under similar conditions might lead you to Ⓑ behave exactly as you did at your last job even though you swore you weren't going to

Ⓐ Reviewing a memo from your boss might prompt you to Ⓑ do extra research about the topic at hand

Ⓐ Past experience with corporate initiatives might trigger you to Ⓑ say that you think the newest initiative is just a "flavor-of-the-month"

Ⓐ Reading this book might prompt you to Ⓑ apply some of the tools and techniques you are reading about to your personal or professional life

Multiple Antecedents Can Trigger the Same Behavior

Clearly understanding the antecedent-behavior relationship is your first step in understanding why behaviors occur. Multiple antecedents can combine to trigger behaviors, too. The following figure shows some examples that illustrate this very point.

Antecedents and the Behaviors They Trigger

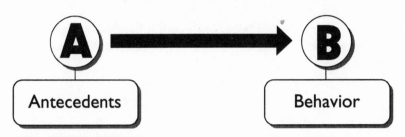

Antecedents	Behavior
• Declining results in detergent sales for three successive quarters • Observing more meetings between sales and advertising in past when sales were declining • Team critique of promotional campaign used for detergents	Hold a one-day meeting to discuss the cause of slumped detergent sales and the advertising plan for the rest of the year
• Deadline tomorrow for the revised proposal • Previous good suggestions from direct reports	Leave voice mail for direct reports announcing a 4:00 meeting to review the revised proposal
• "To do" list sitting on desk • Completed item	Cross item off "to do" list
• End of first quarter • Thank you from department members for previous updates • Data received	Leave voice mail update for the department on financial statistics for past quarter
• Back pain • Training on ergonomics	Adjust lumbar support on new office chair

What Are Your Antecedents?

Want a break from reading? Here's an exercise for you. First, think about five things you did today at work. These are **behaviors**. Write each one in the right column.

Antecedent	Your Behavior
Example: Saw date on calendar.	*Example*: Attended meeting.
1	
2	
3	
4	
5	

Now, to the left of each behavior, write the **antecedents** that prompted that behavior. (Use the example as a model for wording.) Some Tips for Identifying Antecedents

Be sure you have a clearly pinpointed behavior.

Ask yourself the following questions. Your answers will most likely be the antecedents you are looking for.

- What happens right before the behavior happens?
- What triggers that behavior?
- What cues prompt your behavior?

When Antecedents Fail

Antecedents are effective in *starting* a behavior. Research in the application of behavioral science, especially in the area of *feedback*, shows that changing an antecedent does indeed change behavior—but only somewhat, and only for a little while.

The fable of the shepherd boy who cried "Wolf!" illustrates this point:

> **The boy had the lonely task of tending the village's sheep while they grazed on the mountainside during the day. The community had arranged a signal (*antecedent*) by which when the boy cried "Wolf!" the village residents would run to protect their sheep (*behavior*).**
>
> **Well, the lonely boy wanted company. So he cried "Wolf!" even though none was present. The villagers raced to his aid, only to find no wolf.**
>
> **Later, the boy did it a second time. And a second time the villagers went to his aid but found no wolf.**
>
> **Then the boy cried "Wolf!" a third time, because this time there truly *was* a large wolf eyeing up the sheep, licking his chops and circling the sheep and the boy, his eyes glowing like hot coals. But this time, the villagers ignored the cry. The wolf dined on mutton and shepherd boy.**

The story's purpose is to teach children about honesty. But it also has a behavioral moral: **antecedents** are effective only when they are backed up by **consequences**. The boy's cry initially was an effective antecedent for the villagers' behavior of running to help. But the **consequences** of doing so proved negative, repeatedly. Villagers ran to help, only to find that nothing was wrong—they wasted their time and energy on a false alarm, twice. So, the villagers' **consequence history** became one of "false alarm, don't bother." And so the antecedent became ineffective for initiating the behavior.

Consequence history

A person's cumulative experience of positive and negative consequences for specific behaviors and/or antecedents. Consequence histories establish people's readiness to perform certain behaviors. If you have experienced negative consequences for a behavior or negative consequences in the presence of certain antecedents, you will be reluctant to engage in that behavior.

The same thing happens in organizations. We issue vision statements about fundamentally different ways of operating . . . getting closer to the customer than ever before . . . investing in our people and their development . . . being better at planning and anticipating so we can be proactive rather than reactive . . . .

All of these antecedents are intended to prompt behaviors, such as demonstrating enthusiasm for the vision, revising our work processes to accomplish the company's goals, and working closely with others to improve how we do our jobs.

But when consequences just reinforce the old ways of doing things, or when they are clearly inconsistent with strong change statements, employees end up with the same consequence history as the villagers: "false alarm, don't bother." Employees say, "The only sign around here we believe is the one that says *WET PAINT.*"

Changing the Consequences

Why do so many organization "solutions" lead to temporary changes in behavior? Because the consequences for behaviors never changed. The old ways of doing things were maintained—even though the *intention* was for things to be done differently. Here is a very bitter example from my own experience . . .

> **In the early '90s I was brought into a manufacturing plant to help implement quality practices and a more "democratic" leadership style. The company made ceramic insulators used on electric utility lines. This plant had a horrible quality record— customers dissatisfied due to product defects, a high scrap rate, and other related quality problems. The employee grievance rate was increasing yearly, just as manufacturing cost and defects were also escalating.**

Employees and management alike were eager to help improve things. Employees were eager to learn quality practices and were grateful for management's commitment to involve them in decision making and running the facility. Based on an early assessment, I predicted close to 50 percent improvement in profitability in three to six months with the application of some basic quality practices and leadership support for new behaviors. I felt certain that with a few new antecedents and changes in some important consequences, new behaviors would quickly emerge and be sustained.

The employees were bright, concerned people. They couldn't get enough of the concepts and ways they could apply them. The managers were also like sponges, soaking up the new tools and techniques. Things looked great . . . until the plans for change were halted at higher levels of leadership.

The employees at this plant were paid for piecework: for each unit produced and packaged, they received x dollars. We saw plenty of evidence that this system worked against "quality" because employees were working to maximize the amount of money they made by producing and packaging as many units as possible, ignoring the quality of the units produced.

Clearly, new behaviors were needed to impact the quality and profitability of this plant. For example, employees needed to shut down the production line if they saw defects of a certain magnitude in the products, and they needed to use the problem-solving process they had learned to analyze quality issues so they could be fixed permanently.

Employees had sustained pretty stable productivity rates for the prior 3½ years that the piecework system was in effect. So, we developed a local agreement between the union and management to continue paying the employees based on historical averages for the next six months while a new compensation system was developed. This way, they would not be penalized (i.e., receive a negative consequence such as reduced compensation) for shutting down the line due to quality issues.

For the first twelve days of implementation, the plant achieved record-low product defect numbers and kept productivity levels within the historical two-year average. Employees were happy and proud. They were successful in improving the quality of the products—and they continued to be paid at their regular levels. But then the international union leadership, together with the corporate leaders, overruled the local decision on pay modification and required management to resume the old piecework system for paying employees.

Almost immediately, product defects escalated and the lines were never again voluntarily shut down. In fact, any discussion that took people off the line, including problem solving on product quality issues, ceased almost immediately. Quality problems continued and customer complaints escalated.

Seven months later, with only a one-week notice, the plant permanently closed. The 300-member workforce located in this small, rural community received neither a severance package nor assistance with finding other jobs.

What's the lesson for us? Antecedents have short-term effects on behavior, and consequences have powerful, long-term effects. In this plant, the desired behaviors were pinpointed. The antecedents were also in place: training, local management commitment to the new approach, and employees excited about their ability to improve performance.

And, management had wisely considered consequences for behavior. They wanted to continue motivating employees, and they did not want employees' pay to suffer because they attended to quality issues. So, they changed the consequences, correctly anticipating that productivity would decline in the short term while they fixed the issues.

Unfortunately, this new consequence system came apart. With the pay system overruled and the piecework pay system reinstated, the powerful consequences of the old system again drove the workers' behavior—and quality slipped. The new antecedents of training and quality were not powerful enough to compete with the consequence system. So, the new behaviors didn't stick. For the manufacturing plant and its employees, the effects of that backslide were fatal.

CYBER Model

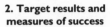

1. Identify business opportunity

2. Target results and measures of success

Conducting an ABC Analysis:

1. Identify antecedents for your pinpointed behavior.
2. **Identify consequences for your pinpointed behavior.**
3. Conduct a PIC/NIC analysis on those consequences.

3. Pinpoint and align behaviors that drive results

4. Understand the influences on behavior

5. Develop, implement, and adjust behavior change plan

6. CELEBRATE achievement of improved results!

The Role of Consequences

There is a *consequence* to *every* behavior—no exceptions. For example, sending an e-mail is a behavior. Every e-mail you send has *some* consequence for you that will affect your future behavior. You may receive a positive response, a negative response, or only the response that says "mail sent" after you click "send." Each of these consequences is a confirmation or rejection, and it strongly affects how you will act in the future.

Remember the salespeople who called customer service reps with orders and questions? What were the consequences of their behavior of calling CSRs?

- They got answers for their customers
- They got current information about pricing
- They got information quickly, while driving or doing other things
- They got to talk with their CSR friends and colleagues

Quite a few very positive consequences. Then, suddenly, they were told to STOP doing those things and start doing the new behavior of logging onto the computer for their information. When this happened, negative consequences replaced positive consequences.

> ## Some Tips for Identifying Consequences
>
> Make sure you have clearly pinpointed a behavior.
>
> Ask yourself:
>
> - What does the performer experience as a result of the behavior?
> - What happens to the performer as a result of the behavior?
> - What events happen immediately after the behavior that are likely to impact the performer (either positively or negatively)?
>
> Your answers will most likely be the consequences you are looking for.

The Power of Consequences

I can't emphasize enough that consequences have the greatest influence on behavior. Consequences *either* increase *or* decrease the occurrence of a behavior. Let's consider each possibility:

Increasing Behavior. At this moment I am typing on my laptop, writing what you are reading. The **antecedents** for my behavior include (1) my commitment to complete Chapter 3 today, (2) a half-completed paragraph on the screen, (3) quiet time on an airplane, and (4) a deadline from my publisher. All of these antecedents are *prompting* my behavior. But it's the **consequences** that *make my writing behavior keep going:*

- Every time I complete a paragraph, I save the file and see one more completed section. So I keep typing (my behavior increases).
- In the past I have helped leaders grow more effective by teaching them how to apply behavioral science. This is something I value greatly. I am excited to be writing a book to help others. So I keep typing (my behavior increases).
- Every time I complete a section, my to-do list of sections to write gets shorter and my tension eases. So I keep typing (my behavior increases).

The lesson is simple: *positive consequences increase behavior!*

Decreasing Behavior. What would happen if I typed, but characters stopped appearing on the screen? I might hit the keys furiously for a short time, but soon I would quit typing. My behavior would decrease, and it might stop altogether. What if I received a call from my publisher canceling my book contract? My behavior would likely decrease (at least temporarily!).

Research on goal-setting and feedback, conducted by myself and others, has documented the relative power of antecedents and consequences:

- An antecedent alone will produce a small, often temporary change in behavior.
- A consequence alone will produce modest, lasting changes in behavior.
- Antecedents backed up by consequences will produce the greatest changes in behavior (either increases or decreases).

My experience in applying behavioral science in corporate settings corroborates these findings. For example, making a big splash about a new product (*antecedent*) will generate a flurry of activity that may quickly die down. From the perspective of consumers, if using that new product is not positively reinforcing (*consequence*), they probably will stop buying it. From the perspective of marketing and salespeople— the folks pushing the new product—if the initial splash is followed by strong sales (*consequence*), their behaviors that led to strong sales will continue.

Consequences have about four times more impact on behavior that antecedents have.

INFLUENCE ON BEHAVIOR

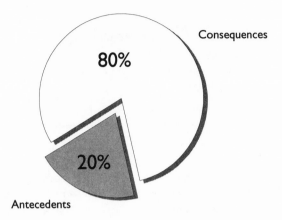

Ironically, leaders spend significantly more of their time and re-sources in the wrong place—on antecedents! They deliver vision state-ments, restructure staff and work processes, and provide training—all of which are important and necessary antecedents to prompt the right behavior. But they leave the critical **consequences** of behaviors unat-tended! To me, it's like watching a gambler put 80 percent of his cash on a good-looking horse that can't run very well! This may make for an enjoyable day at the races, but it's not a good way to make money.

Below are two ABC Analysis tables that illustrate the relative power of antecedents and consequences. The first table shows conse-quences that *discourage* behavior.

Consequences That Discourage Behavior

Antecedents	Behavior	Consequences	Net Result
Manager asks for input	Employee begins to share an idea	Manager takes a phone call while employee is talking	*Discourages desirable behavior of sharing ideas*
Customer smells fresh baked goods in bakery	Customer asks if a muffin can be warmed in microwave	Employee rolls eyes, frowns, says they taste better cold	*Discourages desirable behavior of customer buying*
Employee is trained to smile and greet customer verbally	Employee smiles and greets customer: "How are you today?"	Impatient customer frowns, drums fingers on counter	*Discourages desirable behavior of smiling and greeting customers*
Employee is trained in suggestive selling (to suggest use of *company* credit card)	Employee sees customer using credit card and suggests *company* card	Customer sneers at employee and turns away	*Discourages desirable behavior of suggesting company card*
Sales people are told to work as a team and jointly call on a customer	Sales rep A has serviced account for 3 years and invites sales rep B to jointly call on customer	Customer purchases 80 percent of products from sales rep B and 20 percent from A, reducing A's commission by 80 percent	*Sales rep A will likely not team with another sales rep again!*

Fortunately, we are usually focused on how to *encourage* desired behaviors, which means we are seeking opportunities to recognize and reinforce the behaviors of people making important contributions. The second table shows consequences that *encourage* behavior.

Consequences That Encourage Behavior

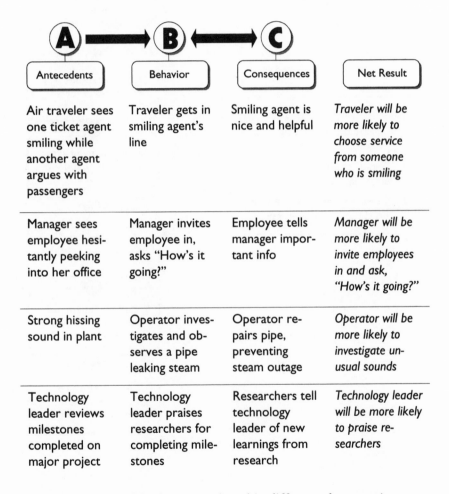

Antecedents	Behavior	Consequences	Net Result
Air traveler sees one ticket agent smiling while another agent argues with passengers	Traveler gets in smiling agent's line	Smiling agent is nice and helpful	*Traveler will be more likely to choose service from someone who is smiling*
Manager sees employee hesitantly peeking into her office	Manager invites employee in, asks "How's it going?"	Employee tells manager important info	*Manager will be more likely to invite employees in and ask, "How's it going?"*
Strong hissing sound in plant	Operator investigates and observes a pipe leaking steam	Operator repairs pipe, preventing steam outage	*Operator will be more likely to investigate unusual sounds*
Technology leader reviews milestones completed on major project	Technology leader praises researchers for completing milestones	Researchers tell technology leader of new learnings from research	*Technology leader will be more likely to praise researchers*

Clearly, a good leader can make a big difference by *managing consequences* for employees—particularly when the consequences that might naturally occur are not positive.

CYBER Model

Conducting an ABC Analysis:

1. Identify antecedents for your pinpointed behavior.
2. Identify consequences for your pinpointed behavior.
3. **Conduct a PIC/NIC analysis on those consequences.**

1. Identify business opportunity

2. Target results and measures of success

3. Pinpoint and align behaviors that drive results

4. Understand the influences on behavior

5. Develop, implement, and adjust behavior change plan

6. CELEBRATE achievement of improved results!

A PIC/NIC of Consequences

I'll provide a full review of consequences and how to use them in the next chapter. But here, let's focus on how consequences either *encourage* or *discourage* behavior. Aubrey Daniels, a pioneer in applying the principles of behavioral science to the workplace, developed a tool called the PIC/NIC analysis. This technique reveals how consequences work.

Every consequence has three fundamental characteristics:[1]

- a consequence can be *Positive* or *Negative*
- a consequence can be *Immediate* or *Future*
- and a consequence can be *Certain* or *Uncertain*

All combinations are possible, like PIU or NFC, but let's focus on two for now:

- *Positive-Immediate-Certain* (PIC)
- *Negative-Immediate-Certain* (NIC)

PICs are consequences that are Positive-Immediate-Certain to the performer of the behavior. An example is knowing from experience that your e-mail will be promptly delivered to the right recipient if you click "send."

NICs are consequences that are Negative-Immediate-Certain to the performer of the behavior. An example is knowing from experience that you will delay the start of a meeting by arriving late.

Why do we focus on *PICs* and *NICs*? Because they are the most powerful consequences for influencing day-to-day behavior. Of the two, it's the *PICs* you want most. And *Positive-Immediate-Certain* consequences for desired behaviors have another terrific benefit: people *feel better* after receiving them. They are motivated to do those be-

---

[1] This concept appeared in Petrock, Frank, "Analyzing the balance of consequences for performance improvements," *Journal of Organizational Behavior Management*, vol. 1, no. 3, Spring 1978, p. 196-205. The concept was further developed by Paul L. Brown (see *Managing Behavior on the Job*, New York: John Wiley & Sons, 1982) and Aubrey C. Daniels in *Bringing Out the Best in People*, New York: McGraw-Hill, 1994.

haviors again in the future. And, since they feel good, they are more likely to perform at even higher levels.

That's what I mean when I say that being reinforced for work promotes more *discretionary effort*. Discretionary effort is the extra effort employees put forth because they want to, rather than because they have to. When employees devote discretionary effort to their jobs, profitability improves. *PICs* are a real win-win.

> ### PIC/NIC analysis
>
> Analyzes the positiveness, immediacy, and certainty of consequences to understand which ones most impact behavior. PICs (positive, immediate, certain) and NICs (negative, immediate, and certain) have the greatest impact on behavior.

PIC/NIC Time

Here's how to do a PIC/NIC analysis. To the ABC Analysis (antecedent-behavior-consequence), simply add columns to indicate whether each consequence is Positive/Negative, Immediate/Future, and Certain/Uncertain.

Important: When you do a PIC/NIC analysis, you must step into the performer's shoes. The performers are the people who experience consequences for the behavior you are analyzing, so you must understand their perspective. Always ask yourself these questions:

- Does the performer experience this consequence as positive or negative?
- Does the performer experience the consequence immediately upon performing the behavior, or is the consequence delayed?
- Is the consequence relatively certain to occur, or is it uncertain?

Back to Our Sales Automation Example . . .

I promised we would return to the unfortunate salespeople and their frustration with having to log onto their computers for order entry and pricing information. Let's apply our PIC/NIC analysis to the situation.

PIC/NIC Analysis: Sales Reps Log onto Network

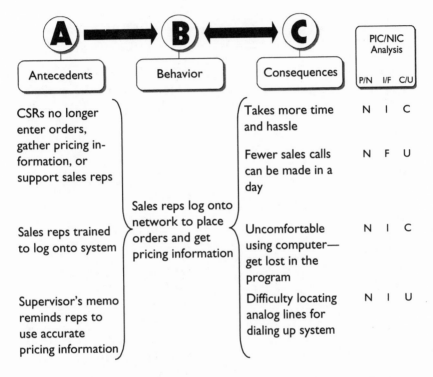

Consequences	P/N	I/F	C/U
Takes more time and hassle	N	I	C
Fewer sales calls can be made in a day	N	F	U
Uncomfortable using computer—get lost in the program	N	I	C
Difficulty locating analog lines for dialing up system	N	I	U

Antecedents: CSRs no longer enter orders, gather pricing information, or support sales reps / Sales reps trained to log onto system / Supervisor's memo reminds reps to use accurate pricing information

Behavior: Sales reps log onto network to place orders and get pricing information

The situation seems grim. Lots of negative consequences. A way to improve the situation is to create positive consequences for the salespeople. This would reinforce the new behavior of using computers to obtain pricing information. A behavior analyst would plan the delivery of positive consequences prior to implementing the new system, anticipating the likely negative consequences for the salespeople.

We can begin by adding new antecedents for the salespeople, like communicating how engaging in the new behavior will benefit them . . .

New PIC/NIC Analysis: Sales Reps Log onto Network

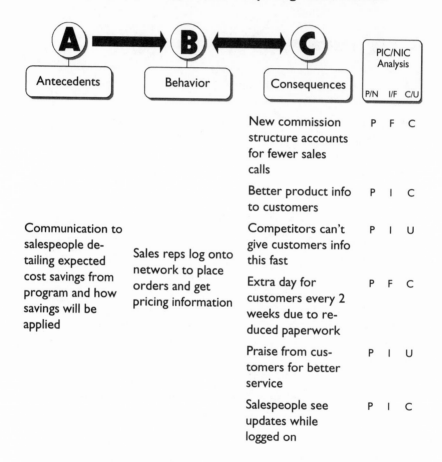

Antecedents	Behavior	Consequences	P/N	I/F	C/U
		New commission structure accounts for fewer sales calls	P	F	C
		Better product info to customers	P	I	C
Communication to salespeople detailing expected cost savings from program and how savings will be applied	Sales reps log onto network to place orders and get pricing information	Competitors can't give customers info this fast	P	I	U
		Extra day for customers every 2 weeks due to reduced paperwork	P	F	C
		Praise from customers for better service	P	I	U
		Salespeople see updates while logged on	P	I	C

Behavioral changes driven by technology and process changes can have negative impacts on the users of those systems. However, if we can understand the significance of the changes, the consequences that drive old behaviors, and the consequences needed to shape new behaviors, we can help smooth the transition.

Consider the PICs and NICs operating in your own life, in your relationship with your spouse, your children, your relatives, your coworkers, telemarketers, and even your car. Do you have new insights into why you do what you do? Do you now know why salespeople might skip out early on Friday for an outing with their friends (PIC), even if means jeopardizing a sales award for the quarter (PFU)? Or why we eat that delicious chocolate brownie (PIC) even though we are trying to lose weight (PFU)? Or why kids continue to act out (NIC) even as we threaten that Santa won't come (NFU) if they continue to misbehave?

It comes down to the power of consequences—and in particular, the power of consequences that are **immediate** and **certain**. Take the time to arrange this type of consequence before seeking behavior change or delivering the consequences, and I promise you a huge increase in effectively obtaining desired behaviors and decreasing undesired ones.

Personal Note: Immediacy of Reinforcers Is Critical, Mom!

I used to ask my four-year-old son to please pick up his toys (antecedent). He would choose not to do it. I would then say, "If you pick up your toys, you can go outside and play." (Playing outside was a desirable consequence.) He would sometimes pick up his toys . . . but more often than not, he'd respond with, "No thank you, mama."

Upon analyzing the situation, I realized that I had the positive and certain aspects of the consequences pretty well nailed. He loved to play outdoors, and he knew that I kept my promises. However, the immediacy part was still an issue. As I considered what consequences I could provide that were more immediate, it occurred to me that more than any other thing, Austin was reinforced by time spent with his mother. So if I used that as a more immediate reinforcer for picking up his toys, it was likely that I would get that desired behavior to occur more reliably.

So, I said, "Austin, let's pick up your toys together so you can go outside and play . . ." to which he immediately responded, "Great! Thanks, mama." Austin and I still pick up toys together and do a lot of other "chores" as a twosome—which ensures we both have plenty of PIC consequences for our behaviors!

The Bottom Line on ABCs

At this point in our journey into behavioral science, we've covered some very important foundation pieces. Here are the top four points I hope you take away from this chapter:

1. To proactively manage behavior and create business results, you must understand the influences on behavior. The ABC Analysis is your key tool for understanding behavior. ABC stands for antecedent-behavior-consequence.

2. There are three steps in conducting an ABC Analysis:

   - *Identify antecedents*—events that come before behavior and prompt behavior to occur.
   - *Identify consequences*—events that follow behavior and influence whether or not that behavior will occur again.
   - *Conduct a PIC/NIC analysis.* Every behavior has a consequence that can be classified by whether it is:
     - *P*ositive or *N*egative
     - *I*mmediate or *F*uture
     - *C*ertain or *U*ncertain

3. Consequences are far more powerful than antecedents when it comes to long-term effects on behavior. If you are going to invest in behavior, invest heavily in positive consequences. And make sure your antecedents and consequences are not in conflict.

4. PICs and NICs are the most powerful consequences for behavior. Find all the PICs you can for a behavior, because PICs lead to increases in discretionary effort—people will *want* to do things, instead of doing them because they *have* to. And tapping into discretionary effort is the secret to unlocking the profitability of your company and of your relationships.

What's Next?

You've nearly mastered the fundamental principles of behavioral science. You are familiar with pinpointing, you can conduct an ABC Analysis, and you understand the importance of PIC and NIC consequences. Because consequences are so important, we need to explore them more thoroughly. In the next chapter, we'll look at the relationship between types of consequences and their effects on behavior.

It's a Matter of Consequences

We were given our choice of how we wanted to be recognized for a job well done. One year I took three extra vacation days, while last year I was able to get a new laptop computer, even though it wasn't my turn to get an upgrade. The best part was knowing that my boss knew about our unit's performance. He always made a point of letting us know how much he appreciated the extra effort we put into our work. Honestly, it was sometimes "little stuff." But big or small, he always made a point of demonstrating his support and encouraging us to keep getting better. The more we did well, the more access he gave us to more interesting and challenging work. He was the best boss I ever had.

—New Managing Director, University Administration

UNDERSTANDING how consequences influence behavior is critical to understanding why we do what we do—and how to change our own behavior. To review quickly, *consequences* are events or conditions that follow a behavior. They either encourage or discourage the behavior from occurring again. As the story above shows us, consequences are powerful. The Managing Director of University Administration was fortunate to have a boss who understood the power of consequences.

He used consequences—"big stuff and little stuff," like feedback, time off from work, computer upgrades, and interesting work opportunities—to encourage behavior. Asking employees how they wanted to be recognized was another reinforcing consequence he used. As a result, people put extra effort into their work and felt good about it. I use the term "discretionary effort" to refer to this. Discretionary effort can only occur when positive consequences for performance are available to the performer.

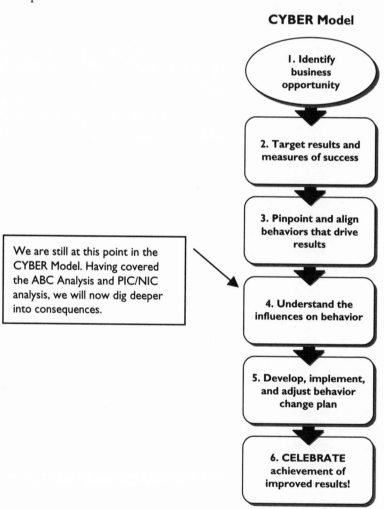

CYBER Model

1. Identify business opportunity

2. Target results and measures of success

3. Pinpoint and align behaviors that drive results

We are still at this point in the CYBER Model. Having covered the ABC Analysis and PIC/NIC analysis, we will now dig deeper into consequences.

4. Understand the influences on behavior

5. Develop, implement, and adjust behavior change plan

6. CELEBRATE achievement of improved results!

More Behavior or Less Behavior?

Behavioral analysis involves breaking into components for study a chain of behavior and its surrounding environment. In particular, we use the ABC Analysis to understand behavior in terms of its antecedents and consequences. The result is a different view of the world—one that provides objective clues to why we behave as we do. The examples below show chains of typical everyday behavior broken down into individual *behaviors* **B** and *consequences* **C**. These examples demonstrate why specific behaviors increase or decrease . . .

B You use a new Web browser on the Internet and **C** find the information you are looking for faster than with your old browser. (This positive consequence will encourage your behavior of using that new Web browser again.)

B You touch a hot stove and **C** you get burned. (This negative consequence will discourage your behavior of touching hot stoves!)

B You drive 60 mph in a 30 mph zone and **C** get a ticket complete with points and fees. (Getting a ticket, paying the fine, and getting points on your license are all negative consequences that will discourage your behavior of speeding.)

B You go into the office early because you want to **C** avoid being unprepared for a meeting with your boss. (You will likely do that again in the future if the preparation time helps make the meeting more successful.)

If **B** you connect to Amazon.com, **C** find the book you are looking for, and **B** order it easily **C** without having to leave your home, you will likely **B** use Amazon.com again in the future.

If **B** you work for days and days on a special report for your team, **B** get it to them on time, but **C** hear no feedback, **B** your behavior of working "extra hard" will probably not occur the next time they ask.

Once a behavior starts, its consequences determine whether or not it will recur.

It's like starting a car. Once the car has started, you must apply your foot to the gas pedal to go anywhere. Consequences are the fuel for behavior. One way we can get behavior started is by using antecedents. Antecedents are like starting the car. They get the behavior going, but they won't *keep* it going. We need appropriate *consequences* to keep it going.

As you saw from the examples above, consequences can either encourage behavior to continue or can discourage behavior from continuing. (No one I know continues to touch a hot stove after they've been burned a couple of times!) In general, we say that if consequences encourage behavior to continue, those consequences are *reinforcement*. But if consequences discourage a behavior, they are either *punishment* or lead to *extinction*.

Four Ways That Consequences Affect Behavior

There are four ways that consequences affect behavior. We'll look briefly at each and then move into more detailed explanations.

1. **Positive Reinforcement (R+).** Positive reinforcement occurs when people experience desirable consequences for a behavior (usually positive, immediate, and certain consequences—PICs). Desirable consequences result in a behavior increasing in the future.

> **Positive Reinforcement (R+)**
> Providing a desirable consequence following a behavior. The purpose is to maintain the behavior or increase its likelihood of recurring. Examples are praise, money, positive feedback from supervisor, or a day off from work.

We abbreviate positive reinforcement R+. The R stands for *reinforcement*, and the + means that a desirable consequence (a PIC) is added. Positive reinforcement is the best way to encourage *discretionary effort* from people, because it creates a situation in which the behavior is followed by a positive (desirable) consequence. Let's look at a quick example of R+.

> Chuck hates to mow the lawn. One Saturday, his wife Maria got out of bed early and mowed the lawn, so Chuck didn't have to. When Chuck realized what Maria had done, he gave her a hug, said "thank you," and took her to lunch at her favorite restaurant to express his appreciation. Maria was so touched that she mowed the lawn for Chuck the following weekend too.
>
> *The behavior:* Maria mowing the lawn.

The consequence: **Chuck's hug, "thank you," and lunch with him at her favorite restaurant.**

The effect: **Positive reinforcement. Maria's behavior increased because she felt good about it. We would say her behavior was positively reinforced.**

Examples of Positive Reinforcement

A ⟶ Antecedents	B ⟵ Behavior	C Consequences	Impact on Future Behavior
Coaching lessons on proper stance in golf	Golfer adopts a new stance	The ball lands on the green and the rest of the foursome applaud	*Golfer repeats the stance on next tee-off*
Sales checklist is used to guide customer product-needs analysis	Sales representative makes cold calls to assess needs	Daily order rate increases, and increase is recognized on sales board	*Sales representative is likely to place more cold calls*
Team identifies how to use a new technique to improve clarity of testing	Research scientist uses the new technique for DNA	Results show a better DNA resolution	*Scientist uses the technique more often in the future*
Coach works with CEO to develop a compelling vision statement	CEO delivers a vision statement	Three VPs tell him it is the most inspirational talk they ever heard	*CEO repeats the vision statement at subsequent talks*
Sales reps review pricing policy and identify pricing strategy for each account	Reps follow pricing strategy during account sales calls	Profitability of daily sales is 10 percent higher, on average, for the week	*Reps follow pricing strategy more closely and more often in the future*

Negative Reinforcement (R-)

Removing or preventing an undesired consequence to increase the likelihood that the behavior will occur in the future. Examples:

- Avoiding being reprimanded (by complying with policies)
- Avoiding a ticket (by driving within the speed limit)
- Avoiding embarrassing lateness (by arriving on time)
- Avoiding nasty notices or interest charges (by paying bills on time)
- Escaping the loud siren of a fire truck (by covering your ears)
- Escaping the sound of your opponent's voice (by walking away from an argument)

---

2.   **Negative Reinforcement (R-).** Negative reinforcement occurs when negative consequences are taken away or avoided. Because of the word "negative," you might think that negative reinforcement would decrease behavior, but it doesn't. It actually *keeps behavior going.* "Negative" simply means that something unpleasant is *taken away* or *avoided.* This removal or avoidance acts to *reinforce* or *increase* the behavior, so we use the term R-.

Have you ever seen people do just enough to get by or just enough to prevent something undesirable from occurring? In everyday language, we say they are "complying." They seek the minimal acceptable standards rather than giving discretionary effort. You can bet that whenever you see "compliance," the consequence responsible for it is negative reinforcement. Let's look at an example.

> **Monthly time and expenses are due to accounting by 5:00 P.M. on the 25th of each month. Accounting prefers to get them in weekly so they can be processed in a more timely way. If time and expenses are received after 5:00 P.M. on the 25th, individual paychecks are held for one week—and expense reimbursements are delayed until the following month. Fewer than 3 percent of the employees send in their time and expenses prior to the 25th. On the 25th, between noon and 4:55 P.M., the other 97 percent submit their time and expenses.**

The behavior: **Employees submitting time and expenses before 5:00 P.M. on the 25th of the month.**

The consequence: **Paycheck is held for one extra week. Expense reimbursements are delayed by one month.**

The effect: **Employees submit their time and expenses before 5:00 P.M. on the 25th to avoid the negative consequences of not getting them in. They do not submit their data every week. Time and expenses are sent in only when the threat of not getting paid is present.**

3. *Punishment (P).* When behavior decreases because it leads to something undesirable—usually negative, immediate, and certain consequences (NICs)—punishment occurs. When people experience punishment, they can feel frustrated or upset. Notice that punishment differs from negative reinforcement: punishment *provides* negative consequences that discourage a behavior, whereas negative reinforcement *removes* negative consequences in order to encourage a behavior. Here's an example of punishment:

Punishment (P)

Providing an undesired consequence following a behavior to decrease the likelihood of the behavior recurring. Examples are reprimands, embarrassing comments, or disappointing someone important to you.

Three-year-old Katherine was excited about her new bike, complete with training wheels. Katherine got so involved in riding her bike that she forgot her mom's warning about riding in the street. When Katherine's mom saw Katherine riding in the street, she ran out, pulled Katherine off the bike, and gave her a stern lecture about the dangers of her behavior. Katherine started to cry because her mom's reaction scared her. Katherine never rode her bike in the street again.

The behavior: **Katherine riding her bike in the street.**

The consequence: **Katherine's mom pulling Katherine off the bike and giving her a lecture.**

The effect: **Punishment. Katherine was upset by her mom's reaction and her behavior immediately decreased—she didn't ride her bike in the street again.**

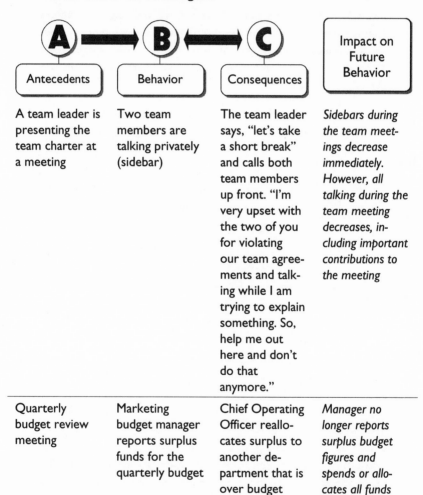

Antecedents	Behavior	Consequences	Impact on Future Behavior
A team leader is presenting the team charter at a meeting	Two team members are talking privately (sidebar)	The team leader says, "let's take a short break" and calls both team members up front. "I'm very upset with the two of you for violating our team agreements and talking while I am trying to explain something. So, help me out here and don't do that anymore."	*Sidebars during the team meetings decrease immediately. However, all talking during the team meeting decreases, including important contributions to the meeting*
Quarterly budget review meeting	Marketing budget manager reports surplus funds for the quarterly budget	Chief Operating Officer reallocates surplus to another department that is over budget	*Manager no longer reports surplus budget figures and spends or allocates all funds before the meeting*

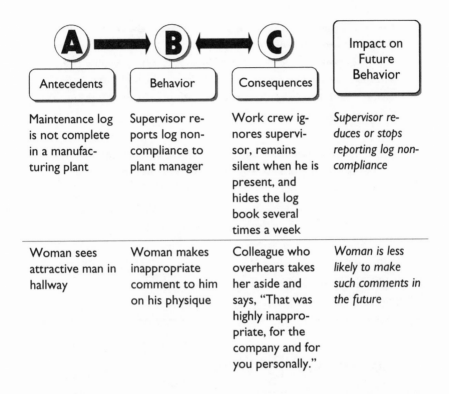

A →	**B** ↔	**C**	Impact on Future Behavior
Antecedents	Behavior	Consequences	
Maintenance log is not complete in a manufacturing plant	Supervisor reports log noncompliance to plant manager	Work crew ignores supervisor, remains silent when he is present, and hides the log book several times a week	*Supervisor reduces or stops reporting log noncompliance*
Woman sees attractive man in hallway	Woman makes inappropriate comment to him on his physique	Colleague who overhears takes her aside and says, "That was highly inappropriate, for the company and for you personally."	*Woman is less likely to make such comments in the future*

4. **Extinction (Ext).** Extinction occurs when a behavior stops because the positive reinforcement that used to sustain the behavior is no longer present. In other words, extinction involves withholding something desirable that was expected.

   Six-year-old Benji loved to tell knock-knock jokes. But no one in his entire family wanted to hear another knock-knock joke. One day, Benji said, "Knock-Knock" to his mom. Rather than saying "Who's there?" his mom said, "It's time for dinner." Benji tried again, "Knock-Knock." His mom answered, "Would you like peas or carrots?" Benji tried again, "Knock-Knock." His mom said, "Peas or carrots?" Benji sighed, "Peas, I guess. Hey, guess what Ms. West said at school today?" His mom said, "Tell me all about it, honey."

   The behavior: Benji telling knock-knock jokes.

The consequence: In the past, his family always answered "Who's there?" to Benji's "Knock-Knock." Their attention positively reinforced Benji's joke–telling. This time, Benji's mom withheld her previous response of "Who's there?" Rather than saying, "Who's there?" she asked Benji questions about a different subject: dinner.

The effect: Extinction. After several tries, Benji stopped trying to tell his mom the knock-knock joke and moved on to other things.

Extinction (Ext)

Withholding a desired consequence to decrease the likelihood that a behavior will continue. Examples:

* Withholding attention for inappropriate comments
* Withholding praise for work accomplishments

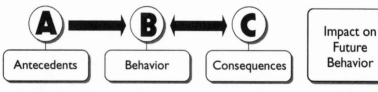

Antecedents	Behavior	Consequences	Impact on Future Behavior
Staff memo from boss asking you to present a report at the staff meeting	Stay late to complete report	Boss does not ask for report in meeting	*After a temporary increase in asking boss if he wants to see the report, you stop asking him. Decreased probability that you'll stay late to finish reports in future*

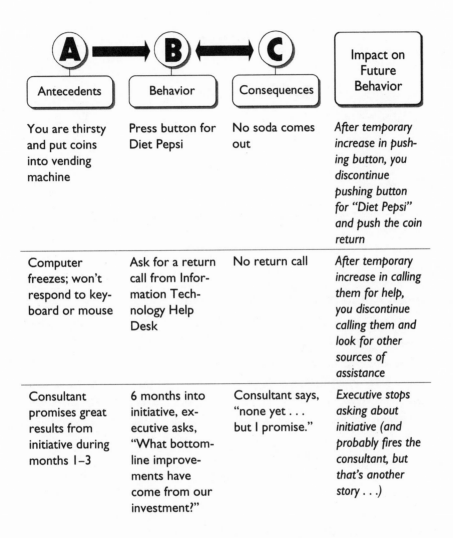

A → Antecedents	**B** ← Behavior	**C** ← Consequences	Impact on Future Behavior
You are thirsty and put coins into vending machine	Press button for Diet Pepsi	No soda comes out	*After temporary increase in pushing button, you discontinue pushing button for "Diet Pepsi" and push the coin return*
Computer freezes; won't respond to keyboard or mouse	Ask for a return call from Information Technology Help Desk	No return call	*After temporary increase in calling them for help, you discontinue calling them and look for other sources of assistance*
Consultant promises great results from initiative during months 1–3	6 months into initiative, executive asks, "What bottom-line improvements have come from our investment?"	Consultant says, "none yet . . . but I promise."	*Executive stops asking about initiative (and probably fires the consultant, but that's another story . . .)*

That's our quick tour of the effects of consequences. Let's take a closer look.

Consequences That INCREASE Behavior: Positive and Negative Reinforcement

The first two consequences I introduced were positive reinforcement and negative reinforcement. Positive and negative reinforcement have something in common: they both **maintain** or **increase** the probability that the behavior they follow will occur in the future. Remember our examples? Maria continued to mow the lawn for her husband as a result of positive reinforcement.

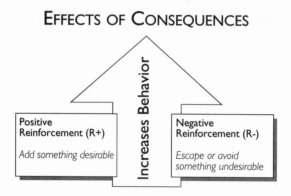

EFFECTS OF CONSEQUENCES

More About Negative Reinforcement

I have found that negative reinforcement is one of the trickiest concepts in behavioral science. For that reason, I'd like to spend a little more time explaining it and sharing examples.

The technical definition of negative reinforcement tells us that it involves "removing or preventing an undesired consequence," which maintains or increases the likelihood that the behavior will continue. What does that mean, exactly? First, it means that a behavior can remove an undesired consequence—in other words, people can behave in order to escape something negative. It also means that behavior can function to prevent an undesired consequence—people can behave in some way to *avoid* something negative. So, we have to look at both "escape" and "avoidance." Let's start with escape.

In some instances, negative reinforcement is a matter of escape—getting away from something unpleasant. The examples in the figure show how escape works to increase a behavior in the future. In each of these examples, the consequences of escape will likely increase the future probability of the behaviors they follow.

Examples of Negative Reinforcement in Escape

Antecedents	Behavior	Consequences	Impact on Future Behavior
Alarm clock sounds at 5 A.M. Joe is still tired	Joe hits snooze button on the alarm clock	Joe escapes annoying sound of alarm	*Joe will hit snooze when alarm goes off if he is still tired*
Claire sees a person who has nagged her in the past walking down the hall toward her office	Claire closes the door to her office	Claire escapes having to talk to the person who nags her	*Claire will close her door to avoid having to talk to the person who nags her*
A writer has trouble writing the opening paragraph of a report and feels stressed	Writer leaves desk and takes a walk	Writer reduces stress of "writer's block" by escaping the place where the problem is occurring	*Writer will likely leave desk temporarily when she experiences "writer's block"*
A director needs to prepare a budget. To do so, she has to untangle three sets of conflicting reports	Director chooses to spend time working on the annual plan (due in two months) rather than the budget (due in two days)	Director makes progress on an important work task (annual plan) and escapes contact with difficult work (budget)	*Director will work on "easier" work versus more complicated or aversive tasks*

In other cases, negative reinforcement is a matter of avoidance—keeping something unpleasant from happening. As a result, the behavior is more likely to be repeated. With avoidance, a threat exists, and the person acts in a way that reduces that threat.

Examples of Negative Reinforcement in Avoidance

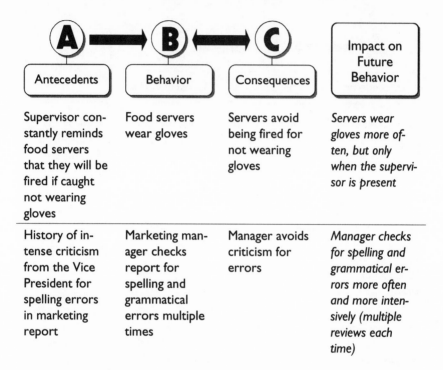

A Antecedents	B Behavior	C Consequences	Impact on Future Behavior
Supervisor constantly reminds food servers that they will be fired if caught not wearing gloves	Food servers wear gloves	Servers avoid being fired for not wearing gloves	*Servers wear gloves more often, but only when the supervisor is present*
History of intense criticism from the Vice President for spelling errors in marketing report	Marketing manager checks report for spelling and grammatical errors multiple times	Manager avoids criticism for errors	*Manager checks for spelling and grammatical errors more often and more intensively (multiple reviews each time)*

In the examples above, the threat comes from the chance of being fired (in the first case) and frequent feedback from a highly critical boss (the second case). In both examples, the presence of the threat triggers avoidance behaviors. These avoidance behaviors are followed by an immediate decrease in the threat. This "relief" is a powerful motivator for increasing the behavior that produces the relief. Negative reinforcement increases the behavior, but it requires a threat so that relief is possible. Otherwise, the motivation isn't strong enough to make the behavior worthwhile. Therefore, negative reinforcement reinforces a behavior *only as long as the threat is perceived.*

Negative reinforcement and discretionary effort seldom occur together. When the consequence for a behavior is negative reinforcement, people often perform a task *only* because they will be criticized if they don't. In other words, they will exert only the necessary effort to avoid criticism. Such conditions rarely produce the highest quality performance that a person can achieve. Managers must create conditions where best efforts occur, and this can best be accomplished through consistent use of positive reinforcement.

In large organizations, managers face many important priorities that compete for their time. This means that finding time to provide the consistent positive reinforcement needed to create an optimally productive work environment is sometimes not easy. However, for any manager, no other activity is more important for the long-term success of the company.

Consequences That DECREASE Behavior: Punishment and Extinction

With positive reinforcement, we saw how behavior would continue or increase by adding something desirable. With negative reinforcement, we saw how behavior would continue or increase by escaping or avoiding something undesirable. Similarly, behavior will *decrease* when something undesirable is added (punishment) or when something desirable is withheld (extinction). Let's take a look at examples of punishment and extinction.

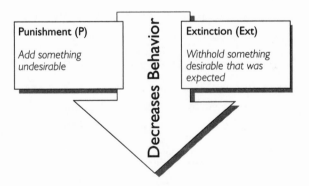

Punishment

Punishment often affects much more than just the specific behavior being targeted. In an example we saw earlier, the punishment eliminated sidebar talking, *but also decreased useful contributions to the meeting.* Therefore, when using punishment, it is essential to first pinpoint the behaviors you are punishing and then apply consequences appropriately. Later, you can find opportunities to reinforce *desirable* behavior.

Both of these practices will help you demonstrate that you are punishing *behavior*, not *people*.

Caution: The Side Effects of Punishment

Punishment certainly affects performance, and it can work quickly. Often, behavior decreases immediately when it is punished. But relying only on punishment is not the best technique for trying to change behavior. This is because punishment tends to produce undesirable side effects:

- People may become frustrated or unhappy
- People may feel embarrassed and stop participating altogether
- People may focus only on their own performance and not their team's
- People may avoid contact with you
- The frequency of similar, desirable performances may also decrease
- Desired behaviors are not encouraged
- Retention of employees, quality of work life, overall productivity, etc. may suffer

Positive Reinforcement Is an Alternative

Positive reinforcement, when used appropriately, can affect performance without the negative side effects of punishment or extinction. Here are some of the effects of positive reinforcement:

- Positive feelings about work and capabilities
- Examining not just own performance, but also team's performance
- Contact with providers of positive feedback
- No reduction in related desired performances—in fact, increases are possible
- A positive, proactive organizational culture of managing performance

Personal Note: Punishment and Parenting

I see the greatest potential for misuse of punishment in parent-child interactions. Sometimes, when children misbehave repeatedly and seem not to care that their parents are furious and frustrated, techniques like "time out" or describing the wrong behavior feel inferior to spanking, threatening, or returning the obscenities or unkind words the children are using.

However, I caution you . . . be certain you are punishing *the unwanted behavior* and *not the child*. Not speaking to the child, not making eye contact after the dispute has been settled, and not engaging in a "normal" conversation after the end of a behavior mishap are common examples of punishing the person and not the behavior. Children need to know you still love them—and that they are not "bad people" just because they exhibited some bad behavior. As parents, we need to be careful to effectively punish unwanted behavior and reinforce other, preferred behaviors. And we should just as actively and effectively demonstrate our love and positive regard for our children as people.

Extinction

Behavior also will decrease when something *positive* is *removed*, in which case we call it **extinction**. The sequence of events for extinction is a little trickier. In all of the previous examples, a person did something and a consequence followed immediately. In extinction, a person is accustomed to receiving something positive, but then the positive consequence stops.

With extinction, behavior sometimes does not decrease right away. The behavior may actually increase immediately after the reinforcement stops. In fact, the strength of the behavior may be greater than ever before. However, after peaking, the behavior decreases irregularly and ultimately disappears altogether. A few examples will help you understand extinction.

> *Example 1*: For three months, an employee got a cranky copier to work by opening the output door and slamming it shut. Then, one day, slamming the door no longer worked. The employee slammed it several times—harder and harder. Finally, he stopped slamming the door and called the repair service. For a

while, he slammed the copier door whenever the copier mal-functioned. Eventually, he stopped slamming the door (extinction) and went directly to call service.

Example 2: A software development team in a major software company created a wonderful team culture. The team leader was very effective; she regularly provided feedback and prompted the team to celebrate milestones. Halfway through the project, she was promoted and moved to another position. The new team leader was much more outcome-focused and did not provide feedback or prompt celebrations. The team performance graph showed a consistently high level of milestones achieved by month (95 percent achieved) under the original leader. After the change in leaders, the trend stayed high initially and even peaked at 100 percent for two months. However, for months 3, 4, and 5, the trend dropped steadily from 90 percent to 85 percent to 75 percent, an all-time low. Team performance was extinguished by a lack of feedback.

Example 3: BioLabs hired a new research scientist whose graduate school advisor provided lots of personal attention to students who worked hard. During his first months on the job, the new scientist stayed late and worked weekends to perform extra assays. But no one ever expressed appreciation of the extra work he did. Pretty soon he stopped doing the extra work.

What Happens When We Don't Reinforce Behavior?

When a behavior occurs and reinforcement does not follow, eventually that behavior will no longer occur. It is tempting to say that performance has been punished, because the rate of behavior decreased, all the way to nothing!

However, not providing reinforcement is NOT the same as punishment. Punishment involves *providing* a condition that an individual considers aversive or undesired. *Withholding* reinforcement is therefore not the same thing as punishment.

When reinforcement is not provided, and the rate of behavior decreases to nothing, the process is called **extinction**. Extinction of a performance follows a unique pattern.

The rate of performance change is different when reinforcement is withheld, or not provided, compared to punishment:

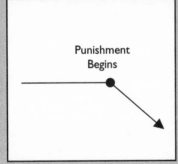

When punishment is applied, there is an immediate decrease in the rate of behavior, usually until the behavior stops.

When reinforcement is withheld (extinction begins), an immediate increase in the behavior rate will occur. This is called an "extinction burst." Once the extinction burst has subsided, the behavior rate tends to reduce as rapidly.

The extinction burst is the most difficult part of the extinction process. Often, people notice the initial behavior rate increase and abandon the extinction process because it appears to be encouraging the behaviors. But if the extinction process is allowed to continue, the behavior will eventually decline.

So, What Do I Do with Consequences?

After people understand the effects consequences have on behavior, they often ask, "So, what do I do now?" I often answer the question like this: It is important to recognize that consequences—positive reinforcement, negative reinforcement, punishment, and extinction—happen *every day for every behavior*. And leaders are often the sources of those consequences. Said another way, we often positively reinforce, negatively reinforce, punish, and extinguish behaviors. As leaders, each of us should become aware of how we choose to use consequences.

The Flogging Will Continue Until Morale Improves!

Leaders are defined by the consequences they choose. A leader who chooses punishment and extinction is clearly a coercive leader—hunting down unwanted behaviors and stamping them out. A leader who uses negative reinforcement also gets things done by threat and coercion, because, to provide relief from a threat, the leader must first create a threat and then remove it. When employees work with leaders like these, they will do only what they have to—they will comply only enough to avoid the negative consequences.

Contrast this with a leader who reinforces behavior. Employees who work for this type of leader will perform above and beyond the base level of expectation because they *want to*. *This is the secret to unleashing discretionary effort in your organization!*

In reality, leaders choose all types of consequences. The real issue is the *balance* they choose among consequences. I know many leaders who think they are positive managers, but who really use negative reinforcement or punishment as their primary leadership style. Here's a case I encountered in one company ...

Juan had a great track record as CFO. Every executive wanted Juan to run his or her financial systems. In fact, everyone said, "You won't have to coach Juan—he has it all down." I hoped for the best and set up some coaching meetings and plans to observe Juan in his team meetings. At first, Juan *did* seem to have it. His meetings were well-organized, and he often commented on the good things he heard or saw when his team reported on their progress. Then I began to notice a subtle behavior pattern. Several times during the meeting, Juan would stop, summarize the successes, and congratulate the team. Then he would say something like the following:

"We had a great month, and I am looking forward to another one coming up. All of you have done a wonderful job, and I congratulate you. But—*and I do mean but*—we are not across the finish line. We have to do what we did this month and more to make our quarterly numbers, and the next quarter is even more challenging. Celebrate, but don't rest on your laurels too long. We have a lot to do."

I quickly looked around the room and observed the faces. Like many of us during a long week, they showed the signs of a stressful job. But something else was there. In spite of their success, they seemed down. I stayed for a few minutes after the meeting and asked a couple of team members for their reactions. They both told me that Juan was "never satisfied." They explained that the goals kept getting higher and higher and that the pressure was subtle, but always there. The only relief from the pressure, they told me, occurred when the quarterly results went 20 percent above the goal level.

I went to see Juan for our regular coaching session. I described what I had observed about the meeting and the impact of

his behavior on the team. He looked shocked and told me his version.

"I want to be positive, and I try to tell them how much I appreciate what they do. I really do appreciate it, you know. But I just can't seem to trust that they won't let down their guard. I guess I'm afraid that they will take my positive feedback to mean they can relax. And, you know, I can never relax—they can never relax—we can never relax. It is a competitive world out there. I have to live with it, and they have to live with it too!"

You don't want a "great, but . . . "

Juan's "*great, but . . .* " behavior in verbal communication is one of the most frequent missteps leaders exhibit. In an effort to avoid misrepresenting a situation and to not leave people feeling as though everything's "all right," leaders (and parents!) have a tendency to say things like . . .

- "You did a great job in organizing the celebration with our key customers, but I had expected more of our customers to be present."
- "Our performance during the first quarter was on target and on budget, but I'm not sure we'll be able to pull it off two quarters in a row."
- "I'm pleased with your performance overall, but it's not quite where you need it to be if we're going to promote you. Keep up the great work—but you need to try harder."
- "I'm really proud of you, sweetheart. A 96 percent on your geometry test is a super grade. But what happened to the other four points?"

A way around a "great, but . . . " is to separate your feedback with some time, if possible. At the very least, you need to separate your statements. Here are a couple of the examples from above, reworked:

Example 1.

Less preferred: "You did a great job in organizing the celebration with our key customers, but I had expected more of our customers to be present."

Preferred: "You did a great job organizing the celebration with our key customers. I was very pleased with how it turned out. Did you expect that number of attendees? I thought the theme was just excellent and the booths were very effective for showcasing our new products . . . "

Example 2.

Less preferred: "Our performance during the first quarter was on target and on budget, but I'm not sure we'll be able to pull it off two quarters in a row."

Preferred: "We did a wonderful job during the first quarter. Our performance was on target and on budget, which pleased me greatly. This quarter is going to be a tough one, though. I know it will take everyone's maximum efforts to hit our numbers. How are you all feeling about it?"

A Lesson to Remember

The story and examples I just shared have a hidden lesson in them. People who provide consequences for behavior are also impacted! Remember Juan? He very much wanted to positively reinforce the team's efforts that led to great results, even though he needed to challenge the team to work even harder. As a result of his "great, but" statements, the team actually felt their behavior was being punished. No matter how hard they worked, they felt they couldn't please Juan and couldn't receive positive consequences for their efforts. What Juan didn't know was that his pattern of providing consequences—the "great, but"—was impacting his team's morale and perception of him. And that was a strong negative consequence for Juan!

Let's take a look at the impact of consequences, both on the person receiving them and on the person giving them . . .

Consequence	Effects on the Receiver	Effects on the Giver
Positive Reinforcement (R+)	Behavior will occur more often in the future	The giver is reinforced by strong business results
Increases performance by adding something desirable	Performance can be optimized by R+	If R+ is used often enough, the giver himself or herself is seen as reinforcing and is sought out as a colleague
	Consistent use of R+ creates an environment that in itself becomes reinforcing—in other words, working in the environment is reinforcing	
Negative Reinforcement (R-)	Task is made aversive by R-	The giver is reinforced by strong business results
Increases performance by escaping or avoiding something undesirable	The performer does only enough to avoid or escape the undesired consequence	If R- is used often enough, the giver himself or herself is seen as a threat or punisher and is avoided
	Performance levels can never be optimized and are typically 30-60 percent below levels attained with R+	
	Using R- as an ongoing strategy creates emotional undercurrents and discontent	
	Using R- makes employees and colleagues feel devalued	

Consequence	Effects on the Receiver	Effects on the Giver
Punishment Decreases performance by adding something undesirable	Punishment causes the performer not to do the behavior but does not teach the performer what to do instead The person receiving punishment often experiences strong emotional effects of frustration, fear, or aggression	The giver experiences negative consequences of weak business results If punishment is used often enough, the giver himself or herself is seen as a threat or punisher and is avoided
Extinction Decreases performance by withholding something desirable that was expected	The receiver often shows a burst of the behavior Because the positive event is withdrawn entirely, extinction can decrease a wide range of behaviors, including desired ones The person receiving extinction often experiences strong emotional effects of frustration, fear, or aggression	The giver is not likely to be reinforced because behavior change takes a long time with extinction The giver can be perceived as failing to keep promises

As you can see, consequences not only have important effects on the receiver, but also on the giver. Positive reinforcement (R+) optimizes performance, encourages discretionary effort, creates a rewarding work environment, and has great effects on the people you work with—and on you!

It's a Matter of When, Not If

You might be asking, "But aren't there times to use negative reinforcement or punishment?" Yes—in instances when you may need to affect a behavior very quickly. For example, punishment is appropriate when you see someone engaging in dangerous or illegal behavior. It also might be appropriate when an employee is systematically undermining an important initiative or work process. If you must resort to punishment—*and it should be only a rare occasion*—you need to do so within a supportive relationship. (There will be more about that relationship in the chapter on feedback and coaching.)

Negative reinforcement might be appropriate when you need to get behavior started quickly and positive reinforcement has not been effective. For example, let's say you are interested in having a manager in your finance organization work closely with the marketing manager to straighten out budget issues. Your requests (*antecedents*) and words of encouragement (*intended positive reinforcement*) have so far not resulted in their working together. This means that your efforts have *not* functioned as positive reinforcement. In this case, you may need to apply negative consequences like scheduling a meeting of them with you to inquire about how they would like to work together. They will likely choose to meet on their own to avoid the embarrassment and aversiveness of their boss sitting down with them to discuss the matter. You can offer to cancel the meeting if they show evidence that they have met and have resolved the budget issues. In all likelihood, they will have done this.

The Four Types of Consequences

Every behavior has a consequence. And every consequence has an effect. As you've seen, the effects a consequence can have on behavior include positive reinforcement, negative reinforcement, punishment, and extinction. Now it's time to turn our attention to the types and sources of the consequences that affect behavior.

Every behavior we perform—speaking, breathing, blinking, saying "thank you," writing, reading, closing a sale, walking, praising performance, turning a valve, thinking, holding a performance review—has an immediate consequence. Sometimes the consequence is quite subtle, as in feeling pressure on our fingers as we hold a tool. Other consequences are not so subtle, as in when we receive a bonus for completing a project on time and under budget. The importance of such a consequence, however, becomes clear only when it is lost.

Let's look at the four ways consequences are provided:

1. *Feedback*—information about a performance, words of praise, applause, frowns, smiles, measurement data that allow you to evaluate performance, etc.
2. *Tangible items*—things that can be physically touched, held, or exchanged for other physical items, such as money, trinkets, plaques, letters of commendation, movie tickets, etc.
3. *Activities*—the opportunity to participate in a desirable activity as a result of doing another behavior. Examples of activity consequences include preferred work activities, company-sponsored recreation activities, conference attendance, training, etc.
4. *Work processes*—the next step of the work being performed. For example, if an order is entered into the computer system, the next step is that it will be shipped later that day.

Let us look at each of the four ways to provide consequences.

1. Providing Consequences Through Feedback

Feedback is a flow of information about a *behavior* or its *result* back to the performer. In the context of ABC Analysis, providing feedback means providing information to a person who then adjusts his or her behavior accordingly. Normally, we talk about positive feedback and constructive feedback.

- Positive feedback provides performers with words of praise and commendation that result in their repeating the rewarded behaviors in the future.
- Constructive feedback is more complex. It not only includes providing information designed to discourage an undesirable behavior that has occurred, but also specifying and encouraging a different, preferred behavior.

Positive feedback is easy for most folks to deliver. However, it is tough for some. I have worked with leaders who believe that positive feedback makes people think they've done enough and don't have to do any more. Others believe that people who need positive feedback are weak. Still others believe that people know what they need to do and don't need feedback about their performance. Whatever their reasoning, these managers are not comfortable delivering positive feedback, so they rarely provide it.

For most of us, delivering *constructive feedback* is more challenging. It involves pinpointing the behaviors we wish to discourage, while also pinpointing preferred behaviors. Constructive feedback *can* be done well, with grace and style, and can leave someone quite confident and able to change his or her behavior.

I have found that the most effective feedback, whether positive or constructive, is NORMS-based. Remember that NORMS is a tool to help you state your observations about behavior objectively (N=Not an interpretation, O=Observable, R=Reliable, M=Measurable, S=Specific).

I saw a wonderful example of constructive feedback when a manager spoke to a direct report following a meeting on discretionary bonuses ...

George, I wanted to share some feedback on the meeting. Having participated in these sessions for three years, I can say it was our best one yet! We had everyone there, which required good scheduling on your end. Plus, the questions sent in advance allowed everyone to be a meaningful contributor. I think that went a long way toward helping the session.

The thing I would do differently next time is to ask people to put in writing who they felt should receive bonuses and why. When we went around the table, some people went on and on, while others had no data to back up their recommendations. It struck me that we never specified what we wanted them to tell us about their nominees.

To ensure it doesn't degrade into a popularity contest, maybe we could add a template to our pre-work that would clearly specify what data we were seeking—and would serve as a prompt for folks to submit the data in advance. What do you think?

The manager did an effective job pinpointing what went well, what didn't go well, and what she would prefer to see again in the future. The feedback was objective and NORMS-based, not personal. The manager used "we" to share ownership of the situation, rather than blaming George for any problems. Finally, she asked questions, rather than acting like "the expert." As a result, George felt good about the session and knew precisely what to do next year.

You'll learn a lot more about feedback, both positive and constructive, in Chapter 5.

2. Providing Consequences Through Tangible Items

Tangible consequences can be physically touched and held. They include trophies, pictures, mugs, commendation letters, money, movie tickets, nicer offices, lunch, etc. Tangible items are ubiquitous in corporate settings, especially if they carry the company logo. (My company uses jackets, lunches, nice dinners for families to enjoy privately, flowers for employees or their spouses, fruit baskets, etc.)

Tangible consequences can be very effective *if they are seen as positive in the eyes of the receivers.* I was at one company sales meeting where, in recognition for the record sales achieved that quarter, the top 200 sales people received tickets to the hottest running Broadway show. Now, while I would personally love such a gift, many of them did not. Instead of positively receiving them, most salespeople said things like, "I'd rather have the $250 . . . or "Who on earth came up with this hare-brained reward?" It was a tangible consequence meant to positively recognize the top performers, but instead it had a negative effect on many people in the group.

So, tangible reinforcers are tricky. The key thing to remember is that "beauty is in the eye of the beholder," or "reinforcers lie in their effect on the behaviors of the performers." A tangible item is only a reinforcer if the behavior it was intended to reinforce continues. One size does *not* fit all, and tangible reinforcers for one group could be judged as junk by others. One easy solution to this potential problem is to ask employees what tangible items they would appreciate receiving.

3. Providing Consequences Through Activities

Long ago, behavioral scientists discovered that an easy, preferred task will positively reinforce the completion of a harder, less-preferred task. Some people just love to do certain types of things. Some people love brainstorming; others hate it. Some people love working out all the details of a project; others prefer to focus on the big issues. So, an employee's favorite activity—such as being part of a planning team—will positively reinforce a less preferred one, such as preparing all the materials for an audit.

This is hardly breaking news: the power of *activity consequences* has long been known by parents and grandparents the world over. "Would you like dessert? You have to eat your peas." "Want to go outside to play? Finish your homework." "You'd like to invite your friends for a sleepover tomorrow night? Clean your room first."

Activity consequences can work the same way in business. One supervisor I knew had a team of about 12 people performing telemarketing work. They were on the phone all day long making cold calls, which was very punishing work because so few contacts resulted in a sale. Well, the supervisor discovered that the telemarketers preferred working on special teams over their daily work. In fact, so many people in her group were signing up for special teams that properly staffing her shifts was becoming difficult.

She could have decided to be on special teams herself away from the telemarketers, which would have forced them to stay at their desks. Instead, she went for a win-win approach. She made participating on special teams contingent upon telemarketing activities. In other words, the telemarketers had access to a preferred task (participating on special teams) based on their performance on a less-preferred task (making cold calls). She saw gains in productivity, and the employees were happy because they continued to participate on special teams.

4. Providing Consequences Through Work Processes

A specific form of activity consequence occurs within work processes themselves. Think of the different ways you approach work that gets harder and harder as you approach the end, versus the way you approach a task that gets easier and easier. When each step of the work gets easier and more pleasant as the process moves along, the later steps positively reinforce completion of the earlier steps. Whenever I help companies design work processes, I try to create a process that has easier tasks at the end. That way, the performer has some built-in positive reinforcement.

Creating a memo on the computer is an example of a work process. It has a starting and a stopping point, along with a series of steps in between. How many of you remember working on WordPerfect™ in the "old days," before it became the sophisticated product it is today? I sure do, and I remember how difficult it was to create a memo. The work process consequences I experienced with the old WordPerfect™ were very punishing. When I wanted to save my work, I had to remember which combination of <Shift> <Alt> <Function Key> would do it for me. When I wanted to boldface a word for emphasis, I had to experiment with a sequence of keys to do so. I felt more like I was trying to fly a jet airplane than writing a simple memo! The consequences of creating a memo in that program were punishing—the process was time-consuming, confusing, and difficult to remember. At first, I gave up trying to use boldface for emphasis—I simply couldn't remember how to do it. Eventually, I avoided writing memos altogether—I just made phone calls.

As soon as Windows-based word processing software became available, the work process consequences for creating a memo changed dramatically. I am now able to save my work by pointing and clicking on a single icon. I've even found that I can use **boldface**—not to mention *italics*—with ease.

The Importance of Consequence Alignment

One of the most common issues I see in companies is misaligned or nonaligned consequence systems. An example is when work processes are redesigned to promote collaboration and teamwork, but the tangible rewards remain individualized. Another example is a supervisor who positively reinforces preventive maintenance and proactive intervention before equipment failure, but who is later punished at bonus time because his expenses for the quarter are too high.

It's essential to align the consequences for behaviors you need for your company to be successful. Otherwise, you will be led into antecedent-based fixes to try and correct a problem that ultimately lies in the consequence systems.

Here's a quick test for you. See if your department's or company's consequence systems are aligned:

1. Do your employees receive positive feedback and tangible rewards for putting in time, rather than for exhibiting desired behaviors?

2. Can your employees engage in preferred activities by avoiding or handing off less preferred activities without experiencing negative consequences?

3. Do you deliver "tangible" rewards, such as trips and tickets, for desired behaviors without consulting with employees about their preferred reward?

4. Does your "vision statement" or "values for the organization" conflict with how employees are paid or recognized?

A "yes" to any of these items should be a caution that you most likely have a misalignment between the behaviors you desire and the consequences that impact behavior.

Given the influence that consequences have over our behavior, a lack of alignment of consequences can create inconsistent patterns of behavior that will be difficult to change unless the consequences are aligned.

Which Consequences Do YOU Provide to People?

The typical corporate leader relies on consequences such as bonuses, promotions, and reward systems to recognize desired behaviors. These consequences usually require little personal effort to deliver.

Leaders who rely on these positive consequences are underestimating the power and effect of *their words* and *their behaviors* on others. Money and promotions may be an important motivator for some behaviors, but research tells us that while it's a necessary source of reinforcement for us to work at all, it is not sufficient to motivate us to higher levels of performance. Feedback, especially from supervisors and peers, is the way to motivate our highest levels of performance.

This is why it so important to seize the opportunity to reinforce specific behaviors that are important to you and to the success of your organization. Get out and talk with your people. *Work with them to identify the consequences that will increase the key behaviors they need to exhibit to attain your desired business results.*

Positive Reinforcement Tips

How do you increase your use of positive reinforcement and help ensure that the consequences you arrange have the intended positive impact?

1. **Being there helps**—Positive reinforcement works best when delivered immediately after the behavior. Being present to observe the behavior and deliver the consequences makes immediate reinforcement possible.

2. **The receiver judges impact**—The receiver of consequences is the ultimate judge of whether or not the positive reinforcement was used. Asking people to describe how they are affected is one way to determine what happened. Also, subtle signs of impact can be sensed by directly observing the reactions of a person (facial expressions, comments, reactions of others, etc.).

3. **Consistency counts**—Effective positive reinforcement requires repeated delivery of the consequence following the pinpointed behavior across days, weeks, and months.

4. **Variety counts**—The same positive reinforcer may lose its value if it is delivered the same way over and over. Develop a collection of consequences that are likely to have positive effects and vary the ones you use. For example, you might deliver praise by e-mail, face-to-face, or through a note.

5. **Combine short-term and long-term consequences**—Immediate consequences such as praise, public recognition, and short celebrations are more effective if they are linked to long-term consequences such as performance appraisal results, merit raises, resources for individual or team projects (e.g., computers) and broad public recognition (e.g., award given at a corporate quality conference).

6. **Monitor the 4:1 ratio**—A good rule of thumb is to deliver four times as much positive feedback as constructive feedback. Keeping track of your record and making adjustments to maintain the ratio helps to meet this goal.

7. **Ask people what they like**—Positive reinforcement includes any consequence that increases the strength of a behavior, but in many cases, the effect of a consequence can't be confirmed directly. In this case, asking people what they like and what they feel is a positive reinforcer for their behavior is a good approach. Most people know what they like and are willing to talk about it.

8. **Watch carefully to create a list of positive reinforcers**—Nothing works better for identifying positive reinforcers than careful observation. Anytime you are around peers, team members, or supervisors, keep a close eye on the kinds of foods they like, how they use their break time, the reading materials they prefer, and so on. Develop a list using your observations and surprise them by picking just the right consequence to celebrate success.

9. **Teach others to positively reinforce**—Teaching team members to use positive reinforcement with each other is a good way to expand its use within your team. Reinforce the use of positive reinforcement by others.

One More Time: Consequences Drive Behavior

If you harbor any doubts that consequences drive behavior, read this dismaying story, told to me on a flight home one night. This fellow had worked for 12 years at a major heavy equipment company, but now was bailing out. Here is his story . . .

I once would have stood in front of a train for this company! I felt that much devotion to who we are and what we do. And I still feel that devotion to our *customers*, but I no longer feel it for the *company*.

They just kept demanding too much. You know, they never once bothered to say "thank you." My marriage is on the line, I have a young child who barely knows me, and I travel almost every weekend. I fly to Tokyo, make a sale, and fly back.

I would do anything for this company because I believe in our products, I believe in what we do, and I know that we can help our customers be even more successful by using our products.

All it would take is for them just to say "thank you"—for them to tell me that my work matters—to show they care.

But I am leaving this company. Next week I begin working elsewhere, and you know what, the company will never understand their role in my decision to leave. I'll tell them in my exit interview tomorrow morning. I will tell them they are losing good people like me who would kill for this company. Simply said, they just don't give a darn about people.

What saddens me most is that the people at the top of this organization have no clue. They make short-term decisions. They rob people of $500 and $1,000 bonuses that to them make all the difference. Last year we really earned our bonuses, which are contingent on whether we stay beneath an inventory target. For eleven straight months we celebrated coming in under our targets. Then, around the end of the tenth month, a new general manager came in.

You know how the game is played. The new GM comes in and has to make the prior numbers look bad, especially since it's the end of the year—so he can turn it around and show that it looks so much better the following year because of him. That's the game, everybody knows it, everybody plays it, that's how it is.

So he comes in and starts saying that it doesn't look like we are going to make our bonus this year. And I say, "What the hell do you mean we are not going to make our bonus this year? We've been within our inventory limits for eleven straight months!" And he says, "No, I just don't think we'll make it; we are way over our inventory this month." The corporate controller is sitting right there. I look him straight in the eye and say, "What the hell are you talking about? What numbers are you showing him?"

The controller squirms in his seat and says, "Well, it does look like what he is saying is true. It doesn't look like we are going to make those targets for the year because of this month's miss." Well, I am furious. I tell the controller that we should recalculate the numbers to be sure they are correct—because they don't seem right from my data set.

I then say, "We should do whatever is in our power to make them right because those people have been busting their butts for eleven months straight. They are counting on that $1,000 bonus, and it means the world to them. For them to have to go home now and tell their families that they didn't make it would not only be morally wrong, but it would devastate the 320 people in this little town who count on that money. You've got to be crazy!"

Well, the new GM says, "Hey, if we pay out $1,000 in bonuses to all of those people, we won't make our operating revenue targets and we'll be in trouble." He goes on to say that the decision was made and the numbers had already been submitted to corporate. And in fact they ended up not paying the $1,000 to the lower-level people!

Now I have to look them in the eye and tell them that they're not getting a bonus, that it makes sense, and that it is the right thing to do! It just makes me sick!

I have made my numbers every year that I have been there. I have always been in a turnaround business, and I have made

**great things happen. But it happens because I know how to mo-
tivate my people—and show them that I care and that their efforts matter.**

**You know, I went to the Naval Academy. That is how I got
through college. They worked me as hard there as I possibly
could have worked. But you know what, I could keep up that
pace for the rest of my life because it was physical labor, and
we're talking about getting physically tired and straining mus-
cles and running hard. But that is nothing compared to the
stress, the mind games, and the feeling that you are inadequate,
that you don't matter, that you are expendable, and that people
just don't care. That is the kind of crap I just can't take.**

**I go home after busting my butt every single day. I know I am
making a difference to the people who report to me, but you
look upward and you see people who worry only about flying on
their corporate jets and beating the system so they can make
their six-figure bonuses. Frankly, I've had enough.**

This story reminded me of the power of consequences. This manager had valuable discretionary effort to give to his company—he
looked for ways to contribute by flying overseas, making sales, and
spreading the company's name. Unfortunately, his behavior was extinguished. No one ever recognized his behavior with a "thank you." Not
only did he have discretionary effort to give, but his people did too. As
a leader, he recognized his role in providing consequences to other
employees. He established relationships with them and made a promise
to reward their work with a year-end bonus. But when that promise
was broken by someone else in the organization, he knew the company
had blown it. They had an opportunity to demonstrate their values for
hard work and for employees, and they failed. They also missed an
opportunity to tap into employees' discretionary effort—why would
employees continue to "bust their butts" for consequences the
company yanks out of their hands?

One of the many sad parts of this story is that leaders in the organization did not realize their impact on behavior. Did they intend to
make people feel taken advantage of and cheated? Probably not. But
did they actually make people feel this way? They certainly did. It goes

to show you that *you can have good intentions when it comes to motivating employees, but intentions don't guarantee you'll succeed.* How you manage consequences and their effects on behavior is the true test. Employees are motivated when the *effects* of the consequences you provide are reinforcing.

The Bottom Line on Consequences

We've covered some very important foundation pieces—especially the role of consequences in influencing behavior. Here are the top four points I hope you take away from this chapter.

1. *There is a consequence for every single behavior.* Every consequence affects behavior. We don't need to be aware of what's going on for consequences to influence behavior.

2. *There are four effects consequences can have on behavior:*

   - *Positive Reinforcement (R+)*—adding something desirable to increase the likelihood behavior will occur again
   - *Negative Reinforcement (R-)*—escaping or avoiding something undesirable to increase the likelihood behavior will occur again
   - *Punishment (P)*—adding something undesirable to decrease the likelihood behavior will occur again
   - *Extinction (Ext)*—withholding something desirable to decrease the likelihood behavior will occur again

3. *The primary tool for unlocking discretionary effort in your organization is the application of positive reinforcement for desired behaviors*—those behaviors that lead to important business results.

4. *Consequences come in different forms:*

   - *Feedback*—a flow of information about behavior or a result, back to the performer
   - *Tangible Items*—items that can be physically touched or held

- *Activities*—arranging activities so that having access to an easier or preferred task is contingent upon completing a difficult or less-preferred task
- *Work processes*—Performing the task is reinforcing in and of itself

Do recognition programs lead to better organizational performance, employee satisfaction, or customer satisfaction?

Recognition is intended to influence people to do their jobs in a way that has a positive business impact. The wide range of behaviors, results, and events that can be recognized include service anniversaries, attendance, customer service, revenue generation, project completion, safety, and collections. Unfortunately, many recognition programs fail to have a business impact. This happens because they are not integrated with strategic planning or operations. Thus, they often send mixed messages to the organization.

Successful recognition resides in the organization's behaviors and consequence system. Start by integrating recognition with strategic planning and operations. You can do so by recognizing critical behaviors that are likely to impact important business results. This helps your organization know how it is getting results, and rewards how those results are achieved. You use recognition systems to shape desired behaviors to get those results.

As our CYBER model shows, you must be clear about the business opportunity and the critical results you seek. Then, you must pinpoint the behaviors that drive those results. Place recognition systems where they can help your organization reinforce those pinpointed behaviors and achieve strategic results.

What's Next?

Now that you are grounded in the principles of behavioral science—including the importance of consequences of behavior—it's time to look at how to apply the concepts you've been reading about.

So far, our journey has taken us through Steps 1–4 of the CYBER Model. In particular, I shared with you the contribution of behavioral science to Steps 3 and 4. I shared with you the science and art of pinpointing behaviors that drive organizational results. And I shared with you the fundamental tools for understanding the influences on behavior—the ABC Analysis and the power of consequences.

The next chapter, on feedback and coaching, begins our journey into the *application* of behavioral science. Step 5 of the CYBER Model tells us to Develop and Implement a Behavior Change Plan. The best place to start is with feedback and coaching, since they are such powerful consequences for influencing behavior.

CYBER Model

1. Identify business opportunity

2. Target results and measures of success

3. Pinpoint and align behaviors that drive results

4. Understand the influences on behavior

5. Develop, implement, and adjust behavior change plan

6. CELEBRATE achievement of improved results!

Feedback and Coaching: Your Secret Weapons!

I listened in awe to the Vice Chairman of a major oil company as he keynoted an international petroleum conference. He revealed the company's major strategies in intimate and remarkable detail—where they were drilling and expanding wells, seeking wealth in new areas of exploration—verging upon giving away the store, it seemed to me.

Then he revealed an even more remarkable thing. "What we are doing on the people side is where our real success is going to come from. This is how we are going to make a real difference in our performance as an organization. It is one of the most exciting things that I have been a part of. But, you know what? I'm not going to tell you about it! The reason I am not going to tell you about it is because we believe it is our secret weapon."

THE VICE CHAIRMAN'S "secret weapon" for success was not better geology, drilling, or chemistry. He was referring to **feedback and coaching**, and he was absolutely right. They are the most underutilized levers for encouraging the heart, the mind, and the contribution of discretionary effort.

Feedback is information given to an individual or a group about their behavior and its impact. Powerful and supportive feedback is given sincerely, without trepidation, and is in the spirit of helping, not harming. Effective leaders are comfortable delivering and receiving feedback. Feedback is the most powerful consequence you can deliver as a leader and shaper of performance—much more powerful than money. When used well, feedback and coaching are indeed your secret weapons!

If it is important to sustain or improve performance, to encourage outstanding performance, or to develop a more loyal crew that feels free to speak up, then performance feedback is the answer. The key is to do three things:

- *Coach people with objective feedback*: use things you have directly observed or directly heard others say (good or bad).
- *Coach people by sharing the effect of their actions, good or bad, on yourself and others in the organization.* Don't leave them wondering what you think of their performance.
- *Coach people by demonstrating your desire to help and not harm.*

> *As a leader, you can use feedback and coaching as a powerful consequence to influence performance. Research has shown time and again that money is necessary but is not sufficient to motivate performance. Feedback, especially your feedback as a leader, is the most powerful motivator of performance.*

It is critical that you understand the power of your feedback. It can build people up or tear them down, in part because people listen to and analyze much of what leaders say. In this chapter, I will present to you the tools for using feedback and coaching effectively. I will share with you the proven techniques I use with executives—the same techniques you can use to become a champion coach who develops people by giving feedback that matters.

Why Performance Appraisals Aren't Enough

"Leadership 101" always talks about the importance of evaluating performance. In most companies, leaders are asked to fill out those tedious evaluation forms, evaluate their people's performance, and assign ratings. Then they call in the individuals for a meeting to get "performance discussions" over with. The process takes time, it doesn't work very well, employees hate it, and leaders hate it. Often, this poor process sends the wrong signals despite the good intent. The unfortunate effect is that top and above-average performers often go unrecognized or are encouraged only by a "Keep it up!" or "We need more of the same." And poor performers remain uncoached and ignorant of how they might improve their performance.

In fact, as I work within and across large and small corporations, the complaints I hear most often are about poorly conducted performance reviews. Here are three recent examples:

My performance review was done in an elevator. My boss said I was doing a fine job and hoped I understood that she'd let me know if there were any problems. Oh . . . and she mentioned that we both were so busy that we needn't waste time going over that ridiculous HR form. We both could better spend our time on real work.

—*Executive Vice President of Marketing, Fortune 100 company*

You know, Leslie, I was in this office [the CEO's corner office] only once before I took this position—and that was when they told me that I had been selected as the new Chairman! I was dumbfounded. I hadn't been given any feedback in over five years. I always thought I was doing a good job, but I sure never heard words to that effect. I was never told that my contributions were valued or that I was even considered as a candidate for a job like this!

—*CEO of a major company*

I'll never forget my first performance review! I'd been here four months. My supervisor said I was doing great and everything was fine, and I was given my six-month bonus early. I was thrilled—until the next day—when our entire department received a shutdown notice, and we were all told to apply for new positions within the company! Those who couldn't find a job within six weeks would receive a severance package with one month's pay. I make six figures! This isn't supposed to happen to an engineer with a graduate degree and over ten years of experience!

—Engineer leading software development for a technology company currently trading with a 40 P/E ratio

These stories demonstrate lost opportunities to reinforce desired behaviors and provide continuous feedback that will help good performers see what they need to do to improve.

Let's look at performance appraisals from a PIC/NIC viewpoint:

Consequences of Performance Evaluations	P/N	I/F	C/U
Performance description given was vague and addressed events not under performer's control	N	F	U
Evaluations did not consider antecedents or consequences	N	F	U
Information shared during performance evaluation was tied only loosely to everyday performance	N	F	U

At best, the *consequence* to the person whose performance is being evaluated is negative, future, and uncertain. In other words, performance evaluations have relatively little influence over the day-to-day activities of employees. They are simply too far removed from the performance.

Even without this PIC/NIC analysis on the effectiveness of traditional performance appraisals, high-performing leaders do not rely solely on traditional annual performance reviews. Instead, they invest their time selectively by providing *frequent, pinpointed* feedback and coaching to their direct reports and to the organization at large.

The Link to CYBER

CYBER Model

```
      ┌─────────────────────┐
      │    1. Identify       │
      │     business         │
      │   opportunity        │
      └─────────────────────┘
                 │
                 ▼
      ┌─────────────────────┐
      │ 2. Target results and│
      │ measures of success  │
      └─────────────────────┘
                 │
                 ▼
      ┌─────────────────────┐
      │ 3. Pinpoint and align│
      │ behaviors that drive │
      │      results         │
      └─────────────────────┘
                 │
                 ▼
      ┌─────────────────────┐
      │ 4. Understand the    │
      │ influences on behavior│
      └─────────────────────┘
                 │
                 ▼
      ┌─────────────────────┐
      │ 5. Develop, implement,│
      │ and adjust behavior  │
      │     change plan      │
      └─────────────────────┘
                 │
                 ▼
      ┌─────────────────────┐
      │   6. CELEBRATE       │
      │   achievement of     │
      │  improved results!   │
      └─────────────────────┘
```

Step 5 is where feedback and coaching come in. Once you know which behaviors lead to business results and understand why the behaviors are occurring or not, it is your job to influence those behaviors. One of your primary tools for doing so is feedback. Systematically providing feedback about the behaviors that matter is one of the best ways I know to create results.

Just What Is Feedback?

Have you ever rehearsed a speech by presenting it to a mirror? If you have, you know the power of instant feedback. Every nuance of your behavior is reflected back at you, enabling you to see clearly what you're doing right and what you're doing wrong. This immediate feedback is invaluable in improving your performance.

Key points about feedback:

- Feedback is information you receive—somehow—about your behavior.
- Feedback is a **consequence** of your behavior.
- Feedback is most powerful when it is specific and is received immediately following the behavior.
- Feedback is a way of shaping desirable behaviors or changing less effective behaviors.
- Feedback helps a person know whether he or she is on the right path toward achieving a goal.

Feedback is a highly effective coaching tool because it focuses attention on critical performance. It is especially valuable during times of change. It is also the most underutilized tool in many leaders' toolboxes.

Managers and other coaches of performance (including parents) want to see an increase in desired behaviors and a decrease in undesired ones. Feedback is an important tool for encouraging these changes, because feedback can maintain, increase, or decrease behavior, depending on the kind of feedback given. The three kinds of feedback are (1) positive feedback, (2) constructive feedback, and (3) no feedback.

EFFECTS OF FEEDBACK

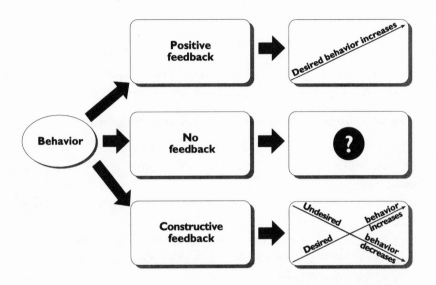

We deliver *positive feedback* to encourage desired behavior. We use *constructive feedback* to discourage undesired behavior and to encourage desired behavior.

If no positive feedback is given for effective or appropriate behaviors, they are likely to decrease. If no constructive feedback is given for ineffective or inappropriate behaviors, those behaviors are likely to continue or may even increase in frequency.

The absence of any planned feedback can be very damaging because it leaves the performer wondering, and it can send unintended (and untruthful) messages to the performer. This is a highly preventable situation! We can avoid unproductive time spent wondering, worrying, feeling bad without cause, or feeling positive when we shouldn't (ignorant bliss).

What about you as a leader in your organization? Do you effectively solicit and receive feedback about your own performance? Because of the nature of many leadership positions, leaders often become isolated, removed from situations in which they receive feedback naturally. It is critical that you find ways to keep in touch and to *solicit* feedback as well as deliver it.

Let me emphasize that the success of feedback is not guaranteed. Its success depends on how the feedback is given and on the relationship between the giver and the receiver. (I'll return to this point a little later.)

*So, feedback is information you receive—somehow—about your behavior. Feedback is a **consequence** of your behavior. And feedback is most powerful when it is specific and you receive it immediately following the behavior.*

Positive Feedback Powerfully Reinforces Behavior

When leaders use positive feedback, they intend to increase or maintain the likelihood that a desired behavior will occur again. Positive feedback, when delivered effectively, also leaves a person feeling good about his or her accomplishments. For these reasons, positive feedback is the primary way effective leaders reinforce behavior.

How do you give positive feedback? This may seem obvious, but in the hustle of your hectic days, you may not think about it. You give positive feedback through . . .

- Your words ("Excellent project summary! It is precisely what the customer asked for. Thank you!")
- Your gestures (smile, handshake, pat on the back, thumbs-up)
- Your symbols (gift, lunch, humorous award, time spent with the individual)
- Your concern and compassion (acknowledging difficult accomplishments and challenges)
- Your actions (invitations to events, taking someone out to lunch)

All of these are ways to sincerely communicate your perception of the goodness and the contribution of behaviors you want to reinforce. We use positive feedback as a way to reinforce behaviors that we want to continue or increase in frequency. It is a wonderful way to demonstrate our sincere interest in the behavior and in the performer.

We All Need Positive Feedback

So often people assume that others do not need positive feedback. In fact, *all* of us do. Our behavior is impacted most when we receive positive feedback promptly. Positive feedback has its greatest impact when it is delivered immediately after the behavior occurs. The shorter the delay between behavior and feedback, the greater the impact of the feedback.

Here is a story about a highly effective leader who had to wait a bit too long for his feedback. I supported this CEO, whom I'll call Mark, during his final years at the helm. I had the good fortune to attend his retirement dinner . . .

> **One by one, Mark's direct reports and peers shared their appreciation for his leadership and entrepreneurial spirit as he led the way for corporate and industry transformation.**
>
> **Mark's direct reports thanked him passionately for his sensitive coaching and commitment to leadership, which he demonstrated by his relentless pursuit for continuous improvement and stretch objectives. His boss, the Board Chairman, told of the Board's faith in him and how he would be missed.**
>
> **After the party, I met with Mark for our final coaching discussion. He shared how he was taken aback by the specific, personal, positive feedback he received at the dinner from all levels of the organization. *Then he told me that he had received virtually none of this feedback during his 33 years with the company!***
>
> **In fact, he continued, were it not for our coaching relationship, he probably would have abandoned some of the new behaviors he was trying because they seemed unappreciated and unimportant to the folks he wanted to affect. But, after hearing the feedback that evening, he recognized that his behavior changes *were* appreciated and important to the success of the business.**

It was unfortunate that more of that feedback hadn't been delivered to Mark when he needed it most: during the previous third of a century! *Positive feedback needs to be timely to help others succeed.* Imagine how much more powerful the feedback would have been if it had been delivered earlier! I wish this story were unique—but it is all too common that I hear executives share their frustration with insufficient feedback.

What should you take away from this story?

- Feedback is vital to personal development and effectiveness.
- *Positive feedback* is rarely provided. Either we think people don't need positive feedback or we are uncomfortable providing it. And I've heard people say, "No one gives me feedback, so why should I bother providing it to someone else?" The truth is that each of us needs positive feedback—especially when learning a new behavior or making an effort to change old behaviors.
- *Specific feedback* on new and desired behaviors is rarely provided. If you provide positive, specific feedback for behaviors that matter in your business, I assure you it will have a significant impact on your people and your results.

Feedback takes time (for folks who have little or none to spare). Feedback requires thought (by people racing from one task to the next). Feedback requires you to have knowledge of what the performer did. For these reasons, feedback gets put off the "top 10" list and relegated to a when-I-have-time priority. Don't let this happen to you! Take charge and establish yourself as a positive reinforcer for things that matter to you and your business.

Why Don't We Give More Positive Feedback?

There are several reasons why we don't provide more feedback. In fact, there are some common objections to using praise or positive feedback:

1. Our culture doesn't do a good job of teaching us how to give or receive positive feedback. We are often more comfortable using sarcasm or negativity.

2. Some people believe we shouldn't be praised for performance that is "expected."

3. Individuals need positive feedback at different intervals and detail levels. (This applies to teams as well.) In general, we need frequent and detailed feedback when we are learning a new task or behavior. As we become more proficient in the task, we need less frequent, less detailed feedback.

4. Often we think that only our top performers deserve feedback. If we tell our "mediocre" or average performers that we are pleased with what they did, are we sending the signal that everything they do is OK? No, not if we pinpoint specifically the behaviors for which we are providing positive feedback.

Positive Feedback Delivery Skills

Effective delivery of positive feedback is tricky. Not only must your delivery be effective, but you also must manage the receiver's reaction to your words. The following tips will help you provide positive feedback with confidence. I have separated them into "basic" and "advanced" techniques to signal progression toward excellence in feedback delivery.

Basic Techniques
(Must-Haves for Good Feedback Delivery)

1. Describe the performance objectively, specifically, and sincerely. Rely on the NORMS of objectivity to help you specify the behaviors you particularly liked. (Comment on specific actions or events. What was the performance? How did you learn of the performance?)

2. Deliver feedback as soon as possible after performance.

3. Don't wait until the performance is perfect. People need positive feedback when their performance improves. Provide feedback for small improvements in behavior. (We call this "shaping" performance—the next chapter covers the ins and outs of shaping.)

4. Make sure your feedback was a reinforcer by observing whether performance improves or stays the same and whether the person or team is more effective.

5. Don't say, "Great! . . . but . . . " (Don't mix positive and constructive feedback—feedback intended to stop a behavior.)

Advanced Techniques
(Used by Highly Skilled Feedback Providers)

1. Tell the person how you felt about the performance and the positive reactions you observed by others in reaction to the performance.

2. Talk about any other positive effects the performance might have on other people or the team. (Describe how the person's actions create positive results for themselves, the team, or the organization.)

3. Get input from the person. Ask the following:

   - What did you think of your performance?
   - Has anyone else noticed?
   - Has this improved your ability to be successful?
   - How did you feel about that?

Sincerity Is Important

People have a special radar that senses the absence of sincerity when positive feedback is delivered! Your feedback will be viewed as insincere when:

- You provide feedback only when you have hard data
- You know very little about the person or the performance
- You make general statements like "great job" or "good work" or deliver an aerosol spray of positive feedback to everyone
- You don't allow time for questions or discussions
- You provide only positive feedback and never provide constructive feedback
- You provide feedback immediately after meeting the person
- You praise one person in front of others, with the goal of punishing those who haven't done the desired behavior

Create Winners!

Across time, try to deliver positive feedback four times for every instance of constructive feedback (4:1). Please refer to Appendix C for more detailed guidance on positive feedback delivery.

Precision Is Important

Let's look at the content of some statements to contrast their effectiveness. Please take this quick test. Below are statements of expectation or feedback. Statements on the right have a greater impact on behavior than statements on the left. Can you see why?

Less Impact	Greater Impact
"Your customer satisfaction numbers are unacceptable."	"I want your western sales region to increase customer retention by at least 20 percent beyond current performance."
"The joint venture with Wystat Corp. has really worked out for us."	"As a result of our joint venture with Wystat, revenues and operating margins are up over 16 percent, utilization rates are 22 percent better, and both companies report increased earnings per share."
"Jerry is an inspirational leader."	"Several employees told me that when Jerry shared his vision for the new organization, he excited folks and led to their approaching group meetings completely differently."
"You own information technology for our company."	"I expect you to develop our company's IT strategy to align with our business strategy. You are accountable for the success of all IT purchases and implementations, except for our LAN/WAN system, which will be run out of corporate."

The primary difference is that the statements in Column A are vague and unspecific. Those in Column B are more focused and identify specific behaviors.

Behavioral descriptions that relay specific expectations (Column B) are more likely to prompt desired behaviors than general descriptions (Column A). This is especially true in times of uncertainty or change, or when a performance is inconsistent with what is needed and behavior needs to change. People can more easily change their behavior when they clearly understand the antecedents: specific expectations and communication of what is desired or needed.

Similarly, when the consequences (like feedback) are precise and sincere, they have a stronger effect on the behaviors they follow. Being told you did a "great job" has low impact. But suppose your boss is specific: "Your sales presentation to XYZ company was fantastic. It led to a $3.2M sale of our products over the next year. That puts us over the top for our revenue target for the quarter. Congratulations!"

When you hear that, it's hard not to feel good! Each of us, and leaders especially, has an amazing power to reinforce desired behaviors—through our words, our attention, and our acts of support. Said behaviorally, by providing clear and necessary antecedents for the desired behaviors, and ensuring that the desired behaviors are reinforced by consequences, we can create an environment that enables each employee to be more successful. And if each of us performs well on strategically critical tasks, the company will perform well. Everyone wins!

Constructive Feedback Intends to Improve Behavior

People learn faster when they receive a mixture of consequences. In the 4:1 ratio, the 1 (constructive feedback) is very important. But positive feedback is often easier to give because it does not threaten. Plus, less-than-positive feedback can be touchy. The problem is that it has a negative aspect emotionally—telling someone that things aren't right and need to change. At my company, we have come to call it **constructive feedback** and intentionally distinguish it from negative (or corrective) feedback or criticism. Constructive feedback is a gift people give you when they want to help you be successful.

My distinction between *constructive feedback* and *negative feedback (criticism)* is deliberate. Negative feedback focuses on the "bad side" of performance and does little to help others improve. It simply points out the behaviors you no longer want. An unfortunate side effect of negative feedback is that it is often directed at the *person* rather than the *behavior*.

Constructive feedback, on the other hand, is more developmental in nature. It is intended *to discourage an undesired behavior and to replace it with a preferred behavior.* Unlike criticism, which is intended to harmfully stop a behavior, constructive feedback replaces the undesired behavior with a more effective behavior to decrease the likelihood that an undesired behavior will occur again.

Constructive feedback has two components that operate together:

1. *Punishing the undesired or less effective behavior* by describing what was wrong with it and the negative impact it had.
2. *Specifying a preferred behavior* so you are sure the performer has knowledge of the desired behavior.

Please note that I am using the word "punishing" in the technical sense. Punishing simply means using consequences to decrease the frequency of a behavior. In the case of constructive feedback, we use consequences to decrease the undesired or less effective behavior, so technically, we punish that behavior. Then, when you observe the new (preferable) behavior, be sure to provide the person with positive feedback.

Constructive feedback is extremely effective when you recognize that you are replacing one behavior (undesired or less effective) with another behavior (preferred). For the new behavior (preferred) to really take hold, the performer must receive positive feedback about that behavior. This means that your job is to "catch the person doing it right" and to encourage his or her behavior by delivering sincere, positive feedback.

Remember, always pinpoint the undesirable behavior(s) as well as the desired behavior(s) when providing constructive feedback.

> *Use only NORMS-based observations and descriptors to provide good constructive feedback! Avoid subjective language. When giving feedback, be as pinpointed and NORMS-based as possible.*

As an illustration of the effective use of constructive feedback, let me share with you this e-mail I received from Joseph, operations manager for the specialty chemical plant of a Fortune 100 company.

Dear Leslie:

Here are my thoughts on Jane's coaching and feedback skills. There have been some pretty significant shifts in the past six months (largely due to your effective coaching and her commitment to improve, I think).

Yesterday was my performance appraisal. Nothing she said surprised me. She has given me pretty regular feedback—at least twice per month—and she has direct access to what I do.

She said my unit's productivity rate was 92 percent, below our stretch goal of 105 percent. But she congratulated me on the 92 percent and commented that I wouldn't have achieved that level if I weren't committed and working hard. We had a good discussion about why our unit didn't hit the stretch goal of 105 percent. Jane suggested that part of it was beyond my control due to the types of projects we are doing.

The other part, maybe 7 percent, we agreed was within our control and could be improved. She shared observations of three instances where I did not follow through on commitments I had made. And she pointed out where my time could be more productively spent.

I felt really good about our discussion. As I said, it wasn't a surprise because we frequently discuss my performance, both good points and where I need help. She cited specific instances of how I've contributed to the work team. For example, our team

had completed **97** percent of my preventive maintenance tasks. I'd forgotten some of that stuff and was amazed that she knew it.

Another thing Jane did, which made me feel great, was pass along compliments others have made about my work. I could tell it was important to her that I knew how others felt.

Leslie—what else can I say? It's 180 degrees from where we were a year ago, and it's made the world of difference for our entire unit. Thanks for your role in helping Jane make the transition. I know she trusts you a great deal, and I can see why.

Regards,
Joseph

What is it about Jane's feedback that makes Joseph feel good about his accomplishments and areas for growth? You can see that Jane provides NORMS-based feedback about behaviors within Joseph's control, and she provides frequent feedback about behaviors, not just results. She also suggests specific behaviors to change to increase productivity. *Feedback can act as both a consequence (by increasing or decreasing the likelihood of behavior in the future) and an antecedent (as information that guides future behavior).* Let's take a detailed look at Jane's behavior and its consequences for Joseph's behavior.

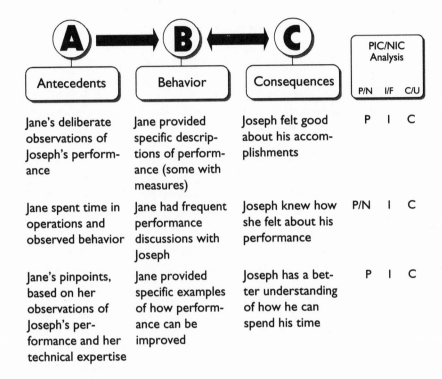

			PIC/NIC Analysis		
A Antecedents	**B** Behavior	**C** Consequences	P/N	I/F	C/U
Jane's deliberate observations of Joseph's performance	Jane provided specific descriptions of performance (some with measures)	Joseph felt good about his accomplishments	P	I	C
Jane spent time in operations and observed behavior	Jane had frequent performance discussions with Joseph	Joseph knew how she felt about his performance	P/N	I	C
Jane's pinpoints, based on her observations of Joseph's performance and her technical expertise	Jane provided specific examples of how performance can be improved	Joseph has a better understanding of how he can spend his time	P	I	C

Joseph is not left wondering what he should be doing, or what behaviors are valued by his supervisor and others.

Constructive Feedback Delivery Skills

Since constructive feedback can be especially challenging, the following important tips can be used for delivering effective, constructive feedback. Again, I have divided these tips into two levels, basic and advanced.

Basic Techniques
(Must-Haves for Good Feedback Delivery)

First, evaluate the following:

- Whether you've clearly stated your expectation *(antecedents)* and provided direction on how to meet the goal or performance expectations
- Whether you have provided the proper tools for the person to perform the expected task
- Whether you have given timely, relevant performance feedback
- Whether you have reinforced the person for making progress toward the goal *(consequence)*

If you haven't done these techniques first, don't try to correct the other person's performance by providing constructive feedback. Rather, correct your own performance—you have not given him or her what he or she needs to be successful!

If you have clearly stated your expectations, provided direction and tools, and given feedback and reinforcement for improvements in performance, use the following techniques for providing constructive feedback:

1. Discuss the performance privately.
2. Don't provide constructive feedback when you are angry (unless behavior is life-threatening).
3. Talk to the performer as soon as possible after the performance occurs—do not store up or postpone feedback.
4. Be specific and objective when discussing undesired performance. Use the NORMS of objectivity when describing the behavior. What was the performance? When and where did it occur? How did you come to know about the performance?
5. Describe the desired performance specifically. Again, use the NORMS of objectivity to describe what you would prefer to see the person do.
6. Talk about behavior, not the individual's personality traits.

7. Catch the person doing it right. Look for opportunities to reinforce behavior change and improvement.

8. Remember that when it's over, it's over. Don't punish the person. Focus on the behavior and support evidence of desired behaviors.

9. Use "I" statements—own your message. Rather than saying, "*You* need to improve," try saying, "*I'd* like to see you try . . . "

Advanced Techniques
(Used by Highly Skilled Feedback Providers)

1. Give the feedback in a climate of trust and support.

2. Describe to the person the consequences of undesired performance for you, others, the team, and the organization.

3. Describe how you felt about the performance.

4. Get the person to participate and talk.

5. Get the person to agree that a problem exists.

6. Get the person to offer solutions.

7. Agree on one solution and have the person summarize your discussion.

Create Winners!

Provide constructive feedback even though it might be uncomfortable for you.

I have included more detailed tips in Appendix C if you would like to examine the finer aspects of delivering and receiving constructive feedback.

Most of Us Avoid Accepting Constructive Feedback. Why?

- It is often difficult to own your developmental needs. And it is even more difficult to acknowledge your needs in the presence of another person.
- We are often afraid to find out what other people think about our performance.
- Dealing with a developmental need forces us to examine an aspect of our behavior that we may be aware of but prefer to avoid discussing.
- We think that our situation is unique and cannot be understood by anyone else.
- It is often phrased in a blaming manner instead of in a concerned, suggesting way.

In general, it comes down to more subjective and person-specific things such as pride, self-evaluation, and desire for success. This is why effective delivery of feedback, which we call "coaching," can be tricky to do well.

No Feedback at All
(Doing Nothing Actually Is Doing Something!)

In the case of feedback, not saying anything about a person's performance is really saying a lot! When you don't give people positive or constructive feedback for desired behavior, they develop all sorts of (mis)interpretations about why you are silent.

Commonly, if you fail to give people positive feedback, they think the worst: they think you are displeased. As a result, they often stop behaving in desirable ways! In other words, without positive feedback, desired behaviors may undergo extinction and eventually stop.

Conversely, when people don't receive constructive feedback, they may assume their undesirable behavior is acceptable and continue to behave that way.

You can see that *doing nothing* actually is *doing something. The absence of a consequence can be the most powerful consequence.* When people do positive things but hear no feedback or feel that what they did doesn't matter, these consequences may drive their behavior in the wrong direction! This is why you just can't leave behavior up to chance—especially behaviors needed for driving an organization's profitability.

So, my number-one recommendation is to *increase your feedback, both positive and constructive.* Don't leave behavior to chance. When it is left to chance, we often see a decline in desired behavior and a continuation or increase in undesired behaviors.

Sharing Feedback: The Fine Art of Coaching

Feedback is an essential part of applying behavioral science, but the "how" of delivering feedback is a fine art. We deliver feedback through coaching.

By now you should have a good feel for feedback—what it is and why it is important. Your next question is probably, "How do I bring feedback to life?"

Feedback Comes to Life Through Coaching

Each of us has a consequence history with coaching, so coaching means something slightly different to each of us. For me, coaching is a "caring sharing" of feedback in a relationship of mutual trust and respect. Coaching integrates all the NORMS-based data to help the coachee attain better performance. To bring coaching to life, I will share my coaching model with you.

Coaching has three steps: *observing, analyzing performance, and delivering feedback.* Whether I am coaching you, or you are coaching a direct report, all three steps apply.

Observing. Gathering NORMS-based data on performance begins with observation. This step involves accompanying the individual and observing his or her behavior (or reviewing written products) to understand the effects of the person's behavior on others. The objective is to sample accurately the individual's behavior.

Ideally, I would videotape the person's behavior and we would view it and analyze it together. This would be the equivalent of watching oneself in a mirror. But that's unrealistic. Instead, I do nonintrusive direct observation and take scrupulous notes on what the person says or does. (This builds a valuable database of specific examples to which I can refer when I deliver my feedback.) I also speak with others who directly sample a person's behavior, so I can obtain additional (and often historical) examples.

Analyzing Performance. From my observations, I pinpoint specific behaviors and the context in which they occur. I then analyze why the behaviors occur. I look to see what is prompting them—and what is reinforcing them. I am especially looking to see if the person is receiving sufficient positive reinforcement for desired behaviors. (After all, I could be sampling behavior in the middle of an extinction burst—which means I'm observing a temporary increase of a behavior that's really on the decline.)

Delivering Feedback. This is where one-on-one feedback, both positive and constructive, is shared. (This also can be done with a team.) During the coaching discussion, several things should occur:

- The performances, either desired or less preferred, need to be identified specifically (either by you or by the person receiving the coaching).
- Your observations should be communicated along with your qualitative impressions about the behaviors you observed.
- The individual should develop an understanding of the need for some behaviors to remain constant or increase, or the need for some behaviors to decrease.
- Antecedents and consequences needed to change and/or sustain behaviors should be talked about and planned.

In actual coaching, these steps recur, sometimes fairly seamlessly and rapidly. A good coach maintains a 4:1 ratio of positive to constructive feedback over time. This does not mean you should always give four pieces of positive feedback and one piece of constructive feedback in every coaching session. If this were the case, the feedback would probably look mechanical and insincere, because people can easily spot patterns, and the receiver would come to expect feedback on at least four good behaviors.

The goal is to look for opportunities to provide more positive feedback than constructive feedback during the coaching period. This will encourage the performer, maintain excitement about improving performance, and further develop trust in your coaching relationship.

Coaching, Feedback, and the Labor Shortage

In today's competitive market for good employees, coaching can be a valuable tool for retaining your people. Individuals want to feel valued; they want to make a difference. People have more choices today than ever before as to where they work and what they do. Individuals are choosing to stay with companies where they see growth and development opportunities. People want to know what's *in it* for them, not just what's *expected of* them.

Companies with feedback-rich environments help people feel valued and appreciated. People choose to be there and give their discretionary effort freely. Organizations with little or no feedback or one-way feedback tend to have higher turnover, lower overall morale, and more *compliant* behaviors than *commitment* behaviors (or discretionary effort).

Here is a quick test of whether feedback and coaching can be a power tool in your company's culture:

1. If your company uses an employee commitment survey, are the lowest scores in provision of feedback, listening to employees, or discussing career development plans?
2. Do you often hear people complain, "I'm not sure what's expected of me?" or "I don't know what they think about my performance?"
3. Do supervisors resist completing performance reviews?

If the answer is "yes" to any of these questions, your organization most likely needs more feedback and coaching.

Executive Coaching

We are seeing a tremendous increase in executive coaching. Why? It is because:

1. *Sustained levels of high performance within organizations begin with the effectiveness of executive leadership.* Executive leaders need to establish an environment where people understand business priorities and values, have the necessary resources to perform, and most importantly, want to perform

at high levels. Their performance is critical to the success of the organization.

2. ***Executives rarely get feedback.*** Most organizations today are a hotbed of politics. Evaluation of an executive's behavior may not be well received—particularly if the evaluation is unsolicited. Thus, the use of an outside coach provides a safe haven where executives get feedback, talk about their own insecurities and needs, and have available an objective, caring resource whose main concern is that executive's success—unencumbered by any personal agenda the coach might have.

3. ***The tenure of an executive has never been shorter or more performance-dependent than it is today.*** Executives have no room to deliver below expectations. Combine this with the typical dearth of feedback, and you have a potentially combustible combination. The use of an outside coach cuts the cycle time of feedback from the critical players—if delivered by an effective behavioral coach.

Seek and Ye Shall Find

Leaders have power, and this, combined with their formal positions, often isolates them from honest feedback, even if they report being comfortable receiving feedback. The truth is, many people have grown up in organizations where they tell leaders what they think the leaders want to hear. They have seen these behaviors heavily reinforced within their organizations.

Don't let this be you! Feedback is critical to your own growth and development, and it's necessary for you to understand the environment accurately enough to make good business decisions. Successful leaders seek constructive feedback and realize it is necessary for their personal development and their organization's development.

Personal Coaching Style: The Importance of Relationships

Your personal reinforcing power is very important in establishing and maintaining an effective relationship during coaching. If hearing your voice or seeing you is an antecedent for a person's stomach to churn as he braces to hear what he is doing wrong, you might explore career options other than coaching!

That is not to say that you should lurch to the other extreme and exaggerate the positives. In fact, ensuring that pinpointed behaviors for coaching are the ones that drive organizational success and profitability is one of the toughest parts of the initial coaching process.

Researchers have explored two critical components for establishing an effective coaching relationship. You need to analyze *what* you talk about and *how* you talk about it.

Coaching is usually characterized by immediate feedback, describing specific target behaviors, objective observation, relationship building, active listening, sharing a climate of support and trust, frankness, and building of performance through shaping. We can look at this from two vantage points: *what* gets discussed and *how* it is talked about.

What you talk about	How you say it
• Sharing your observations of NORMS-based, pinpointed behaviors that are critical to the person's job or role in the organization	• Providing the information immediately is critical
• Offering concrete observations related to the pinpointed behaviors	• Discussing information in an honest, caring, supportive, and sincere way
• Identifying (jointly) possible antecedents and consequences contributing to the desired and less preferred behaviors	• Use of NORMS-based descriptors of what was observed as opposed to loaded language that might trigger an emotional reaction
• Inviting the coachee to suggest his or her personal observations or impressions of the data you are sharing	• Encouraging the performer to elaborate on the behavior, possible improvements, and the consequences that would encourage new behaviors

More on Delivering Feedback

I could write a whole book on the how-to of delivering effective feedback. Earlier I referred you to Appendix C for tips on developing your feedback skills. I ask you to visit Appendix C again for a helpful presentation of FAQs (frequently asked questions) on feedback. For positive feedback, these questions include the following:

- How can I ensure that my positive feedback is sincere?
- How often should I give positive feedback?
- What if others do not accept my positive feedback?
- Is it possible to provide too much positive feedback?

For constructive feedback, the FAQs include the following:

- Why is it so hard to give constructive feedback?
- How can I use constructive feedback to help and not harm others?

- What should I do if the receiver gets defensive?
- How can I be less defensive when receiving constructive feedback?

I'll close this chapter on feedback and coaching with a great story told to me by a direct report of one of my coachees . . .

I'll never forget the first time I met George. I was sure he would be our future chairman, and I still expect that to happen. George's enthusiasm is almost tangible. His excitement is infectious. When we talk about my role as Division President, he not only cares, but he also supports me in a way that leaves me wanting to do better. He also discusses the less successful parts of my business candidly and directly but with no less concern and sensitivity. He does all of the things we're taught to do when we first become managers but lose in the face of profitability, shareholder value, promotions, and opportunities. In sum, he's a great coach. He cares, and he shows it. He notices things, he pays attention, but he doesn't micromanage. His feedback is sincere and direct—and his praise is frequent. He's one helluva leader—and I've been around long enough to know a good one!

—Division President during an executive coaching interview about his boss

The Bottom Line on Feedback and Coaching

Here are the top three points I hope you take away from this chapter:

1. *Feedback is one of the most powerful consequences for behavior.* Feedback is most powerful when it follows behavior immediately and certainly (in other words, it is used as a PIC or even a NIC). Providing feedback about behaviors that create business results is the secret of some of the best leaders I've known.

2. *There are three types of feedback you can put into your leadership toolbox:*

- *Positive feedback.* Positive feedback is used to maintain or increase the frequency of behavior. When delivered effectively, positive feedback also leaves a person feeling good about his or her accomplishments.
- *Constructive feedback.* Constructive feedback is used to decrease the frequency of a less desired behavior and replace it with a preferred behavior. When delivered effectively, constructive feedback helps individuals understand how to be more successful while making them feel good about their accomplishments so far.
- *No feedback.* The absence of feedback affects behavior. When a desired behavior is not followed by feedback, it might decrease. When a less effective behavior is not followed by feedback, it might keep going. The point is that providing no feedback leaves behaviors—and business results—to chance.

3. *Feedback comes to life through coaching.* Effective leaders establish coaching relationships with their direct reports, peers, and supervisors to help them be more successful. They provide feedback about behavior in the context of a supportive relationship. They focus on providing objective, specific feedback targeted to behaviors that create business results.

What's Next?

We will continue to focus on Step 5 of the CYBER Model in the next chapter. We will also explore the shaping process in the next chapter. Shaping is about building behavior to highly successful levels through the systematic application of feedback and coaching. Shaping is an important skill for leaders—it's about growing people.

6

Shaping Up the
Right Stuff

*Of all the behavioral science tools I've learned, "shaping" is the one
that helped me become a better teacher to my children. When I saw
its emphasis on reinforcing progress toward a desired goal, I realized
that I was probably unintentionally holding back my children's
development because I was so quick to point out what they were
doing wrong. I truly am a better parent today.*

—Executive and father of three

How DO WE get good at what we do? Excellent behavior doesn't
happen overnight. Think back to when you learned how to do something new. Did you learn to play the piano overnight? Did you ace your
serve the first time you played tennis? Were you a successful business
executive when you received your MBA?

So, how do we learn complex, advanced behaviors? Conventional
wisdom tells us that "Practice makes perfect." But we all know that
isn't necessarily the case. If you grip your tennis racket incorrectly and
bend your wrist while hitting the ball, all the practice in the world won't
help your game. So sometimes we say, "*Perfect* practice makes perfect."
But that really isn't the case, either.

Behavioral science tells us that practice—even perfect practice—is
not really the main ingredient for developing behaviors. The recipe is a

complex process called "shaping." Its ingredients are *behavior, feedback,* and *increasingly challenging behavioral goals.*

Let me share a story about shaping. Randy is an engaging and energetic public speaker. He makes eye contact with everyone in the room, smiles, rarely relies on notes, and uses humor at appropriate points. After watching Randy deliver a presentation at a company conference, I complimented him. But he smiled shyly and said, "You know, it took me a long time to become this comfortable in front of a large group of people." I asked him to share his story . . .

> I started my career in technology, and my job was to interface with our customers and understand their issues with our products. I had a wonderful supervisor. We used to have long talks about the issues in the department and how we could address them. One day he asked me to organize some of my thoughts and present them at a staff meeting. I was terrified! There were only five people in the meeting, but it felt like 500! I scripted my presentation and read it word-for-word as fast as I could. I don't think I even looked up from my paper.
>
> My boss Karl approached me a couple of days later. In a very caring way, he complimented the thoughts I shared at the meeting and then asked me why I was so nervous in front of the group. We had a great talk. Karl told me that he thought my ideas were great—and went precisely in the direction our department needed to go. In fact, he suggested I could play a major leadership role in helping us get there. But it would require me to become more comfortable with public speaking and communicating to groups. So, I began my journey with Karl's help.
>
> In our company, technology and product sales folks gather for a two-day conference every year. Karl and I set a goal for me to give a short presentation to a group of approximately 50 people at one of those meetings. I had six months to prepare. He let me know that my content was on target and didn't need much coaching. We decided that I should focus on three areas: use of notes, eye contact, and voice projection. We also looked for

relatively safe opportunities for me to get in front of people to speak, such as weekly staff meetings, customer calls, and so on.

It wasn't easy, but with Karl's help, I made a lot of progress. I went from scripting and reading my presentation, to putting key points in large type on paper, to using overheads with note cards. Karl was always there to provide feedback.

I'll never forget the meeting when I actually looked up at the audience and saw my coworkers smiling. What a rush! I felt they were really on my side. A little later, I took a risk and told a joke during my presentation. People laughed! I couldn't believe it. I started to get hooked. People were actually listening to me and appreciating what I was saying.

Well, I gave my presentation at that yearly conference. I couldn't even eat for two days before the presentation. But I did a good job. My goal was to use overheads and only look at my note cards if I absolutely needed to. In fact, I only brought two note cards to the presentation. After my presentation, Karl went wild—he was so proud of me. And the head nods throughout my talk were reinforcing as well. Since then, I've really worked on my presentation skills. I've learned to identify an area to work on and then take it slow. I've used coaches to give me feedback. And I always look at the audience to see if I'm getting a positive reaction to what I'm doing. It's made all the difference in the world.

Clearly, Randy was not a born public speaker. He had to *shape* his presentation skills. No wonder he is now such an effective speaker! He applied shaping and worked on his skills over time. Here are some of the things Randy did:

- *Bits and Pieces.* He broke the complex behavior of speaking at the conference into "behavioral chunks," or bite-sized pieces he could work on. He focused on his use of notes, eye contact, and voice projection.
- *Just Within Reach.* Randy set a goal for himself. He wanted to give his presentation using only overheads. That was a stretch

for him, considering his starting point was reading his presentation from a script. But he didn't make the mistake of leaping toward his goal all at once. He set small, attainable sub-goals toward which to work. He put his key points on paper in very large type to help him see his notes easily, so he could turn back to his audience. Later, he started to use overheads with his notes on note cards. Eventually, he used fewer note cards and referenced them less often.

- *Practice and Feedback.* Randy and Karl identified plenty of practice opportunities. Randy received feedback during and after every opportunity. He saw people smiling and nodding their heads—a natural consequence of making eye contact with the audience. He also experienced a very powerful natural consequence when people laughed at his joke. In addition to natural consequences, Randy received social consequences from Karl in the form of feedback. And Randy provided himself with feedback about his performance.

- *Upping the Ante.* Randy kept pushing himself. Once he reached a goal, he raised the bar a little more and found ways to get feedback about his performance.

The Science of Shaping

Shaping is both science and art. The science lies in having proven behavioral science techniques to isolate and reinforce the right behaviors. The art lies in knowing when and how to apply those techniques. Let us take an everyday example to further understand the science of shaping:

Teaching Austin to Ride

Many of us have had the delight of teaching a child to ride a bicycle. We know the ultimate goal is for our son or daughter to be well-balanced, to pedal properly, to steer correctly, and to smile the whole way! But getting there requires a deliberate sequencing of events and reinforcement for each step in that sequence. Let's look more closely, using my four-year-old son Austin as our example.

Our first step is for Austin to understand the key parts of the bike and what successfully riding a bike *looks like.* (Based on Christmas and birthday requests, I'd say that knowledge almost always precedes having the bike!)

Our second step in teaching Austin to ride is to have him sit on the seat without sliding off. The first time Austin sits on the seat, he smiles, giggles, and maybe slides a little, but eventually he feels confident and balanced. Of course, we are providing support by holding the bike until he gets that sense of comfort and balance. Austin's behavior of sitting properly in the seat, not sliding too much to the left or right, is very reinforcing to him. So are our smiles and words of praise and pride.

But Austin will not progress toward the goal of riding his bike if he is content just to sit on the seat and do nothing further. So, the third step is that he has to *stop* receiving reinforcement for just sitting well-balanced on the seat and has to *start* receiving reinforcement for progress—like extending his arms so they touch the handlebars at the right place.

The fourth step is that Austin has to *stop* receiving reinforcement for just holding the handlebars while sitting balanced and has to *start* receiving reinforcement for even further progress—like extending his legs to the pedals.

The fifth step is for him to *stop* receiving reinforcement for just extending his legs and to *start* receiving reinforcement for moving the pedals with his feet while the rear wheel is off the ground. This allows him to experience the natural reinforcement of moving the pedals, spinning the tires, and hearing the sound it makes.

SHAPING AUSTIN'S BEHAVIOR

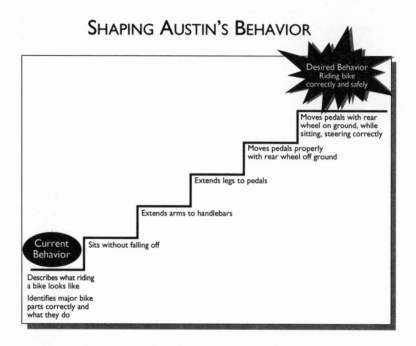

The sixth step: Austin has to *stop* receiving reinforcement for simply moving the pedals and spinning the rear wheel without moving. He has to *start* receiving reinforcement for actually moving the bike as the result of pedaling. To do this, I lower the rear wheel while he continues to pedal (training wheels on, of course), and away he goes, with me running along at his side, cheering, clapping, and smiling.

At this time, I'm excited too, so the pitch of my voice changes and the rate of my encouragement increases. Both Austin and I are reinforced for our behaviors in this shaping process.

And so on . . . until his proud parents' assistance with balancing is no longer needed and he can sit properly, hold the handlebars correctly, move his feet on the pedals, and ride his bike safely! (Of course, that's when mommy and daddy's worrying really begins . . . but that's another book!)

Shaping Behavior from the Current to the Desired

Here is the behavioral science version of Austin's story: "describing what riding a bike looks like" is a

> ### Shaping
> The process of differentially reinforcing successive approximations of behavior toward a goal.

current behavior. Austin's "safely riding his bike without assistance" is a *desired* behavior. And the steps I outlined are *behavioral steps* that move Austin from the current state to the future desired state. *That's what shaping is all about—moving from the current behavior to the future behavior.* Shaping is one of the most important components of behavioral science.

What does shaping really mean? Let's examine each piece of our scientific definition:

- ***Shaping is a process,*** and a process is a set of steps. The steps get you from where you are to where you want to be. Shaping is a set of steps that develops a behavior from its current state (describing what riding a bike looks like) to a desired state (riding the bicycle safely without parental assistance).

- Shaping is a process of ***differentially reinforcing***. Shaping requires the performer to receive positive reinforcement for a behavior. It also requires that the performer NOT receive positive reinforcement for other behaviors. Differential reinforcement simply means that behaviors are distinguished from one another—some behaviors are reinforced and others are not. How are those behaviors differentiated? Let's look at the last piece of our definition.

- Shaping is a process of differentially reinforcing ***successive approximations of behavior*** toward a goal. Behaviors are differentiated by how close they are to the final behavioral goal. In our example, sitting on the seat without falling off was reinforced *verbally* by the parent and reinforced *naturally* because Austin wasn't sliding to the ground. Then, to move closer toward safely riding the bicycle unassisted by a parent (the goal), Austin had to hold the handlebars. He received verbal praise and eventually physical comfort (reinforcement) for holding the handlebars, but the verbal reinforcement he received for simply sitting on the seat and not falling off was no longer provided.

As you can see, *shaping behavior is about perfecting a* **chain** *of behavioral steps through the systematic application of positive reinforcement.* To progress up the behavioral chain, behaviors closer to the goal need to be more positively reinforcing than earlier behaviors. Providing positive reinforcement for behaviors earlier in the chain will only sustain those behaviors, which are just stepping stones toward the goal. But we don't want those behaviors sustained in isolation; we want to promote the *next* behavior in the chain.

Now that you've seen the details about how shaping works, let's take a look at some everyday examples in action.

Shaping Consumer Behavior

Successful sales organizations use shaping to influence consumer behavior without even knowing it. Any organization that sells products to consumers can use the concept of shaping to great advantage. Understanding behavioral shaping can help the salesperson progress through the sales cycle, from the introduction to the customer, to getting the first sale, to building a lasting relationship.

Here is an example of how this process works. We'll look at how Ginny, a Technical Sales Representative for WaterChem, shapes consumer behavior in her interactions with Dave, a Maintenance Engineer at PaperCo.

Shaping Step I. Ginny sends some written marketing material to Dave with a cover letter saying that she will follow up with a phone call to discuss the materials and to gain a better understanding of PaperCo's water treatment needs.

Dave's Response. **He reads the material and cover letter. If some features of WaterChem's products address his needs, natural positive reinforcement occurs for Dave when he reads the literature. (A first shaping step has been accomplished.)**

Shaping Step 2. Ginny makes a phone call to follow up on the written materials and to request an opportunity to visit Dave at PaperCo's facility.

Dave's Response. **Dave requests that Ginny just send more materials. But she does not want to reinforce this level of consumer behavior again, so she suggests that she will be able to**

bring value if she visits PaperCo's facility and better understands their water treatment needs. Dave agrees to the meeting, Ginny reinforces his decision, and they agree on a date for
the visit. (A second shaping step has been accomplished.)

Shaping Step 3. During the visit to PaperCo's plant, Ginny offers to collect water samples for fluid analysis studies to identify
opportunities for optimizing performance and minimizing total
cost. She explains that, following this work, WaterChem will
recommend a water treatment protocol. They will also outline
PaperCo's benefits from using WaterChem's water treatment
products and from signing a fluid monitoring and maintenance
service contract.

Dave's Response. Dave is not immediately comfortable com-
mitting to the next behavioral step of allowing WaterChem
to collect the samples. He suggests that Ginny make a return
visit or send him more materials. Ginny then outlines more
specifically the anticipated benefits (reinforcers) to PaperCo
of agreeing to the fluid analysis studies. Dave agrees to the
study, and Ginny reinforces his wise decision. The fluid analysis
provides valuable information (another reinforcer) to Dave
about PaperCo's operation. (A third shaping step has been
accomplished.)

Shaping Step 4. Based on the results of the fluid study, Ginny
presents the water treatment protocol recommendation and a
formal fluid monitoring and maintenance service contract. The
report and contract outline the benefits of PaperCo's using
WaterChem products and services. This is potential positive
reinforcement for Dave if he decides to work with WaterChem
to meet PaperCo's water treatment needs.

Dave's Response. He signs an agreement for a term of service
and products from WaterChem. PaperCo experiences good
order placement and delivery service, as well as documented
savings from WaterChem's monitoring of fluid levels. All of
these benefits reinforce Dave's behavior of signing with Water-
Chem. His continuing experiences of fine support will produce

the long-term relationship Ginny is looking to build. (Shaping mission: accomplished.)

Throughout the series of interactions with Dave, Ginny provides *antecedents* by describing the benefits of working with WaterChem. She provides *consistent reinforcement* each time Dave agrees to another step in the sales process, while avoiding reinforcement of steps in the sales behavior chain that already have been passed. Finally, and most importantly, Ginny ensures that Dave's decision to do business with WaterChem is continuously reinforced.

Shaping on the Internet

The Internet is also a wonderful example of shaping in action, with all the powerfully reinforcing aspects of information right at your fingertips. The Internet offers easy access to product visualization and ordering, visual and auditory prompts that cue your next click, etc. In fact, in the past decade, technology developers have demonstrated a striking awareness of how to shape human behavior. Their programs guide us very effectively toward certain outcomes and purchasing behaviors—behaviors that otherwise would not occur.

The next time you are on the Net, study the Web sites and links and note how they smoothly prompt you along—powerfully shaping you all the way!

Here's the important thing to remember:

- If the shaping steps are too big (like ordering a product online when you've never used a computer), the behavior will cease mid-chain.

- If the shaping steps are too small (like clicking on links that lead only to more lists of links, which lead to more links, taking forever to reach the information you seek), the behavior will cease mid-chain due to the delay or absence in reinforcers for those additional "clicks." Careful sequencing and provision of reinforcement for new behaviors is critical for shaping to work.

The Art of Shaping

Shaping is a scientific process, but it has a strong artistic side. Let's look at the art of shaping—applying your behavioral skills to the shaping process. As with any process, shaping requires that you have an end in mind. *What is the behavior you'd ultimately like to see?* This is where you call upon your pinpointing skills. Start by identifying those key behaviors that lead to results.

Once your goal is clear, examine where the performers are right now. *What behaviors are they currently exhibiting that could be shaped toward the desired end state?* Use what you've learned about ABCs to pinpoint the current behaviors.

Let's look at an example with the following goal: *improved accuracy in budgets and operating profit forecasts submitted by General Managers.* Here is the current situation:

- GMs routinely are late in submitting budgets and profit plans
- GMs submit budgets that do not include all planned costs from product specialists at the plants
- GMs submit profit targets that do not align with those of Sales and are generally not within 10 percent of actuals
- Management often does not understand or follow budgets and forecasts
- GMs submit funding requests for additional projects that arrive after budgets are approved. Although those projects were not included in original budgets, they appear to be legitimate

What Shaping Steps Are Needed?

Now that you know where you want to go and where you will begin, you need to develop a path—a chain of steps—for getting from here to there. *What behavioral steps can the performers make to move from where they are to where you want them to be?*

1. Communicate the business case. In this instance, it's the need to achieve improved budget adherence and improved operating profit through forecasting accuracy.

2. Communicate the goal of getting budgets/profit plans submitted on time, improving cash flow through lower inventory levels, and increasing accuracy through communication among key groups. Reinforce evidence of these behaviors when they occur.

3. Hold meetings for finance staff members, general managers, business managers, sales managers, product specialists, and plant staff. Share information and update forecasts. Reinforce attendance at the meetings and information sharing when these behaviors occur.

4. Have GMs conduct a comparative review with the Divisional VP to ensure accuracy of numbers across the different groups who are reporting. Reinforce behaviors that lead to accuracy of numbers.

5. Have GMs understand the fluctuations between expected and actual monthly financial results and the business plan commitment. Engage the original group (GMs, business managers, sales managers, and product specialists) in identifying root causes of inaccurate or inconsistent data in developing process or behavioral change plans to prevent future occurrences of these same issues.

6. Implement the corrective actions and align information-sharing to improve accuracy of financial reports. Ensure that contributions get properly recognized and positively reinforced.

7. Monitor progress and communicate the trend data regarding actuals and forecasts to ensure that all parties recognize their roles and contributions to the measured improvements.

8. Track the percent reduction and the gap between expected and actual financial results. Reinforce contributors if the data trend in the right direction.

9. Incorporate the new learnings into revised work processes, training, communication, etc. so they become a regular part of how forecasts and budgets are determined.

10. Use a discretionary recognition/reward process for participants who help achieve improved outcomes. Give written

praise so you can discuss it during performance review. Encourage team members to praise one another for progress.

Size of Behavioral Steps Is Important

It is important to identify accurately the size of the behavioral steps. This is one of the trickiest, but also one of the most crucial, parts of the shaping process. If you make the behavioral steps too big, the performers are less likely to succeed. Most people find that failing to reach a goal is very punishing, so they quit trying.

This Behavioral Step Is Too Big—

Remember Randy's public speaking dilemma? If his boss, Karl, had tried to encourage Randy to go immediately from reading his scripted notes word-for-word to presenting with overheads and no notes at all, Randy probably would have failed. His behavior would have been punished. In all likelihood, Randy would have been too frustrated to try again.

This Behavioral Step Is Too Small—

The flip side is making the behavioral steps too small. Imagine creating so many sub-goals for behavior that you have trouble telling how much progress you really make from one step to the next. It would be difficult to know how to differentially reinforce behavior. If one behavior is almost the same as the next, when do you start providing reinforcement for the next behavior in the chain and extinguish the previous one?

Returning to Randy's situation, he could have set goals that were way too small. For example, imagine if his first step had been merely to type his notes on paper in larger type so he could read them more easily. Then, imagine that he moved to typing only one paragraph per page in large type. Then, he shortened each page to contain only the key points of the paragraph, and so on. It would have taken a long time for Randy to reach his goal. He would have lost interest.

This Behavioral Step Is Just Right—

When behavioral steps are just right, they are challenging but realistic:

- *Challenging.* When people first try a new behavioral step, it should feel a little uncomfortable. They should feel like they need practice at the behavior.
- *Realistic.* While the behavioral steps should be challenging, they should also be realistic. In other words, the performer should be able to do the behavior—even awkwardly—on the first try. That way, the performer will receive some reinforcement for the behavior. If the performer tries the behavior and fails, he or she is punished for the behavior—a step backward. If the performer does not receive reinforcement for behavior, that behavior will extinguish and shaping will stop.

Turning Behaviors into Results

My point throughout this book is that you can create significant business results by systematically focusing on behavior. This means that once you have a behavior in mind, you must shape it to ensure results! Let's review what we've looked at so far:

CYBER Model

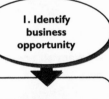

1. **Identify business opportunity**

2. **Target results and measures of success**

3. **Pinpoint and align behaviors that drive results**

4. **Understand the influences on behavior**

5. **Develop, implement, and adjust behavior change plan**

6. **CELEBRATE achievement of improved results!**

1. Identify desired business results.

2. Identify which behaviors lead to the desired results (pinpointing).

3. Determine which current behaviors can be shaped into behaviors that drive results and which ones need to be eliminated. Then identify the behavioral steps that lead from current to desired behaviors.

4. Understand what motivates current and desired behaviors (ABC Analysis).

5. *We are here.* Determine how to manage antecedents and consequences for each behavioral step in the chain. By systematically managing the antecedents and the consequences, you can grow the behaviors that lead to business results!

A Leader's Role in Shaping

When I talk with leaders about shaping, the most common responses I hear are, "It makes sense; the process sounds straightforward; I see how it can work. But, Leslie, I don't have *time* to manage antecedents and consequences that systematically!"

On one hand, these leaders are correct. Their busy schedules afford little extra time. On the other hand, they have more opportunities available for shaping than they realize. Here is an example from a recent conversation with a client:

Paul: I think I understand the shaping process. I want to try it, but honestly, Leslie, I don't think I have the time!

Leslie: Paul, I understand your schedule. Your calendar is full. But what I think you can do is leverage the time you already have booked. For example, you're going to see the general managers next week at the quarterly reviews. Why not use that as an opportunity for shaping their behavior?

Paul: OK, but what would I do?

Leslie: Start by looking at the behavioral pinpoints you have for each general manager. Look at the data you have about their behavior. My guess is that you have some information now, but you probably need more to have a meaningful conversation about their performance. Am I on target?

Paul: Absolutely. Take Hal for example. My shaping target for him is this: get him to identify *honestly* the factors contributing to his making or not making his numbers. I feel like I'm getting a snow job about his division's operating performance. I learn about incidents long after the fact—generally from one of Hal's direct reports—and I rarely get the full story on the root causes.

In our last quarterly review meeting, I saw numbers indicating we were going to make only about 82 percent of our target for the quarter due to "unforeseen changes in the market." That's not good enough for me—especially when our other divisions are affected by the same market conditions and are making 100 percent or greater of their target. Plus, an 18 percent deficit should not come to my attention for the first time in quarterly reviews!

Notice that Paul just gave me information about several behavioral pinpoints for Hal that would directly impact business results. Those pinpoints included (1) giving Paul advance knowledge of the operating performance of Hal's division (especially when it is below forecast), (2) sharing a root-cause analysis of incidents that occurred within his division (including their effect on operating performance), and (3) detailing what factors impacted divisional performance, including marketplace changes, etc.

Leslie: OK. That tells me you need to know more about the general performance of Hal's division, outside the quarterly reviews as well as within them. Now that we've identified the desired behaviors, let's see if we have the proper antecedents to prompt them and the consequences to reinforce progress toward them.

Notice that I encouraged Paul to consider the current antecedents and consequences to ensure they wouldn't encourage undesired behaviors or unintentionally prevent the desired behaviors he was looking for.

Paul: Great. Let's start with the antecedents. *(He handed me a three-page memo.)* Here is the memo I send out one month before the reviews. It details what I expect in the quarterly review meetings. The same memo goes to all of the GMs. See where I ask them to explain deviations and root-cause analysis on incidents?

Leslie: Looks pretty thorough. Let's talk about past reviews. Consequence histories are pretty powerful antecedents. What happened in past quarterly reviews when Hal failed to share the information you requested?

Paul: Well—nothing, I guess. I mean, I ask him where it is—but he glosses over the whole thing. To avoid getting behind, I usually let it go and move on to the next GM's report. It's a lot more reinforcing for me to hear from my other GMs, because they *do* give me all of the information I need.

Leslie: Well, we might have just identified a powerful consequence that is maintaining the very behavior you DON'T want! Sounds like Hal gets reinforced for the way in which he provides his data. He gets to sit down quicker, he doesn't have to explain why he didn't make his numbers, etc. The absence of any constructive feedback from you just reinforces the old behaviors you want to change. In fact, he might begin receiving punishment if he details all the problems he finds.

It is always important to examine the consequences that may be sustaining current behaviors—especially if they are behaviors you wish to shape toward new or different ones. As I mentioned, the current behavior need NOT be reinforced, while a newer behavior DOES need to be reinforced.

Leslie: Let's detail behaviors you need from Hal that you can support through positive reinforcement.

Paul: I guess I would begin by asking detailed questions about his division's performance. Then I'd indicate that I need such information in the formal quarterly review reports. I could also ask him to review why they made their numbers, or didn't, and be sure not to jump down his throat, even if I think he screwed up. I should reinforce his telling me—and calmly work through the content of what happened at a different time. Does that sound about right?

Notice that Paul picked up on the fact that he needs to withhold any punishment for the new behaviors of sharing information on why operating problems occurred—despite the fact that it might be frustrating for him to hear! The behavior of Hal's sharing openly and honestly what is happening with his unit will be fragile at first and will need to be reinforced. The content of his message should be handled separately so that Hal does not feel Paul is "shooting the messenger."

Leslie: **Yes, that sounds right. Also, I recommend that we look at your calendar for the next 60 days to identify other times when you will have contact with Hal, so you can reinforce the behaviors we've pinpointed. We can evaluate whether you have enough opportunities to shape the behaviors you need from Hal or if you need to add some shaping time into your calendar. We can repeat this process for the other GMs as well.**

Notice we are arranging a system that allows Paul to keep in touch with the progress his folks are making on strategically critical areas. He will be able to reinforce or shape evidence of desired behaviors if he is seeking opportunities to do so.

Paul: **Sounds good. Here's my calendar . . .**

When I have these conversations with leaders, my goal is to emphasize three key points:

1. *Every opportunity you have to interact with performers is a shaping opportunity.* You should look at all the time currently booked on your calendar and ask how you can leverage the time to shape behavior that creates business results!

2. *You need to gather information to maximize your shaping effectiveness.* You probably don't know enough about the performers' behaviors or the results they are producing to provide specific and meaningful feedback. One of the best ways to gather this data is to talk to people who have access to the performers' behaviors and results.

3. *You need to develop a plan for shaping behavior.* It's not enough to look at your calendar. You have to organize the information: who the performers are, what the shaping targets are, when you'll see the performers next, and what information you need to provide feedback. You can use a simple table to help organize the information. I call it a Shaping Opportunity Grid. For each event on your calendar, map out the following:

Shaping Opportunity Grid

Target Audience	Opportunity	Purpose	Plan and Approach
Who will be influenced through the contact?	Events available for use as shaping opportunities	Business objectives, focus of reinforcement	Actions you will take, things to look for, how you will get information prior to the contact
Hal	Quarterly review meetings Weekly phone conferences Lunch next week	Encourage honest reporting of factors that contribute to his division making its numbers	Prior to quarterly review, ask Hal for a preview of his report. Clarify what I'm looking for during the review
		Encourage advanced reporting of operating performance	Ask Hal problem-solving questions about problem areas
		Encourage sharing of root-cause analyses of incidents	Reinforce Hal's sharing of information with me, even if it's bad news

Then you need to ask, "Who performs behaviors that are critical to the success and profitability of the organization, but is NOT on my calendar?" Can you access that person's behaviors (and thus provide reinforcement) through telephone conversations, e-mail, or voice mail? The Shaping Opportunity Grid has become a standard part of my Executive Coaching technique.

The typical executive becomes boxed into certain patterns of action, based on what people *think* the executive wants to hear or see. Generally, the result is a dog-and-pony show that takes weeks of preparation by the field people (time taken from work they *should* be doing). You can halt that dog-and-pony routine by working through the Shaping Opportunity Grid. The results? Your employees will actually *know* what you want to hear and see, so they will better utilize their time. And you can use the grid to prompt yourself, to think through how you can reinforce their desired behaviors. Together, you'll be able to shape the organization's progress toward aggressive, strategic, and profitable performance.

Here's a Shaping Challenge

Now that you know the fundamentals of shaping, here's a shaping challenge. Read this real example and we'll work through the questions you need to develop a shaping plan.

> I recently coached Maria, VP of Sales. Three people had transferred from her team. She requested coaching because she knew her relationships were suffering, but she did not know what to do.
>
> After my initial meetings with Maria, I interviewed her direct reports as part of the coaching process. Maria's team members overwhelmingly viewed her as a very autocratic decision maker. Here are a few of their comments:
>
>> "Maria means well, but she just doesn't listen. She asks for input, I give it, and she tells me why my idea won't work! It's so frustrating. I think she's already made the decision before she even asks."
>>
>> "I don't think my opinion matters. Maria simply tells us what we're going to do, and that's that. Even if it doesn't make sense for the business, we are expected to march to her orders."
>
> It became clear that a coaching target for Maria was her *decision making*. Her decision-making behavior needed shaping. I shared the interview results with her. She said, "I think my team is on target. I tend to make decisions and go with them. I don't want to appear wishy-washy. *But*, it seems they perceive my style to be frustrating and autocratic while I would have described it as decisive and clear! OK. It's obviously an area I need to work on. What should I do?"

I introduced the concept of shaping, and she liked it. I suggested that we work together to develop a shaping plan for her decision-making behavior.

Here are the questions for developing a shaping plan. If you were in Maria's position, how would you answer them?

Question 1. How do you currently make decisions? What behaviors do you perform?

Question 2. When making decisions, what behavior would you ultimately like to see yourself doing?

Question 3. What behavioral steps toward your desired behavior feel challenging to you, yet realistic?

Question 4. What antecedents and consequences do you need to support behavior at each step of your shaping process?

Here's the discussion Maria and I had, using those same questions:

Question 1. How do you currently make decisions? What behaviors do you perform?

Maria: **I gather as much information as I can. Then I analyze it and decide which direction to head. I dislike wasting time. In this business, if you don't move quickly, you lose opportunities.**

Leslie: **What role does your team play in helping you make decisions?**

Maria: **I often ask them for input. Sometimes I use it and sometimes I don't. There are times when I don't have time to ask. I need to make a decision quickly for the good of the department.**

Leslie: **How do you think your team perceives your decision-making style?**

Maria: Well, it sounds like they think I don't listen to their input, that I'm autocratic.

Leslie: It seems to me that this is one reason why your relationships are not where you want them to be. Basically, people feel punished when they offer you input because you ask for it but don't take it. Why should they keep trying?

Maria: You're probably right. I hadn't thought about it that way. I thought I was being a good leader—strong and decisive. But I can see how my style has been hurting my relationships with people.

That's the kind of insight I listen for when coaching!

Leslie: It's not easy to change your decision-making style—especially if it's something that clearly has led to your success as a leader. So let's talk about how you might include your team in making decisions while maintaining your leadership effectiveness.

Question 2. When making decisions, what behavior would you ultimately like to see yourself doing?

Maria: I'd like to make people feel they play a part in the direction of our business. If they don't feel included, they're less likely to follow—and at this level of management, they're likely to leave, eventually.

Leslie: Good point. Let's talk about what it means to include people. You tell me that sometimes you consult people and sometimes you don't. I've also heard from your team members that they don't always feel you consider their input—that you make up your own mind. When I think about alternative decision-making styles, I come up with three options:

- You could consult the team members after you've made a decision to hear what they think.

- You could consult the group before you've made a decision and then consider their input as you make the decision.
- You could work with the group and make the decision together.

Maria: Well, I think each of those approaches makes sense under different circumstances.

Leslie: Yes, they do. Since your people seem to want more input on decisions, let's talk about the types of decisions in which you could further involve them.

Maria: Ok, I often agree to implement new initiatives brought to my boss and my peers but without consulting my own team members. And they are the ones challenged with implementing them. They have been unhappy about this in the past.

Leslie: Ok, so why don't we start there?

Question 3. What behavioral steps toward your desired behavior feel challenging to you, yet realistic?

Maria: First, telling my team members that I will bring recommendations on new initiatives to this team for their input, and then following through on that.

Leslie: Good. Let's focus on getting them involved in decisions on implementing new initiatives. Let's look at the shaping steps needed to go from where you are now—essentially making most of the decisions with little input—to where you want to go—acting as an advisor to a team that has final decision-making authority. You could go with a three-step process:

1. *You could work with the team to review proposed new initiatives.* You could hear their input, make the decision, and communicate how the team's input influenced your decision.

2. *Then you could work with the team to review proposed initiatives, and then work the issue as a team.* You could evaluate

the upsides and downsides of the proposed initiative, become a voting member of the team, and support the team's decision.

3. *Finally you could work with the team to review proposed initiatives and provide input to the team.* You could provide the information and advice you feel they need, and then step back and let them decide.

Maria: Well, one and two sound okay—but I'm not ready to commit to step three yet. Letting them decide makes me nervous because I don't want them to make mistakes. I have more experience, and I know the landscape better.

Leslie: The truth is that you <u>will</u> be uncomfortable at points along the way. But unless you have the support of your team members on new initiatives, they won't be implemented successfully anyway. And you will actually be a better manager because you will be investing in developing your people's skills in analyzing options, benefits, and obstacles. This will strengthen the long-term success of any initiative. If you don't give them access to the issues, options, and decisions, how can they get the experience to make your operation stellar?

Question 4. What antecedents and consequences do you need to support behavior at each step of your shaping process?

Maria: As for antecedents, my team members will need background information on the issue we are trying to address. They need to know what other options were considered, the required resources, the timeframe, who is sponsoring, and why. They also need to know what it means to them. What will be expected of them in support of the implementation? That's the part I usually leave out, and it gets me into hot water with them.

Leslie: Sounds like you'll need some feedback along the way to help you keep sight of your larger goals.

Maria: Definitely.

Leslie: **Let's develop a coaching plan, so I can be sure you will have sufficient reinforcement for your new behaviors. Also, I'd like to help make certain you will get feedback from your team members to sustain these new behaviors. You can still count on me for feedback, but it's important that your sources of feedback and reinforcement be in your natural environment and readily available to you.**

Maria: **I'd like that.**

Our conversation continued until we had a plan in place for Maria, and I was sure she would receive enough positive reinforcement to keep her new behaviors going.

Sure enough, after a few months, Maria become more comfortable engaging her team in making decisions, and her team became better decision makers—a huge source of positive reinforcement for her. An unexpected benefit was her organization's improvement in implementation effectiveness for the initiatives already underway. Maria saw dramatic improvement in sponsorship and support from her direct reports because they had greater ownership of the success of the efforts underway. And her relationships improved—another huge source of positive reinforcement. As a result, Maria did not lose any more people from her team—an important business result for her department.

So, that's what shaping is all about: focusing on building the behaviors that lead to business results. Without shaping, we would have great difficulty making progress in strategically critical areas.

The Bottom Line on Shaping

Shaping is critical because it pulls together the theory of behavioral science into a practical application: influencing behavior. Shaping is about pinpointing desired behaviors—those that lead to business results—and then applying antecedents and consequences to build up those desired behaviors. Here are six key points to remember about shaping:

1. Shaping is "the process of differentially reinforcing successive approximations of behavior toward a goal." Shaping behavior is about perfecting a chain of behavioral steps by systematically applying positive reinforcement. To progress up the behavioral

chain, behaviors closer to the goal need to be more positively reinforced than earlier behaviors. Providing positive reinforcement for behaviors earlier in the chain will only sustain them, and they are just steppingstones toward the goal.

2. The first step in shaping is to carefully pinpoint the desired behavior. It's important to use your pinpointing skills to identify a behavior that will drive important results.

3. Use your pinpointing skills to identify the behavioral steps between the current behavior and the desired behavior. Remember, the size of those behavioral steps has to be challenging and realistic. If the steps are too big, the performer is unlikely to meet the goals you set. If the steps are too small, the performer is likely to become confused or frustrated.

4. Use the ABC Analysis to identify the antecedents and consequences required to influence the selected behaviors.

5. Use your feedback and coaching skills to see every interaction as a shaping opportunity. Feedback and coaching are the primary tools for shaping behaviors.

6. Rely on the Shaping Opportunity Grid to help you organize your feedback and increase the likelihood that you will successfully shape behavior.

What's Next?

You have reached an exciting point in your journey into applying behavioral science. You now have the tools to effectively influence behavior for business results. You probably have a new perspective on why some organizations can execute strategies, implement change, and maneuver in the marketplace when others cannot. *It comes down to behavior!*

Next, I'll share some important lessons about business execution from a behavioral perspective. I think you might see yourself or someone you know in the stories in the next chapter. I hope you can also see yourself applying the principles and tools in this book to avoid the traps you'll see in "Great Ideas: Lousy Execution."

7

Great Ideas: Lousy Execution (Why?)

Our transition from a functional organization to integrated business units was a great idea, but it nearly brought us to our knees. I thought we had done an excellent job identifying new roles and responsibilities, changing our financial reporting processes, altering our organizational structure, etc. We did all of the things the books tell you to do. We involved people. We transitioned in a planned, phased manner. It really was a world-class plan. But the execution tore us apart for almost a year as we struggled to make the implementation work.

Knowing what I now know about behavioral science, I can say that our problems came down to the fact that old patterns of behavior prevailed. The new ones we expected from the managers and leaders were fragile and went unreinforced and ultimately underwent extinction. In addition, we underestimated the impact of our discretionary bonus plan, which depended on the old criteria. Now I say, how dumb were we not to have seen and planned for all of these things?

—Chief Operating Officer

Many ORGANIZATIONAL LEADERS hit the proverbial wall because they try to implement too many programs and find that none sticks for long. I believe that a *focus on behavior* can overcome this problem. My company and I have enjoyed most of our success by sweating the details at the behavioral level. We have learned that we must address four major issues to successfully implement sustained change:

1. the strategic *goals* of the business,
2. the *processes* needed to make the business work,
3. the *behaviors* required to make strategy and processes work, and
4. the consequences needed to support the behaviors that drive all key outcomes.

Initiatives that focus only on strategy or processes, but omit behavior, will fail to make change a reality. Initiatives that focus only on behavior may lead to change in actions, but will fail to influence anything important to the business. Only initiatives that address the "what" (changes needed to help the business) and the "how" (the behaviors of key people needed to make it all happen) will lead to meaningful and sustained change.

We have also found that, even years after implementation, programs that are not working often can be unlocked by adding behavioral technology. Total Quality Management (TQM) is a good example. Many companies spent millions on TQM between the mid-80s and the mid-90s, but found that it fell short of their expectations. The cultural and economic value promised in the design stage never materialized. This failure often was the result of incomplete implementation.

TQM programs had many of the key ingredients for successful implementation, including a compelling case for change, a clear vision, leadership support, and training for key people. Teams were chartered, process changes were made, and resources were provided to support projects. However, most TQM programs did not follow through completely at the behavior level. Few, if any, managed consequences differently than under the old systems. And few pinpointed the specific behaviors needed to make a difference.

Ideas are not worth much if people don't change what they do along the way. *Effective organizational change requires effective behavioral change.*

In this chapter, we'll focus on the problems that result from the failure to implement change. We'll look at how you can overcome such problems for yourself and for your business.

Flavor-of-the-Month: Bitter

Failure to implement effectively has created a "flavor-of-the-month" problem in many companies. A constant stream of initiatives feeds the need to know more and do more. Yet few initiatives are ever implemented as intended. Why? You can easily understand this failure with your new understanding of antecedents, consequences, PICs, and NICs.

- *Today's businesses are under pressure to perform.* Do more with less. Increase profitability. Improve shareholder value. Grow market share. Innovate. Outperform your competitor.
- *Executives are constant targets of influence.* They read a lot. They listen to voices of wisdom. They learn. They continually seek new ideas and approaches to improve the current state. But alas, executives are affected (or afflicted?) by antecedent-heavy sources that promise positive consequences upon implementation, but have trouble delivering it. Antecedents surround executives like bees buzzing around a hive. The antecedent might include a *Harvard Business Review* article, a Conference Board presentation, a *Fortune* cover story on "Why CEOs Fail," a meeting with a consultant or faculty member, or a discussion with the CEO of another corporation. If any of these antecedents is convincing enough, executives will support it.
- *Numerous consequences support executives and leaders who try new things.* The consequences of flavor-of-the-month, however, tend to be short-term. And they tend to be linked to the verbal behavior of the implementers (promises of what will be), rather than to long-term, measurable improvements.
- *Support means education, sponsorship, and investing time and dollars toward the overall improvement of the organization.* Of course, the initiative *must* start with the executive—start at the top and cascade it

downward—if it isn't modeled up above, it won't stick below. Right?

Well, partially—except the "cascading down" model lacks a key ingredient: *consequences* for the executives who sponsor this new effort. Here's how it usually goes, using the hypothetical example of an initiative called *New Breeze* . . .

Implementing *New Breeze* . . .	Behavioral Analysis . . .
A bright, bottom-line driven, shareholder-sensitive senior executive busts his butt daily to lead his organization. Someone sells him some magic *to help improve his organization's performance.* Perhaps it's a general "change the culture and the results will follow." Or maybe it's a more direct hit, like "if we streamline x, y, z processes, we will save so many dollars." Either way, the guy at the top (usually it *is* a guy) buys a strategy—hook, line, and sinker—on the promise of bottom-line impact. Let's call it "Project *New Breeze*."	The reinforcers for the executive's behavior of supporting the new initiative are both *natural* and *externally provided.* To the exec, the promise of improved performance is naturally reinforcing. It *feels good* to do these things (positive-immediate-certain, PIC).
The consultants tell him that, as a good sponsor, he must "model the way." So, he and his senior execs participate in the training; they issue the power memos; and their ghostwritten article gets the front page in the company newsletter. *New Breeze* starts out blowing hard, fanned by the consultants.	The consultant or support person who assists with designing or implementing the effort is a strong source of positive feedback and praise. Plenty of PICs for the execs' behaviors! Sweet dreams . . .

Implementing *New Breeze* ...

Unfortunately, several weeks pass before the executives have a scheduled opening for the training (which is condensed to just a few hours, of course).

But the training happens, and the cascading begins. Direct reports are trained more deeply than the execs, which requires more time and generates schedule conflicts and delays. A few more weeks pass. The field implementation work is juggled with a jillion other demands. Everyone promises to approach things using their new toolkit—as time permits.

New Breeze continues to cascade downward in the organization. More time passes, and now the winds of change almost reach the bottom of the upper third of the organization!

Behavioral Analysis ...

The positive consequences for executive sponsorship of the effort become a *little more delayed*—and the words of "promised improved results" *begin to lose some of their naturally reinforcing qualities* because they are not paired with improved results . . . at least not yet.

Negative-immediate-certain con-sequences (NICs) occur, includ-ing time consumed by the effort and ongoing operational or per-formance problems.

PICs occasionally come from direct reports and colleagues, who praise the executives for their support of this effort.

Implementing *New Breeze*...

Six months or more have passed. Executive sponsorship continues, but begins to fray: *"We've worked with New Breeze a while . . . I'm not sure I'm seeing much benefit . . ."* Five-figure invoices arrive monthly from the implementation consultants. The execs begin calculating the cost of people being off-task to participate in the process. However, they rehearse the mantra in their minds: *"if the targeted (improved) new results are achieved, New Breeze will pay for itself in a heartbeat."*

The cascading continues downward. Excitement grows within the organization—the winds of change now have reached the middle of the organization. The weeks and months pass. People try to practice the new tools.

But the passage of time cools passions. The executive memos and newsletter columns dwindle. The initiative is barely mentioned in the 40-minute CEO videoconference. During a field visit, New Breeze isn't mentioned until someone from the field asks a question.

Behavioral Analysis...

Few PICs encourage executives to demonstrate sponsorship behaviors, except for continued praise from consultants—which grows stale.

Improvement in results has gone from positive-future-certain (PFC) to positive-future-uncertain (PFU) as doubt grows—will this intervention really make a difference?

The NICs from investing time and money in the effort are increasing their impact on executive sponsorship behaviors. Improved results have become PFUs for executive sponsorship.

Implementing *New Breeze* ...

Nine months have passed—three whole seasons of the year, and three quarterly dividends to shareholders. The executives are questioning why they invested hundreds of thousands in actual cash (called "green" dollars) and in cost of time and resources (called "blue" dollars) with no bottom-line change, except for the expense of the effort. Original doubters are saying "I told you so . . ."

Ten months into implementation, *New Breeze* has finally blown down to the bottom third of the organization (middle managers and first-line supervisors). Here is where it can strongly impact profits and losses.

The anniversary of the initiative arrives! Finally, *New Breeze* has reached the part of the organization where the rubber meets the road—front-line sales, operations, customer service, etc. They love it!

Behavioral Analysis ...

The NICs are growing stronger from current performance issues.

"I told you so" comments are painful NICs. Supporters criticize executives for not showing more sponsorship. NICs abound, and the whole enterprise has become quite aversive.

Just *talking* about the effort has become a NIC for executives. Few measurable results exist. A LOT of money has been spent (NIC), and the CEO's tenure has been potentially damaged by his support of the initiative (NFU). Promised results improvements remain PFUs.

Implementing *New Breeze*...	Behavioral Analysis...
However, front-line folks are not sure how committed leadership is, so some parts of the organization give lip service to the effort and abbreviate the implementation.	Because employees have a consequence history with flavor-of-the-month, they are skeptical about the staying power of New Breeze. They are used to seeing leadership roll out the next "most critical thing for the success of our business."
Meanwhile, the frustrated CEO begins hearing about a new approach that has worked—and worked quickly—at some other companies. It's called *"Second Wind."* He reads about it and makes some calls: After all, he has poured several million into this other thing, and the only ones who see a lasting payoff are the consultants!	Learning of a new or improved alternative serves as a PIC for him. Talking about *New Breeze* is a NIC. He feels as though he was had by *New Breeze* (NIC).
Given the increased problems and pressures existing in business (due to growth, expansion, or acquisitions), the executive knows he needs help. And so he investigates that "proven new approach . . . ."	
FLAVOR-OF-THE-MONTH PRE-VAILS AND MORE (NEGATIVE) CONSEQUENCE HISTORY IS LAY-ERED ON! (Return to first step and repeat the cycle.)	

When I share this saga of how flavor-of-the-month works in organizations with my clients, I always get head nods and nervous laughter, followed by, "That's exactly what happened to us!"

Your Takeaways from the Story

What are your takeaways from this? Here's why flavor-of-the-month tends to prevail:

1. *Sponsorship behaviors undergo extinction* because the outcomes promised (improved bottom-line results) either do not occur or are too delayed to reinforce sponsorship behavior.
2. *The natural competing immediate consequences (such as meeting quarterly financial targets) reinforce any behavior used to attain them,* even if the behavior runs counter to the new initiatives.
3. *New antecedents are constantly acting on the behavior of executives,* with new promises of outstanding outcomes (PICs and PFUs).
4. Negative consequence histories, commonly referred to as "resistance to change," occur within the organization because employees see no evidence of sustained focus or consistent antecedents and consequences regarding what's "really important."

What about instances where initiatives DO achieve the desired effect? When we study them, we observe very different behaviors by leaders in those organizations:

- We hear spontaneous (unprompted) mention of examples of the positive impact and success of the initiative.
- We hear praise for the units and people who made it happen.
- We hear leaders asking about the status of the effort.
- We observe leaders displaying a desire to understand what they did differently that led to success. We hear them seeking more information.

In other words, we observe all the behaviors we traditionally refer to as "sponsorship." These behaviors often occur with few special antecedents or none, *because the consequences are **positive** and **certain*** for the "sponsors"—and for employees at multiple levels in the organization.

We need to examine two issues:

1. *How do you understand the consequence history* that gets created from these "flavor-of-the-month" implementations, so your organization can overcome this problem?
2. *How do you implement a strategic initiative* that gets around the issues pointed out in the *New Breeze* example?

I will address both of these issues in the remainder of this chapter.

Antidote for Flavor-of-the-Month

You can break the crippling cycle of flavor-of-the-month by creatively applying the principles of behavioral science. Here are three keys to unlocking the problem:

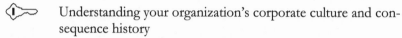 Understanding your organization's corporate culture and consequence history

Using the demand-pull strategy

Aligning consequence systems

 ## Understanding Your Organization's Corporate Culture and Consequence History

The first key to breaking the flavor-of-the-month pattern and effectively implementing change is *understanding your organization's culture*. Most change-oriented leaders, consultants, and implementers will quickly agree that the single greatest problem in bringing about change is *entrenched culture*. Over the years, leaders and employees grow so saturated with antecedents that they are numb to them, and everyone develops a consequence history so powerful—and often so negative—that traditional management cannot overcome it.

Then, in well-meaning attempts to improve the organization, multiple layers of "solutions" like TQM, Empowerment, and Teams are slathered on. The result is a culture of skeptical, cynical people who distrust change. This is what today's executives and leaders are up against—as you well know. *And all of this profoundly affects profitability.*

To solve your organization's problems, you must look hard at your corporate culture. Here is a behavioral definition:

Corporate culture
A pervasive pattern of behaviors that are either reinforced or punished, by the company's systems and/or people, over time.

This definition is true in every way, large and small, from how you treat customers to the company dress code. Let's make this very concrete. Let's look at how different the cultures of two companies can be—at *all* levels:

Cultural Component	Company A	Company B
Real work hours (not the official ones)	People come early, stay late	People are encouraged to work hours that match their personal style
Signature authority	The Chosen Few	Whoever is handy
Dress	Suits, ties, conservative	Business casual (whatever that is!)
Social interaction	Politeness when required	Colleagues are genuinely courteous
Communication	Letters, e-mail	Voice mail, e-mail
Lunchtime activities	Eat at desk while running e-mail	Eat in chatty groups or off-site
Political landscape	Palace intrigue; loose lips sink ships	Say it like it is
Leave policy	Rigid	Lax
Empowerment	As long as you do it exactly my way under my direct view	Just do it
Language	People cuss a lot because the CEO does	People seldom swear because the CEO doesn't
IT	The new version will be implemented if vendor support returns our calls	Buzzy found a cool software patch on the Net

Cultural Component	Company A	Company B
Office noise	*Faintly audible elevator music*	*A boom box in every cube*
Attitude toward customers	*Make them feel privileged to talk with you*	*Everyone deserves a smile*
Restrooms	*Pristine*	*Out of paper again*
Office horseplay	*Office what?*	*Occasional cube-to-cube missiles*
The boss' door	*Open by appointment only . . . and it had better be important!*	*Open to all*

Both companies could be very successful. But just imagine trying to change the culture—the entrenched behavior patterns—in either company! And try to imagine a merger or acquisition between these two outfits! (This is why I have a career!)

The resistance to changing entrenched culture—and the power of applying behavioral science to change it—is evident in this true story from one of my clients . . .

This CEO had a very tough challenge: either significantly reduce operating costs and expense-related practices or face losses from anticipated price erosion in the market. His Cost Team did a corporatewide study on cost reduction and cost management.

They analyzed spending and investment patterns and recommended cost-reduction strategies in every area. The Cost Team worked hard and delivered a plump report detailing observations, findings, and cost-reduction opportunities.

Then they told the CEO the very thing he didn't want to hear: "Our expense issue is really a cultural issue. Our culture doesn't support cost focus and cost reduction. Most of our managers grew up in the growth side of the business. Further, our whole industry has been prospering. So, within the current culture, it will be tough to make inroads on cost reduction . . . ."

The CEO went ballistic. He swore at the Team. "*Culture,*" he proclaimed, "*is a nebulous, fuzzy, and weak excuse for poor performance!*" He ordered them never to mention the "C-word" again. And he told them to find the *real* problem and come back with recommendations that made sense.

Tails between their legs, the Cost Team members scurried forth again and redid their work. The team members *knew* the problem was cultural, but in their data-driven world, they needed scientific proof for the CEO, who hated the very word "culture."

The cost team went back to the CEO, but this time they had behavioral science standing behind them. They sidestepped the word "culture" at first. They pointed out that the needed *behaviors*—those of cost monitoring, evaluation of cost above other factors in decision making, etc.—were not behaviors historically reinforced within their company. In fact, the *wrong* behaviors—those that ignored cost—were being reinforced simply because times were good.

By the way, the name for such a pervasive pattern of *behaviors* reinforced or punished by a company's systems or people over time is called, pardon the word, "culture."

The CEO began to grasp that this was indeed a culture problem, and one that could yield to behavior analysis. If he wanted to change behaviors, he had to

- seek a different behavior pattern than what already existed in the organization,
- understand that powerful reinforcers already existed for the current behaviors, and
- understand that powerful punishers for new behaviors could discourage change.

Thus began a multiyear effort to change this corporation's behavior patterns. The key was to change the reinforcers and punishers provided by the organization's systems and by leaders at all levels—starting with the Big Guy himself.

To my knowledge, this company's effort remains today the single largest systematic and systemic application of behavioral science technology inside a major corporation.

In this story, why did the CEO initially react as he did? Because of his *consequence history*. He had a negative consequence history for issues of "culture"—such a bad history that he detested the very word.

Why did the team respond by turning to science for help? Because of its *consequence history*. The team had a positive consequence history of presenting data-driven decisions: defend your position with data and rigor, and you will win; bring non–data-driven recommendations, and you will be soundly drubbed.

Our consequence histories and our environment of antecedent overload make to-day's landscape extremely challenging for achieving sustainable performance change.

Consequence Histories Revisited

I've really emphasized consequence history, and rightly so—understanding it is essential to understanding, changing, and successfully implementing behavioral change in your organization. If you now look differently at the behavior of those around you—and realize that the reason why Judy won't make eye contact with you in the hallway is because of her consequence history with you—you've got it! You now have the power of understanding behavior, and therefore culture, the first of the three keys to overcoming flavor-of-the-month.

On a Personal Note: Family Cultures

We can extend our definition of culture to our home lives as well. This helps us begin to understand why spending time at our parents' homes may be anxiety-producing, or why our spouses may fall into old behavior patterns (usually unwanted and undesirable) when they are back in the environments in which they grew up.

For starters, every family has its own culture—*its own pattern of behaving that gets reinforced by the people who are part of that culture (e.g., parents and siblings) over time.* Despite the fact that you and your spouse may be meant for each other, she or he may have grown up in a family culture where behaviors different from the ones in your family were reinforced.

For example, stating exactly how one feels may be called "honest," and it may be heavily reinforced in one family. Other families may call this behavior "impolite" or "disrespectful." I'm sure you can think of other examples involving eating behaviors, sleep schedules, TV viewing, game playing, etc.

Why do we fall into behavior patterns in our parents' homes that we don't exhibit in our own homes? Once again, it is *consequence histories*—those powerful antecedents and consequences that over decades have produced behavior patterns for us. Although significant time probably has passed since you played Clue or Monopoly, or since you were in bed before 10 P.M., being in a familiar environment where these behaviors were previously reinforced is probably sufficient to prompt and reinforce them even years later.[2]

---

[2] Interesting research, too detailed for this discussion, explains why the spontaneous recovery of old behavior patterns occurs under similar environmental conditions to those present when the behaviors were first shaped.

Using the Demand-Pull Strategy

Most organizations use a traditional cascading approach when implementing new strategies. As in our earlier *New Breeze* example, changes start at the top with high-level executives and cascade systematically downward into the organization—with the intent of ensuring that the leadership above understands and can model the new, desired behaviors.

In my company, we call this "supply-push," and we think it's a recipe for failure. With supply-push, a group has something it wants others to do—commonly referred to as a new initiative. A supply of new things that need to be done gets pushed throughout the organization, usually in a top-down fashion. Most often, this gets done irrespective of whether people want it, need it, use it, etc. Resistance becomes heavy, and people begin engaging in behaviors just enough to delay or avoid punishment for "not being on board."

You should immediately recognize supply-push implementation as something that is likely to encourage behaviors that will only get *negatively* reinforced. In other words, people will engage only in enough behavior related to the new initiative to avoid being an "opposer" or "non-supporter," but rarely will they engage in enough behavior to really make the thing work. In a couple of my client companies, they refer to this as "dodging the silver bullet." We have been referring to the line between negative reinforcement and positive reinforcement as the point where discretionary effort begins.

So, if supply-push doesn't work, how do you implement a new initiative?

You Need to Create a Demand-Pull

For people to want your new initiative, they must see what's in it for them. How will it benefit their business or their lives? Having the opportunity to decide what is good or not good for your organization is a huge positive consequence for most managers and executives. With demand-pull, you can build this into the process.

Typically, demand-pull *also* begins with top leadership—modeling desired behaviors or processes at the top is still important with demand-pull. However, you need to be concerned with the reinforcers for engaging in the new behaviors. In addition, you need to demonstrate the initiative's goodness to earn the right to implement it across the whole organization.

You demonstrate the goodness by pursuing a dual path of implementation with top leadership and with the organization. While educating, coaching, framing, and learning with the organization's top leaders, you also provide opportunities for key groups lower in the organization to participate in nearly the same activities. If those activities are worthwhile—if they lead to meaningful change and improvement, if they are truly worth the time and dollars people must invest in them—then results will follow. Behaviors will change at the local level, targeted results will improve, and these changes, together with positive reports to senior management, will serve two main functions:

1. They will reinforce sponsorship behaviors on the part of the senior team, which is just beginning its own learning process.
2. They will stimulate demand-pull from other parts of the organization, which will want to sample and eventually embrace what helped other divisions or departments improve.

Demand-pull implementation strategies put the burden on the service providers to be excellent, efficient, relevant, and results-oriented. They also reward the parts of the organization that need assistance and want to improve their performance. Finally, they keep behaviors and results closely linked to ensure that time invested gets returned in the most profitable way possible.

Understanding Consequence History

Can we ask an organization to behave in a new way? No, because *organizations* don't behave. *People* behave. So it is critical to look at the behavioral history of people in an organization. To understand the behavior of the people being asked to follow new processes or to engage in new behaviors, we need to understand the baseline from which we are starting.

What has the consequence history been with respect to the antecedents associated with change initiatives? Here are common consequence histories that many of my clients have:

Antecedent	P/N	I/F	C/U	Common Consequence History
This will be a good thing.	P	F	U	Usually means NFC for some people and PFU for others.
Trust me.	N	F	U	"Trust me" is an antecedent that rarely matches the consequences it promises.
You will be minimally impacted.	N	F	U	Usually spoken by someone who cannot control the consequences for people and who is not accountable for them. Either I will be impacted big time, or I will be left out, which causes other issues.
Your support will be critical to the success of this effort.	N	I	C	Usually means I will have a lot of extra work to do. This antecedent also suggests there will be negative consequences if I don't engage in those new behaviors!
We'd like to understand what got us here so we can learn from it.	P	I	C	Attention to the issue by others could be immediately reinforcing. However, the truth uncovered could mean bad things for me if I appear to be responsible for what happened.

Once we understand our current state, we can develop shaping plans to ensure positive consequences for the new behaviors we will be asking of people. Training, posters, newsletters, and lapel pins are all antecedents. They all prompt new behaviors such as attending training, reviewing manuals, and reading posters. They also prompt a lot of meetings, flipchart writing, and use of problem-solving tools.

The behaviors of executive sponsorship are supported by coaching for a while. *But the behaviors eventually need to come under the control of the natural consequence that the executive finds reinforcing: the bottom-line performance of the organization.* Therefore, if improvement in bottom-line results is not detected within months after implementation, the behaviors we have come to call "sponsorship" undergo extinction. These behaviors fail to get reinforced and thus diminish in frequency and intensity. An executive then reads about a new "silver bullet," and the cycle continues.

Past Consequences, Troubled Future

Here are some initiatives that one of my clients tried to implement. The client was a large corporation comprising several acquired businesses. Each "change effort" had been a negative experience for key groups in the organization. Given that consequence history, how do you think employees will react to an upcoming IT change?

Consequence History

What Preceded	Who Was Affected	Their Key Experiences
A purchasing agreement designed to yield savings based on large orders.	Member companies and local vendors. There had been a relationship between member companies and local vendors. Now, they have to use a national provider.	Told they'd be getting big savings, but savings did not materialize. "The service we receive is lousy."

Effect on Implementation

Based on the above consequence history, here's what must happen for the IT change to succeed: the company must involve "customers" in defining success factors for the new system and its implementation, and then use them with the IT vendor and the communications with the internal customer group.

They must also provide realistic expectations up front about likely challenges.

Finally, they should identify unintended negative effects from the prior implementation and suggest strategies to work through those issues.

Consequence History		
What Preceded	**Who Was Affected**	**Their Key Experiences**
Conversion to standard benefits plan. The initial message promised better service and cheaper rates.	All member companies.	There is no difference between what people had vs. what they have now. Plans may be cheaper, but quality of service is lower.
		Delays in receiving membership cards meant paying for service from their own pockets.
		Difficulty in getting questions answered.
		To some people, the conversion was smooth and seamless.

Effect on Implementation

The company must communicate earlier and better about specific changes.

They must also provide positive feedback for those who "follow the rules" of implementation and consistently communicate the changes and expectations of member companies.

Further, they must provide information early so that people can choose and review the plan information, and they must develop resources and processes to support customers and answer questions.

Aligning Consequence Systems

A third key to avoiding flavor-of-the-month is to align consequence systems with what you are trying to achieve. A critical step in sustaining change, support, and sponsorship at all levels is ensuring that consequence systems (pay, promotion, recognition, development) are not competing with what you are trying to do by reinforcing the wrong behaviors. Here's an example of what can go wrong:

> **One of our clients asked for help in developing leadership skills and processes to improve bottom-line results. We worked hard for 18 months to educate, coach, and support hundreds of leaders, from the company president to the front-line shift supervisors. They learned new ways of managing the business. They were told that future success in the company depended heavily on practicing the new leadership skills and methods.**
>
> **As the leadership and human resources people worked on changing the job selection and promotion processes, teams continued to use policies from the old culture to select people for promotion and high-potential opportunities. The company risked contradicting the new way by continuing to reward and promote the old way. Fortunately, it wasn't long before they implemented, revised, and aligned systems for performance appraisal, compensation, recognition, and job promotion. They also adjusted the requirements for progression to ensure that all promotions, visible and invisible, strengthened the new culture.**

If reward and recognition systems are not adjusted to reinforce the behaviors identified in key initiatives, the initiatives will fail. Behaviors will not be reinforced and sustained in the long run. Repeated failure contributes heavily to the flavor-of-the-month problem and perpetuates the cycle of half-implemented programs.

Realistically, at the outset, you may be limited to assuring that the consequence systems are not working against you by reinforcing undesired behaviors. You can later modify the consequence systems so they reinforce the new or desired behaviors. This can increase the rate of new behaviors and sustain them.

Think for a moment about your own organization. What behaviors are *officially* valued, versus the ones that *actually* get reinforced? Here are some common examples to help you:

What the organization says . . .	What the organization does . . .
"We value diversity"	Promoting white males who have been with the organization a long, long time is the norm.
"Teamwork is valued and important"	Financial incentives and promotions are determined by individual accomplishments and outcomes.
"We care about people"	Bonuses are contingent upon bottom-line results, regardless of how they are achieved.
"Work-family balance is important"	Staying late, working weekends, taking laptop on vacation, and checking voicemail seven days per week is expected. Employees are reprimanded for not performing this way.
"Free checking at our bank!"	No fee is charged for checking at local bank; remote check cashing or ATM usage incurs a service charge.
"Safety is our first priority"	Near misses that allow the line to continue running and don't lead to shutting down are commonplace.

I'll bet you could create a page full of examples from your company!

The bottom line: implementation requires behavior change. Behavior change is a function of what people and systems (pay, promotion, selection, rewards) either reinforce (through positive consequences) or punish (through negative consequences), whether intentional or unintentional.

We get what we reinforce. We don't get what we punish. It's just that simple.

Landmark Gallup Study Links Employee Attitude to Business Outcomes

The Gallup Organization has statistically confirmed a relationship between employee attitudes and critical business outcomes, such as revenue, profitability, customer loyalty, and employee retention. Their study is the first to quantify such linkages across different companies.

Gallup researchers surveyed over 100,000 employees from more than 2,500 business units in 24 companies across a dozen industries. Their research identified twelve specifically worded questions, each of which statistically defines an employee attitude that matters most in managing and improving the workplace.

Their analysis revealed consistent, reliable relationships between each attitude and positive business outcomes. For example, groups where these positive employee attitudes exist are 50 percent more likely to deliver on customer loyalty and 44 percent more likely to produce above-average profitability. In comparing top-quartile to bottom-quartile business units, those in the top quartile averaged 24 percent higher profitability, 29 percent higher revenue, and 10 percent lower employee turnover.

The study found significant variation in these relationships among operating units in the same company. This implies that broad generalizations about workplace quality are misguided. It also indicates that sweeping assumptions about entire industries are even less appropriate.

"A single company does not mean a single culture," notes Gallup consultant Marcus Buckingham. "A company has as many cultures as it has frontline managers. Each of our measurement items points to an attitude that frontline supervisors can impact directly and immediately. Individual frontline supervisors can be extremely effective in building stronger workplaces."

Today's executives and shareholders demand performance measurements that relate to profits and productivity. By tying reliable data on employee attitudes directly to financial outcomes, a productive workplace can be managed by employee attitude as effectively as by financial measures.

Until now, executives have had little help in managing their most valuable asset: their workforce. Executive-level management initiatives like TQM and reengineering often failed because they overlooked essential issues in day-to-day management. Long-term success must be achieved at the front line through employees and their immediate supervisors.

"We are in a new era," says Curt Coffman of The Gallup Organization. "Machines don't matter—minds do. Today's executive has known this for years. What is new is that they can now measure the extent to which their organizations are being successful in this regard."

The Gallup study fulfills an important need for executives and frontline managers. Executives need a scorecard to manage their overall organizations, whereas frontline managers need a metric to build better work units. Employees need their talents properly matched to the demands of their job.

Source: The Gallup Organization

The Bottom Line on Execution

When viewed from a behavioral perspective, organizational change looks very different. It is not only about changing the business or the processes or the culture; it's about changing individual behavior. Why is it so difficult to change behaviors? How can you use the principles and tools from this book to help? Here are the key points I hope you will take away from this chapter:

1. *Many companies face the "flavor-of-the-month" dilemma.* They start to implement one change, but get distracted by another before they see promised benefits from the first one. Why? Senior executives who sponsor change may not receive enough positive consequences (improved business results) from the change quickly enough to hold their attention. In fact, they often experience many negative consequences associated with the change and therefore seek out alternatives that promise more positive consequences.

2. *There are three keys for dealing with flavor-of-the-month:*

- *Understanding your organization's culture.* Entrenched culture is a significant challenge to bringing about change. Leaders and employees have grown so saturated with antecedents that they are numb to them, and everyone develops a consequence history so powerful—and often so negative—that traditional management cannot overcome it. Understanding this consequence history will help you more effectively plan and deliver antecedents and consequences for the new change.

- *Using a demand-pull strategy rather than a supply-push strategy.* Persuade people to implement the change by focusing on what's in it for them and delivering on your promises. Demand-pull usually requires a dual path of implementation with top leadership and the organization. While educating, coaching, framing, and learning with top leaders of the organization, provide opportunities for key groups lower in the organization to participate in nearly the same activities. If those activities are grounded in a strategic business opportunity, if they lead to meaningful change with results improvement, if they are truly worth the time and dollars people must invest in them, then improvements in results measures will be detected. Behaviors will change at the local level, and targeted results will improve. Along with positive reports to senior management, these changes will reinforce sponsorship behaviors on the senior team and stimulate demand-pull from other parts of the organization.

- *Aligning consequence systems with what you are trying to achieve.* A critical step in sustaining change, support, and sponsorship at all levels is ensuring that consequence systems (pay, promotion, recognition, development) are not competing with what you are trying to do by reinforcing the wrong behaviors. In fact, aligning your consequence systems with the desired behavioral changes is a powerful way to increase the likelihood those behaviors will continue.

What's Next?

We've looked at the behavioral side of organizational change. Almost certainly, your organization has recently or will soon undertake major organizational change—a merger, acquisition, or enterprise resource planning (ERP) implementation (Oracle, PeopleSoft, or e-commerce). In the next chapter, we'll take a behavioral view of these and the other powerful "Grand Slam Challenges" facing business today.

The Payoff: Conquering Today's Grand-Slam Challenges

The stock market is exploding. While a downturn in the economy is inevitable, we have never before experienced such growth and prosperity in the U.S. economy. As companies try to hire seasoned talent, candidates are telling them they can make more money by staying at home managing their portfolios than they can by working—even with the signing bonus. The unemployment rate has never been lower . . . a new generation of wealth is being born as young entrepreneurs make it big through IPOs and sales of their companies . . . CEOs are getting younger and younger . . . technology innovations are occurring at light speed . . . college graduates with math, computer science, finance, engineering, and teaching degrees can name their jobs . . . and those without college degrees can make money in factory jobs and positions requiring skilled labor.

What a fascinating time to be alive . . .

Now THAT YOU understand behavior analysis and how it works to support implementation, let's put it to use. In this chapter, we'll address the grand-slam challenges we all face today—and how your newfound knowledge of behavioral science will get you through them. The challenges:

- Merger and acquisition integrations
- Corporate creep
- Supply chain management
- Enterprise resource planning (ERP) implementation
- Employee involvement
- Cross-selling across business units
- Knowledge management
- e-behavior for e-commerce
- Winning the battle for top people
- Successful succession

Merger and Acquisition Integrations

Consider the integration of any two corporate cultures, and it becomes instantly obvious why mergers and acquisitions present such major challenges. Each company has a history of reinforcing certain behaviors and not others. The probability that two or more cultures have identical consequence histories is virtually zero.

Collaboration, teamwork, and sharing ideas in one culture may be seen as wasting time in another culture—a sign of weak individual capabilities or a failure to focus on getting the real work done. Consider the mantra of one company: "Take care of your employees, and they will take care of the customers." This may be viewed as backward by a company that believes leaders and employees exist only for the shareholders. Each of these viewpoints reinforces very different behavior patterns. Thus, each creates and sustains very different cultures related to performance.

Any merger generates hundreds of new documents. Part of this documentation discloses relevant legal and business facts about both companies (this is called *due diligence*). Unfortunately, the documents and the due diligence process don't reveal the full picture—they don't disclose the depth of *cultural* differences. Nor do they reveal how the work gets done in each organization.

In other words, *merger documents rarely reveal the patterns of behavior* that have been shaped over decades by the systems and people within the organization. With a merger, the players abruptly change, consequence providers (a.k.a. leaders) are altered, and antecedents no longer align with the same consequences. Result: the old conditions that allowed desirable behaviors to occur are changed, so behavior becomes less predictable, less reliable, and less aligned with what made the companies so successful prior to the merger.

Having read this book, you understand why the consequences in two merging cultures are seldom consistent. And without consistent patterns of behavior, there are no consistent applications of consequences. Thus, the new culture becomes a collection of subcultural islands, like "the Westinghouse guys" and "the CBS guys" and "the "Viacom guys" or "the Daimler-Benz people" and "the Chrysler people."

What are people really identifying when they use these labels? *They are identifying the behaviors that their leaders predictably and reliably reinforce versus the behaviors their leaders don't reinforce.* And so the subcultures become embedded, and the new culture can't develop for years and years—while profits suffer.

The Elixir for M & A

Here is the elixir: *leaders of both organizations need to come together and pinpoint which behaviors they want to see in the new company. They need to agree upon which behaviors will be reinforced and which behaviors will be discouraged. And then they need to demonstrate those agreements in their actions, through their own consequence provision.*

If this work is done at the outset, consequence systems can be properly aligned, and a new culture can be shaped much faster than if it is left to chance. In fact, the new culture will emerge *even before* any communication efforts or other antecedent events are in place. Employees will observe behaviors either getting reinforced or not getting reinforced all around them, so they will experience the new contingencies themselves. (Remember the 80/20 rule and the power of consequences.)

Leaders can create a new culture and shape new behaviors fairly quickly by aligning antecedents (like a new vision statement) with desired behaviors, and by actively delivering positive, immediate, and certain (PIC) consequences. *Taking the time to do this work is where most mergers fall short.* In the frenzy to get FTC approval and names plugged into organizational charts, and in the race to get results and meet operating targets, it is tempting to view "culture" as a distraction and a waste of time. Leaders usually dedicate their attention to hitting pro forma targets rather than to aligning consequences that would make getting those results more probable in the longer term!

From reading this book, you know the problem: culture is often seen as *future* and *uncertain*, whereas profitability, operating income, and shareholder returns are immediate and (perceived to be) certain.

My one-two punch for smooth M&A is this:

1. *Invest time in clearly articulating to everyone the vision, strategy, and means of success for the future.* In other words, make the antecedents clear and consistent. Encourage new teams at all levels to work together and to review the critical results targets at their levels. Pinpoint key behaviors that need to occur for the results targets to be met.

2. *Invest time to plan and deliver positive consequences for achieving those results* and decide how those who engage in less desirable behaviors will be coached. Shape behaviors that are critical to the success of the organization—don't leave them up to chance! Use a framework like the Shaping Opportunity Grid (Chapter 6) to ensure that every interaction is leveraged as an opportunity to shape behavior.

More About Culture

Many terms are used to describe business cultures. They include "high-performance," "safety-driven," "customer-centric," and "financially oriented." These labels signal the behaviors that are desired and reinforced within a culture. The labels can be powerful antecedents for desired behaviors, if the consequences that support them are aligned.

Here is an interesting example from a post-merger meeting, where I was asked to help with a merger-integration process. I worked with an executive leadership team in the largest operating division of a major corporation . . .

The senior operating officer had been the pre-merger President of the *acquiring* company. He had a history of getting results, was well-respected, and a little feared.

The first leadership team meeting was attended by the new VPs of Marketing, Manufacturing, Sales, Transportation, Human Resources, Finance, and IT. Like the President, the VP of Marketing was highly talented, credentialed, seasoned, and creative, with an impressive record of getting results through positive people practices. He came from the *acquired* organization.

The President welcomed the new team and encouraged them to participate fully, describing his own style as one of open dialogue and communication. He asked them to share their thoughts and speak openly.

The team discussed brand erosion. The President presented unfavorable results from a recent survey, disclosing that brand recognition of their core products had shrunk. Market share had declined three percent. The President had some thoughts about the cause, but he wanted to hear from others.

The Marketing VP sat up, eyes twinkling. He jumped in, describing a similar issue in his company and what they had done about it.

But the President stared expressionless at the VP as he spoke, his head unwavering. Other members of the team began to look down and away from the Marketing VP. In fact, all but one of the six leadership team members broke eye contact with him. (The one person who sustained eye contact was the only other team member from the acquired company.) When he finished his summary of the situation at his previous company, the room fell silent for at least 10 seconds. The team members

continued to look away from him, and a few began peering at the President.

"That was interesting," the President said neutrally. "But I believe our issue is . . . and as a result, I think we should . . . ." He went on to ask the VP of Sales to study the issue—and report back to the team on next steps. He then suggested that the VP of Marketing might want to touch base with the VP of Sales to stay "in the loop" on the issue. Then he proceeded to the next agenda item.

Let's unpack this story . . .

The new Marketing VP barely knew the culture of the acquiring company. At the outset of the meeting, the President said he valued open communication (antecedent), which the Marketing VP naively took at face value. On the strength of that antecedent, the Marketing VP openly shared his thoughts about the brand erosion issue. But his behavior was punished promptly: loss of eye contact with colleagues, absence of head nods or smiles from the President, the President saying that what the VP shared was "interesting" but then explaining the "right" answer, and assigning the issue to someone else who hadn't even contributed in the meeting.

Based on that, what do you predict will occur the next time the Marketing VP has a thought to share? In all probability, he will not risk sharing as openly as he did in this meeting. He experienced the *real* culture, which differed quite significantly from what was described at the outset of the meeting. He also experienced the peer culture: receiving no encouragement from his new team members as he spoke. This will affect his behavior with those peers in the future.

The antecedent "share your thoughts and speak openly" was strong enough to get his behavior started the first time, but that antecedent will not prompt the same behavior again because the more powerful consequences did not align with it (again, the 80/20 rule).

And the Marketing VP probably formed impressions about how others from his acquired company will be treated—which will in turn impact his behavior with others.

Ah, the complexities of being human! In isolation, this short sequence of events might seem unimportant. But over time, thousands of these brief interactions—moments of truth—will occur and will shape the new corporate culture—even if it might be against our wishes or intentions. And without any intervention to prompt an alternate outcome, these brief interactions happen in all parts of newly merged organizations every single minute. It's no wonder "cultures" are so tough to change once they are established.

Corporate Creep

Why is it easier to create life than to resurrect it? Said in an organizational context, why do greenfield start-ups have such higher rates of success than brownfield culture change efforts? Once again, we turn to our behavioral tools for the answer.

With brownfields (organizations that have existed for some time), it is very tough to change all of the consequence systems and contingencies fast enough. So many aspects of how the organization works need to be changed. This requires a highly committed set of leaders with the tools and willingness to give each other feedback.

However, with greenfields (newer organizations), there is no history of consequences, so behaviors are not heavily entrenched or strongly controlled by other variables. They are more open to shaping quickly—in fact, individuals will say they *expect* shaping to occur. Antecedents tend to have a strong effect—at least initially. But can the culture be sustained? Not with corporate creep.

Let me illustrate . . .

I was working with an organization that decided to consolidate its customer service functions. Nine regional customer service centers consolidated into a single location that was closer to the company's major manufacturing sites but was 1700 miles from corporate headquarters. The eight leaders of the new center crafted a vision statement about the level of service excellence their customers could expect, their commitment to empower their workforce, and their desire not to have a single leader, but a team of eight leaders—each to share one-eighth of the President's hat. It was a heartfelt commitment by all.

Within two years, state-of-the-art management practices were in operation. The center's operating costs were well below

budget because of the teamwork and consistent consequences that everyone exhibited. They actively created a plan for positive reinforcement delivery that was contingent upon the occurrence of strategically aligned behaviors. They put into place career ladders to systematically reinforce cross-boundary activities, teamwork, and self-initiated enlargement of job responsibilities (designed to better serve the customer). The leaders taught and modeled leadership behaviors and continuous improvement, and they served as field coaches for the new behaviors to be practiced. It was textbook-perfect.

So, was it sustained? Yes, for a few years. Then, little by little, *corporate creep* began to occur. As locations outside the center were downsized or closed in response to other corporate needs, new managers were imported who embraced philosophies and values inconsistent with the greenfield team.

Some corporate leaders thought the center's culture was strong enough to deal with newly imported managers—even though their performance had been consistently marginal in prior jobs, with no one ever properly owning the coaching and feedback of those individuals. Other corporate leaders were naïve regarding the cultural practices of the center and any relationships between those practices and the business results. The undeniable success of the greenfield organization led senior management to promote its high-potential leaders to other parts of the organization. They then replaced these high-potential leaders with managers from other operating units who did not share the same vision or desired behaviors that had come to define the center. Little by little, the associates' behaviors and work teams' practices that were previously reinforced in the center began to get punished by new leaders who brought with them old ways of managing. Corporate creep was on the march.

The corporate leaders measured the success of the center much like they had always measured success: bottom-line performance. "We don't care how, just get it. Take those high-potential leaders, move them where we really need them, and replace them with people who know the business and won't screw things up." *They never gave a thought to the powerful role that the culture and reinforcement delivery played in getting the impressive business results in the first place.*

It was the employees (often overlooked as important providers of consequences to leaders) who reacted most strongly and consistently to the undesired leadership practices that crept into their center. Things worked for a while, but the organization and leadership consequences became too powerful as they began to punish things like collaboration, teamwork, and shared decision making.

The bottom line held its own for several years, but the initial outstanding performance began to erode. The real impact occurred in turnover numbers, which grew from single-digit to double-digit. In addition, customer and employee satisfaction numbers declined steadily.

Employees and managers would say that corporate creep spread like a weed. In behavioral terms, the pattern of reinforcement changed each time a new leader entered the system and began reinforcing different behaviors. And, perhaps more relevant to this example, new leaders began punishing old behaviors that had reliably led to successful outcomes.

And so the new culture was emerging—one that mirrored an older command-and-control style versus the progressive and highly profitable practices of this center. I refer to this process as *corporate creep*. "Corporate creep" is when the systems of reinforcement from one entity (usually the parent) are different from those operating locally. (In this example, they were built into the very fabric of the organization.) "Creep" refers to the eventual takeover that leaves the original, local contingencies barely operable.

I learned the term "corporate creep" from a senior executive of a Fortune 25 company who had personally designed and led a greenfield site for the first seven years of its existence. In year eight, her division experienced the beginning of "corporate creep." By the ninth year, another major location closed, leading to the transfer of large numbers of people to her center, and the "weed" took over. Little by little, those new consequences contaminated the greenfield's culture. Everyone lost because performance declined rapidly and the new imported leaders undid what they thought was "unnecessary."

The Cure for Corporate Creep

Do you have to keep the original leaders forever to avoid corporate creep? No, of course not. What you need to do, however, goes back to our CYBER Model. Definite antecedents and consequences support behaviors that occur reliably and predictably. Therefore, when you are getting desirable results, you need to make sure you understand the behaviors driving those results. This will help ensure that you do not unintentionally punish those behaviors or eliminate their sources of reinforcement.

As new leaders for a site are selected, you need to ask, "Will they positively reinforce behaviors needed to implement a strategy and achieve our results? Will the consequences operating within the organization reinforce their leadership behaviors?" (For example, some leaders find collaboration or consensus aversive, while others reinforce it.) The key to this situation lies in our ability to analyze it correctly from a behavioral standpoint and then to take deliberate action, and not leave issues of such importance to chance. *Behaviors drive profitability.* We need to ensure that our actions as leaders reflect this understanding.

Supply Chain Management and Behavior

Supply chain is the flow of materials or information from suppliers to customers—typically by way of purchasing, manufacturing, distribution, sales, and marketing.

Studies show that, depending on the industry, top companies in supply-chain performance achieve much higher savings than their median-performing peers. Such results mean that understanding and managing the supply chain with greater efficiency and reliability should be a high priority for leaders.

Supply chain management began in earnest in the late '80s as "brown-paper mapping exercises" in which each work unit would map its process and connect the map to that of the unit receiving its product or service. Breakthroughs occurred left and right as sister units discovered what really happened and what each could do to increase process efficiency and reliability.

What does this have to do with behavior? Everything! Understanding behavior has major implications for supply-chain management.

The Supply Chain Includes Countless Behaviors

Consider the hundreds of process steps that occur from the time a customer orders a product (or even before, when the customer's need arises), until the product is produced, transported, and ultimately reaches the customer. From this, you can begin to see the thousands of behaviors that must occur for that process to work efficiently and reliably. When antecedents are unclear, or consequences are remote or nonexistent, behaviors do not occur very reliably or predictably.

In addition, as projects to improve supply chain management become chartered, insufficient pinpointing of what is expected and how its success will be evaluated often occurs. (I've seen this in every company I've worked with.)

For example, executives often cite a statistic and direct a team to achieve savings through supply chain management. Large figures are thrown around, teams are launched, and savings are expected—with few people really buying into the statistic or the business case.

How could these leaders approach this task differently, using an understanding of behavior?

For starters, they could ask the team to discover specific information about companies or units that have done supply chain management well. They could then compare it with their own organizations to estimate the savings. This would allow them to precisely pinpoint the outcomes they seek and to arrange contingencies for the team that would enhance the probability of success.

They could also ask pinpointed questions about the nature of the savings achieved by other benchmark companies. For example:

- Were the savings achieved through inventory reductions? Inventory turns? Transportation costs?
- How did they manage the successful implementation of their process changes?
- What did people do differently?
- How did they structure themselves for implementation?
- What were some of the problems when implementation did not succeed?
- Was it best to have people on the project team full time or part time?
- What was the percentage of project savings realized?
- How long did it take to reach the desired savings?
- How were the project team members recognized and rewarded?

One company managed a companywide process implementation exceptionally well. They surveyed key stakeholders three and nine months after the implementation to assess the effectiveness of the deployment and the measurable results. Over 94 percent of the respondents stated that this implementation was better than any previous implementation of a new process or initiative. They offered statements such as "there was much better understanding from the get-go due to the planned communications process"; "there was more inclusion/involvement of stakeholders in both the design and deployment stages"; "the roles in the new process were made very clear"; "desired behaviors were clearly emphasized and reinforced when they occurred"; "training was excellent"; and "status of the project and performance feedback were readily available and kept updated."

And the "hard measures" of effectiveness—those on which the executive sponsor was counting—were significant as well. Successes included:

- Process improvement
- Improved timing of stock transfer to terminals
- Significant savings on throughput charges at an outside storage facility
- Reduced freight cost to customers because employees proactively managed the forecast data
- Better demand forecasting accuracy and participation from a better understanding of its effect on the process and business
- Increased purchasing efficiency due to the ability to commit volumes with a higher accuracy, to leverage purchasing volumes, to increase communication, and to clarify roles

This is yet another example of how unlocking behavior directly affects profitability. We see it time and again. Unfortunately, we often say that "people are people" and turn to things like demand forecasting accuracy or supplier-managed inventory without looking at the behaviors and processes required to do the work and achieve results. But we can see why desired and needed behaviors don't occur once we analyze the antecedents and consequences. The good news is that we can change all of this, using our knowledge of behavioral science.

Enterprise Resource Planning (ERP) Implementation

SAP, Oracle, Peoplesoft, BAAN, and J.D. Edwards are credited for tremendous success in some companies. Yet, they are vilified in others. Regardless of which side you fall on, the same statement applies: *the way the ERP solution is implemented determines its success or failure.*

In almost all ERP implementations, a consulting partner is selected to configure and install the system. Typically, the partners bring strong experience in the system design and configuration. Where the trouble begins, and where most partners fail, is in *getting people to use the system.* In other words, users do not behave in a way that corresponds with how the system needs to be followed in order for everything to work properly. Let's look at a couple of examples.

ERP Example 1: The Behavior of Managers Is Critical

This example identifies a very basic behavior that is a major factor in ERP success or failure. I was conducting a one-on-one coaching session with "Karen," a finance department manager for a large manufacturing organization. Karen's boss interrupted us. "Hey, Karen. I need the business summary report by 8 A.M. for a director's meeting. Just leave it on my desk. I really appreciate it, Karen—you always come through for me!" Her boss then walked away.

Karen asked me to excuse her, opened her spreadsheet program, made a couple of changes, and printed the report. While she did so, she muttered, "You know, I probably should try to pull this out of our new ERP system. But that would take too much time, and I still don't know how to get through all of the screens. Plus, I can never find the information I need. Good thing I keep this spreadsheet up-to-date!"

A vicious cycle was in place. People didn't request information from the system because it was incomplete. And because it was incomplete and no one asked for information, no one entered information.

About two weeks later I was asked to meet with a team charged with ERP rollout at the plant in which I was working. They were concerned because most people were not using the system, and those who were using it found the data to be incomplete. The team wanted to analyze the situation from a behavioral viewpoint.

Several antecedents had been used to get people to use the system: training, cheat sheets, newsletters, e-mail messages, etc. Most of these antecedents were well-thought-out. There were no real surprises here. The "ah-has" came when we started talking about consequences.

The most apparent negative consequence was that the system was harder to use than the old system. Users had to go through layers of screens to enter information and print reports. Everyone agreed that this difficulty would diminish as the users got more practice with the system. So then the question became, "How do we get people to become comfortable with the system?"

I shared what happened during my coaching session with Karen. Light bulbs started to go off. By simply asking for the report, the boss had opened the door for Karen to choose her source. Also, by thanking her for the information, her boss reinforced her for using the old system. The group realized that one of the critical leverage points in making the system successful was the *behavior of managers.* Her manager needed to stop reinforcing her use of the old system and start reinforcing her use of the ERP system.

I have seen few, if any, ERP implementation efforts where attention is given to behavior at this level. This is one major reason there are so many problems with ERP implementations!

ERP Example 2: Getting People to Use the Help System

Change efforts like ERP usually include a help desk or other on-line help to answer questions. Typically, an organization sets up a toll-free number or a Web site for help. This client did that. However, people developed "local" help systems—buddies and cheat sheets—as more immediate sources of help, instead of accessing the toll-free number or help desk. This translated into inconsistent information and inefficiency because people were away from their jobs helping others while the intended resources sat idle.

On this project, we provided three waves of support. First was the technical wave, in which new hardware and software were installed. Second was a support wave, in which a team of troubleshooters addressed technical problems. The third and most innovative wave was a small team that *observed people using the system.* When problems arose, the team would guide the person to the appropriate help system. This did two things:

- People learned the help system and were reinforced for using it (PICs for new behaviors until the natural reinforcers—having their questions answered—could take over).

- The support person was able to assess the quality of the help and provide this performance feedback to the help desk team (immediate consequence provision for behaviors that have long delays in performance consequences). This helped assure that people received value-added support. In this way, help desk users received effective antecedents (the prompt to call the help desk) and very positive consequences (getting quality help). And the people on the help desk received additional positive consequences from observing the impact on customers calling in—in addition to their most powerful PICs of simply helping folks on the other end of the call.

The result of our work was one of the most successful IT implementations within the company. It has been benchmarked by dozens of other companies who want to understand what was done and how. The communications effort and the three waves of support were largely responsible for this success.

What the team accomplished was pretty phenomenal: they changed out nearly 40,000 computers in about a year, upgraded their entire IT infrastructure, and will now accrue annual savings in labor and equipment in the ten-millions of dollars.

The Key to Successful ERP Implementation

What many people do not realize is that ERP implementation requires change in people's relationships as much as change in technology. In fact, change in relationships probably influences the success of implementation more than technology.

In one implementation, for example, a major barrier was that the controller resisted the change because the ERP system took away his access to the company's leaders. The ERP system let the leadership team members access reports themselves, so they no longer needed to contact the controller. But the controller wanted to protect this important relationship.

ERP systems change the way people interact at work—they change behavior. For example:

- Instead of calling a clerk, the manager inputs inventory information directly into a new system—a behavioral change.
- Instead of operating at the tactical level checking invoices, the procurement agent needs to work at developing strategic relationships with suppliers—another behavioral change.

And so it goes. Behavior is not an element of change, it *is* the change!

As you know, successfully making these behavioral changes requires careful analysis, planning, and lots of shaping. This means that the success of an ERP implementation depends on:

- Your ability to analyze the type and degree of behavioral changes required by everyone affected by the ERP system
- Your ability to develop a clear case for changing behaviors—including outlining the PICs for individuals making the change
- Your ability to provide training in new skills, not only in how to use the ERP technology but in how to perform new jobs. (The procurement agent mentioned earlier will need to develop negotiation and relationship-building skills to fulfill her new role).
- Your ability to arrange for feedback to performers from supervisors and customers

ERP Implementation Metrics and Behaviors

Much of the fanfare around ERP promises that it will reduce cost and enhance revenue by improving processes and integrating information. The business case for implementing an ERP system often is built on reducing transaction costs, reducing headcount, enhancing revenues through better collection, and so on. These are the ultimate measures of ERP implementation success.

ERP Implementation Metrics

Unfortunately the implementation team is likely to have entirely different metrics than the ones you just saw. The implementation team's success is most often measured by on-time/within-budget performance, and this difference between project metrics and implementation metrics raises serious issues.

First, implementation metrics do not address project quality. On-time/within-budget performance has very little to do with how effectively people are using the system, or how effectively the new system was introduced into the organization. Ironically, on-time/within-budget metrics often drive behaviors that actually work against effective system usage.

Second, implementation metrics are not directly tied to the measures related to the business case. By focusing on on-time/within-budget performance, the project team has no incentive to deliver a quality system, which would entail accountability for the necessary behavior changes and results metrics. Thus, implementation metrics are likely to actually work against the very business case on which the project was sold!

The major issue with the metrics mentioned above, especially implementation metrics, is obvious: *they do not focus on behaviors.* Instead, they focus on results. One of the major opportunities in an ERP implementation (and probably one of the biggest factors in its success) is to pinpoint and shape critical or high-leverage behaviors. By identifying key behaviors for success, you are in a position to analyze and positively influence them—ultimately leading to a successful implementation. The table shows behaviors that are typical of various stakeholders on an ERP project.

Typical Behaviors in an ERP Implementation

Stakeholder	Sample Behaviors
Senior Leadership	• Include ERP information in presentations and communications to field • Monitor progress of project and provide feedback to PMO and Implementation Team
Project Management Office (PMO)	• Review project budgets and timelines weekly (at a minimum) • Provide feedback to project leaders and project team members • Raise issues and concerns to leadership ASAP • Provide leadership with feedback and information about their contribution to success • Report on all aspects of the project: timeliness, budget performance, quality, impact on organization and results
Middle Management	• Articulate business case to organization • Discuss ERP-related news in regular meeting • Specify source of information being requested • Understand how employees should do their jobs and coach them through transitions and difficult times • Ask how people are feeling about the project and how they're being impacted. Give this information to the PMO and implementation teams • Provide feedback to team on system use

Stakeholder	Sample Behaviors
Implementation Team	• Display concern for user community:
	• Answer questions honestly
	• If an answer is unknown, say so and find answer or provide resource for getting answer
	• Measure usage of new system as it gets introduced and shape new behaviors that are needed
	• Send agendas before meetings
	• Frequently communicate meaningful project information to stakeholders
End Users	• Raise issues/problems encountered with system, using established process for resolution of issues
	• Ask questions about the system
	• Attend training sessions, conference room pilots, workshops, etc.

Targeting ERP Implementation Behaviors

On which behaviors should you focus? As always, target behaviors that will have the greatest impact on project success. Since every organization is unique, your target behaviors are likely to be different from those shown in the table.

Again we can turn to the CYBER Model to help us to identify the high-impact behaviors needed for your successful ERP implementation. It starts with the business opportunity and the results you want to achieve:

CYBER Step 1. Start by identifying the business opportunity. What is the entire organization trying to achieve?

CYBER Step 2. Target the business results and measures of success that, if fully realized, will most impact the ultimate result. List the process improvement benefits you are trying to achieve to support the business results. Develop the ERP implementation results you need to achieve.

CYBER Step 3. For each of these "buckets" of results, identify the required behaviors.

Once the behavior driving the results is pinpointed, follow the remaining steps of the CYBER Model. Analyze the influences on that behavior (PICs/NICs), develop and implement a change plan, and celebrate achieved results.

An example of this flow of results and benefits (CYBER Steps 1, 2, 3) from one of my own projects is shown in the figure.

Start with Results to Identify High-Impact Behaviors

I. Shareholder Value

- Earnings per share
- Stock price
- Etc.

2. Business Results/Benefits

- Reduction in bad debt expense
- Reduction in Days Sales Outstanding
- Fixed and variable cost per employee
- Revenue and margin per employee
- Expense to revenue
- Number of cross-serving referrals
- Business generated through cross-serving (dollars)
- Revenue from commission accounting and premium administration systems
- Inventory reduction
- Profitability
- Cash flow

3. Pinpoint Behaviors that Drive Results

(Behaviors)

Process Improvements

- Monthly and quarterly close cycle time
- Bank reconciliation cycle time
- Corp. consolidation cycle time
- Number of manual checks
- Cost per invoice
- Invoice approval cycle time
- Cash and P&L forecasting cycle time
- Utilization of revenue generators
- Demand forecasting accuracy
- Invoice accuracy

(Behaviors)

Project Implementation Results

Budget	Timeliness	Quality
• People and time per project plan • Deliverables • Performance to engagement letter	• Deliverables and milestones	• Employee survey • Training proficiency • Weekly calls to help desk

(Behaviors)

Why Doesn't Employee Involvement Work Like a Charm?

Let's examine how "employee involvement" became the butt of "Dilbert" jokes. In most companies, when employee-involvement efforts began (quality circles, employee problem-solving teams, etc.), they used a separate structure from the normal operational organizational structure. They ran parallel to the normal employee track (a.k.a. the employee's "real job"). Instead of reporting to their normal bosses, employees reported to a steering committee. *This virtually guaranteed failure.*

Those Special Meetings

Employees left their jobs as plant workers, customer service reps, or salespeople for isolation in a comfortable conference room to collaborate with their colleagues on improving processes, product quality, etc. Trained facilitators generally led these meetings, and they positively encouraged employees to be open and share their thoughts. (Talk about being different from their daily jobs!) The facilitators listened to their opinions and jotted them on a flipchart. They thanked the employees for providing input, and the employees were rewarded with nice lunches, participation certificates, and the like—and they didn't have to perform their real jobs for the day. The PICs abounded in the employee involvement meetings.

Then the meeting ended, and the employees would return to their real jobs. There they experienced very different consequences for some of the same behaviors. Back in the natural work environment, they were often managed poorly, supervisors rarely asked for their opinions, resources were scarce, and the focus was only on operating income and business performance—an utterly different environment from the nice cocoon of the Special Meetings.

Employees quickly learned that the way to access stronger and meaningful consequences (such as promotions or results-based compensation rewards) was by doing the *real* work well—not the problem-solving stuff that transpired in conference rooms with flipcharts, notebooks, and warm cookies . . . . They learned that the meetings and invitations for input would pass—and that the organization really valued what occurred as part of their real jobs. Generally, their real jobs lacked positive feedback, requests for input, and warm cookies . . . but it was their "real jobs" with which the major systemic consequences were aligned.

In addition, employees often got grief from their peers upon returning to their jobs after attending one of these meetings. And for understandable reasons: coworkers experienced a multitude of negative consequences as a result of their peers leaving their positions, if only for a short while to attend meetings:

- Peers had to cover for them while they were gone, because in today's lean organizations, extra people are not available. So, coworkers suffered a NIC.

- Coworkers questioned why the attendees were singled out and made so special, and they often made fun of them for being brown-nosers. Another NIC.

- Coworkers demonstrated feelings of envy or distrust toward those who were privileged to attend a special meeting. Yet another NIC.

Thus, employees who tried to help the organization by attending these problem-solving meetings (whose outcomes were PFU's) only continued such actions if they didn't mind annoying their coworkers and disrupting the very work on which they were evaluated and promoted (a big NIC). The contrast and inconsistencies became intolerable.

With all this effort, and with all of these PICs, why didn't quantum gains in profitability happen? You know the answer: problems with pinpointing and problems with consistent and aligned consequences.

Making Employee Involvement Work

You can explain these issues once you understand human behavior—once you understand the strong effects of consequences, the weak effect of antecedents that are not paired with consequences, and the problem with consequences that are misaligned. It's not that employee involvement is wrong. Nor is borrowing people from their regular jobs to focus on improving things. But if you want to tap people's discretionary effort, you must align consequences across all aspects of the work. Otherwise, the result becomes quite the opposite of what you desire.

The most successful employee involvement organizations do not have a separate program or initiative, but rather define everyday behaviors based on "involvement" and "problem solving." These behaviors are expected from employees and reinforced by supervisors and by coworkers. Such companies also have few "facilitators." Instead, they teach their supervisors and managers to actively facilitate as part of their jobs. They have little emphasis on hierarchy or positional power and high accountability and clarity on roles.

If those early employee involvement efforts had been targeted at the natural lines of supervision and work flow, the results would have been more sustainable and more profitable, both in the short term and the long term. The parallel structure would have been nonexistent, and the tougher issues of "employee involvement" behaviors competing with "real work behaviors" would have surfaced earlier and been dealt with from the outset.

Cross-Selling Across Business Units

One profound result of a decade of merger and consolidation mania is that company leaders now expect employees and business units to work collaboratively. This means sharing leads openly, divulging once-confidential and competitive information, and other formerly unthinkable activities.

Can cross-selling work? It comes down to two factors, and I think you can name them without my help: pinpointing desired behaviors and aligning consequences. But knowing this and achieving it are two different things. Pinpointing is not easy when you consider the trade-offs in what people do today. Everything is important. Time constraints are horrendous, whether weekly, daily, or even per sales transaction. Selecting which behaviors are of greatest value for cross-selling necessarily means deselecting other behaviors that may be beneficial, too.

Making Cross-Selling Work

Because cross-selling means having different work units work collaboratively to maximize existing relationships with clients and customers, cross-selling is a perfect example for application of the CYBER Model. Please refer to the figure.

CYBER Model

1. Specify the business opportunity that invites cross-selling.

2. Identify what success will look like if cross-selling is effective and how results will be tracked. Often I see results but no investment in tracking, feedback, and evaluation.

3. Identify critical behaviors that will immediately and strongly affect results if performed consistently and reliably. Examine and prioritize only the key behaviors that drive results.

4. Examine the factors that create natural barriers (time, geography, expertise, etc.). You may uncover competing consequences (incentive structures, data retrieval, etc.) Only through modifying these competing influences will behavior change occur.

5. Implement a plan to extinguish unwanted behaviors (e.g., vertical selling) and to reinforce new behaviors (e.g., understanding customer needs before recommending a solution). A shaping plan to guide the change is critical.

6. Celebrate! (The most overlooked step.) Cross-selling affords the need and opportunity to jointly celebrate progress and milestones.

Knowledge Management

Knowledge management lies dormant in companies today in the same way "quality" did before Edward Deming. Knowledge management is critical to your company's future. In fact, it could be the single process and behavior change that will return an investment hundreds of times over. It will, I predict, be the fundamental differentiator of your company's ability to grow profitably and innovatively in the next millennium. Why is this so?

First, a definition: **knowledge management** is *the system, processes, and behaviors needed to share best practices, to reuse knowledge, and to multiply learning quickly across boundaries among people, geography, or information types.*

Today's corporate fast lane has made imperative the use of knowledge management:

- Business is transacted so rapidly that knowledge demands to be managed.
- So much internal information is available through advanced technology that it needs continual sifting, organizing, access, and security.
- Customer demands and expectations make knowledge management mandatory for service providers.
- If you don't adopt knowledge management, your competitors will, so you'll be behind.
- Pressure to maintain or improve margins is driving companies to eliminate their greatest "knowledge holders" through early retirement or downsizing. No longer will we use the "wise old sage" model of "remembering what we've tried before" and "knowing how it works best."

What does behavioral science bring to knowledge management? If you examine our CYBER Model, you will see that it grounds us in the framework for analyzing knowledge management:

- First, we understand the business opportunities that are necessary if we want to grow profitably in our areas of expertise.
- Second, we target the results and measures of success that would indicate how well we are doing.
- Third, we pinpoint the behaviors necessary to achieve or improve performance in these areas, and what sources of knowledge people require to exhibit these behaviors in the right context.

It quickly becomes apparent that the antecedents and consequences necessary for consistent and reliable behavior do not exist without a formal knowledge management system and a process for knowledge management.

Companies that understand this and organize information, corporate memory, near misses, collateral data, competitor information, etc. will propel themselves into the next millennium on much more solid ground than companies that leave it up to chance.

Prediction: I think we will see a frenzy of investment and flavor-of-the-month mania around knowledge management as companies deal with not having a system in place when they need it. We are already seeing this frenzy among those who sell, buy, or operate groupware, which is the hardware side of knowledge management. So far, I've yet to see a behavioral look at this issue (outside what we are doing with our clients).

My advice: stay true to what you know about behavior, at three levels:

1. *Carefully organize your knowledge management system.* Antecedents must be clear. People need to understand quickly what words and phrases mean, and they must be able to navigate easily through the system. Doing so must be reinforcing for them, or behavior will extinguish.

2. *Integrate your knowledge management system into your business strategy.* Knowledge is power, and converting knowledge into behavior is power made profitable. Analyze how your knowledge management system can create behavior changes for your clients that will differentiate them from their competitors. If you are successful, the reinforcers for you and your organization will be overwhelming, and client loyalty will be increased.

3. *Implement knowledge management within your own organization.* If you go through the CYBER Model, you will pinpoint new behaviors needed—and existing consequence systems that need to be changed to reinforce the new behaviors. Remember the importance of aligned consequence systems—and of the need to shape new behaviors. "Putting it out there" or "telling people to use it" is simply an antecedent, and not a very effective one at that.

e-behavior for e-commerce

The Internet has forever transformed how we behave. Behavior patterns of purchasing, information seeking, and communicating have been permanently altered by the Internet—and this change will continue with more innovations from the Oracles, Microsofts, and Yahoos of the world. How can behavioral science contribute?

For me, this is about the simplest example out there! Success on the Internet depends on understanding human behavior. Companies are faced more directly than ever with the question, "What do my current and prospective customers value?" Said behaviorally: "what behaviors, products, or services should my company offer that will lead to positive-immediate-certain consequences for my customers?"

The answer is obvious: faster, simpler, customizable, and best cost. The barriers of geography, relationships, or brands no longer hinder our finding and getting what we want right away. The Internet is all PICs, PICs, PICs. Don't make me promises (PFU) and don't make me wait (NFU).

The term "sticky" is used to describe Web pages that people visit for long periods. Clearly, in the design and content available at those Web sites, the consequences of navigating them are sufficiently positive to keep people there.

The Dell Experience

Dell Computer is a wonderful example. Dell has taken its entire sales process and put it on the Web—and enhanced it miles beyond the traditional human-to-human sales experience. Dell customizes order and service pages for its larger clients (those with more than 400 employees). These "Premier Pages" have format, content, and language tailored to those customers. Premier Pages are often linked to the client's Intranet site.

This explains why Dell is continuing to rise faster than its competition: the company is providing PICs all over the place! Specifically:

- They have nearly eliminated variability in the customer ordering and buying processes by ensuring *positive consequences* for using their Web-based system. There is no wait time because you go directly to the site (PIC).

- There are no unskilled, uninformed, or rushed salespeople on the other end asking questions and putting you on hold (PIC).
- You can place the order or request service on your own time, at 3 P.M. or 3 A.M. (PIC), as opposed to doing so during normal business hours (NIC).
- As a Premier Page user, you see your name, logo, product, and sales information when you dial in (PIC).
- You get just what you want, not what the local store happens to have on the shelf (PIC).
- The "trust factor," or perceived integrity, is very high, because people know of the quality, timely delivery, exchangeability, and security of personal financial data (PIC).

Understanding what motivates human behavior to purchase one system over another is critical to winning a commodity- or price-sensitive game. Dell is able to execute in a way that reinforces the behavior of buying from them. The magic link between behavior and profits is revealed!

Winning the Battle for Top People and Successful Succession

Recent articles predict a dramatic "senior brain drain" in the pool of executives available to corporate America. This problem is driven by population trends like a slowing birthrate, an aging workforce, and an increasing demand for white collar workers in the new knowledge economy. These trends will intensify competition for the shrinking pool of qualified people and drive diverse ways of attracting and keeping executives.

This situation is made even more serious by the increasing wealth of many younger managers who might otherwise jump at the available positions. The stock market's steep increase over the past 20 years has driven investment portfolios and 401(k)s to record levels, leading great executive candidates to walk away from lucrative offers.

The implications are mighty! Let's roll the clock forward and make some predictions.

Jobs as we know them will be redefined. Employees—not employers—will create the jobs and define their own requirements for staying with a company. A time may come soon when executives will put their resumes on the Internet and accept bids from employers who offer not just money, but flexible benefits and opportunities.

For example:

- Employees may regularly ask for—and get—twice the vacation defined in company policies, or they may simply work only a certain number of days per week, month, or year.
- They may ask for special hours, training, or computer and connectivity equipment.
- They may want the opportunity to write a book and ask for support in achieving this or other personal or career goals.
- They may want to take a year off to start a family (not the typical 5–10 weeks) or to take a year's sabbatical during their first five years with the Company.

I predict that some of you will read the preceding list and think, "so, you're talking about me . . . what's so unreasonable about those things?," while others among you are thinking, "she's really lost it. There's no way a company could be that flexible and still have large numbers of employees." I'll bet that most of you, like myself, nod knowingly at these statements—and remain challenged about how to attract, retain, and develop the very best and brightest employees.

What Other Companies Have Tried

All of this makes succession planning and executive development a hot item, and companies are looking for creative solutions. *Business Week* highlighted best practices by a handful of companies, including Chevron, Prudential Insurance, and Monsanto. Here's what some of these companies have done:

- Review demographic information to pinpoint the location and time of the executive shortage.
- Intensify succession planning to develop younger leaders and target them for high-risk positions.

- Retain retiring senior leaders as consultants and coaches for younger leaders.
- Tailor individualized jobs and working environments to the exact needs of leaders.
- Work with executives to create their "dream job," matching the work to the candidates' needs and motivation.

The Behavioral Solution

All these strategies sound great, and they often work well. But how can we understand this challenge from a behavioral viewpoint? I believe that competition for the shrinking pool of executives can be won by focusing on consequences and, more specifically, on positive reinforcement.

Remember that positive reinforcement is individualized. What is reinforcing for one person is not necessarily reinforcing for another. This means that one-size-fits-all corporate pay, benefit, family leave, and other programs are unlikely to maximize motivation for individuals. Broad programs simply average the reinforcement value across a large number of people, and they fail to hit the mark for anyone. So, how can this problem be solved?

Key People, Custom Profiles

I believe that the solution is a reinforcement profile for each key person, a profile that draws on interviews and reviews of a person's background to identify their reinforcers. This profile can then be used to design a job and career path that maximizes the individual's satisfaction through his or her career.

This is neither easy nor cheap, but it will work. For example, one of my clients needed to retain Jerome, an executive who was of retirement age and had health issues. His experience and knowledge of the technology behind a key line of business was second to none. In fact, he had practically invented it during his 32 years with the company. What Jerome could no longer do, however, was actively manage the way folks needed him to. Travel was difficult, and he was spending less time in the operations where he was badly needed. Jerome wasn't ready to retire, and the company wasn't ready to lose him—but they needed more than he was able to give.

So, the company selected a high-potential successor and put him in charge of the operations, shifting Jerome to a half-time mentoring/consulting role. Jerome's successor is an 80 percent time employee because, at age 42, he has family duties that require him to be home on certain days. Jerome can support and mentor his successor, he can spend time where the organization most needs him, and the operations are not penalized by Jerome's personal limitations.

Continuing Flexibility Is the Answer

The point is clear. Companies who view this as a hassle or annoyance will miss the boat. Look at this type of flexibility as a recruiting and retention advantage, and the light goes on! If you fail to offer flexible arrangements matched to individuals needs, you will probably neither attract nor retain talented people from the pool—people who, frankly, could work for anyone. You want them to choose you. *Day after day, employees must achieve a more reinforcing life with you than with another company.* That's the secret—the behavioral secret—to keeping turnover low.

However, reinforcement cannot be static. People's needs shift, and you will have to maintain open communication with your employees. Thus, good coaching and feedback skills remain important. You will need to regularly assess where your top employees are and adjust each plan to maintain their long-term retention. This is particularly challenging in light of downsizing, which has occurred in most human resources organizations.

Like the other challenges we've examined, overcoming the "brain drain" and becoming the top competitor for top talent is best addressed by using behavioral science. To win and keep people, and to sustain high levels of discretionary performance, the majority of consequences clearly must function as positive reinforcement. It will no longer be simply a financial game (if it ever was). It will come down to the motivational systems and reinforcers people experience within your organization. It will come down to a "want to" versus a "have to." With the demographics and the needs of people in leadership roles, the "have tos" won't cut it. People will go where they want to.

What About the Future?

From reading this book, I hope you'll find it clear that behavioral science offers you the power tools for performance, profitability, and success.

But, you might wonder . . . in a few years, will behavioral science become the old innovation, lying dusty on the shelf, alongside management innovations of bygone days? No way! I am betting my career and livelihood that the laws of human behavior will be the same when my children, grandchildren, and great-grandchildren are adults. These laws hold true, regardless of circumstances or century, because human behavior is timeless.

The topics in this chapter, like M&A and ERP, will be different in five or ten years, but I assure you that the principles of behavioral science will remain unchanged. The future will simply bring new challenges to which we will apply our science, which continues to develop in sophistication. And with you as an expert practitioner of behavioral science, I may one day be reading *your* book!

Epilogue

I F YOU ARE an engineer or linear thinker, you might be wondering, "What happened to CYBER? What about *Step 6: CELE-BRATE achievement of improved results?*"

Celebrations, with liberal use of recognition and positive feedback, are critical to bringing about and sustaining behavior change—at home or within organizations. Plainly and simply—we don't do enough of it in either venue.

Some of the best forms of celebration are done privately, by the team member who made it happen, and simply, where those involved simply take a moment and verbalize out loud their feelings about the accomplishment and what it meant to them.

Celebrations need not be "big" to be meaningful. They only need to be a formal pause to recognize and celebrate the accomplishments achieved.

Celebration Tips

Celebrations need not be initiated solely by managers. Employees at all levels should help decide when and how to celebrate progress and outcomes achieved.

First, decide what is celebration-worthy. Celebrations should be tied to accomplishments when:

CYBER Model

1. Identify business opportunity

2. Target results and measures of success

3. Pinpoint and align behaviors that drive results

4. Understand the influences on behavior

5. Develop, implement, and adjust behavior change plan

6. CELEBRATE achievement of improved results!

- Skills are improved
- A difficult task is completed
- A breakthrough is achieved in teamwork
- A breakthrough is accomplished in process improvement
- A significant result or outcome is achieved

Second, determine *how* to celebrate. Criteria to consider are:

- Significance of accomplishment
- Time available
- People available (for example, coordinating schedules of individuals)
- Consequences preferred by the individuals involved
- Funds available to cover expenses

Here are some of my favorite celebrations that I've seen used in organizations:

- Positive feedback given to individuals for their help in progress made toward team goals
- Simply taking time to applaud the efforts of the entire team. (Positive feedback of this type is best done face-to-face or in a personalized letter. It can also be done during a team meeting or event.)
- A special lunch at the work site to celebrate the achievements of a team, work unit, or location
- A "brag board" used on site for posting announcements of team accomplishments
- A team wish list developed by the team, so that they can identify how they would like to celebrate an important accomplishment

Please keep in mind . . .

Most celebrations can be informal and spontaneous, with minimal planning, rather than formal. When in doubt, just have fun! The most important thing is that you pause to celebrate and recognize progress and improvements.

If you prefer to plan for a celebration, first pinpoint the behavior or result to be reinforced. Then, brainstorm a list of alternatives for celebrations. Identify the pros and cons (or pluses and deltas) of each alternative. If you're working with a team, take action to narrow the list, then make your final choice by reaching consensus. After the celebration, evaluate whether you chose the correct celebration by asking for feedback from those who participated.

Most companies I work with would get low scores in the area of celebration. They run so fast that they start the next project without pausing to celebrate what they achieved! I hope you realize the significance of these lost opportunities. Don't let yourself or your organization miss them. There are enough natural punishers in the world, and there are plenty of events we can't control. Seize the opportunities to celebrate and recognize the accomplishments and contributions in your organization!

Final Thoughts

I wish *all* of our organizational "ills" could be cured by simply increasing the use of positive reinforcement and celebrations. At one time early in my schooling, I believed that to be true. I naively thought, "If we just do a better job of positively reinforcing what is good, the rest will take care of itself." I now know better. And you do, too.

As a final recap on what else you know:

- You know that *without understanding the business context/opportunity, you might erroneously increase behaviors that have no strategic impact.* This would be a grave error.

- You know that *your efforts must be guided by the results targets and measures* that will be the definitive judge of your success or lack thereof.

- You know that *if you pinpoint the behaviors that most impact results—* and ensure these behaviors occur above any others—then you are taking maximum control over whether your behavior impacts the results target.

- You know that *events or environmental influences may act on the very behavior you need to occur.* And you must analyze those events and influences to ensure that your efforts are helped and not unintentionally (or intentionally) hindered.

- You know that *you can put forth effort that will encourage the behaviors you need and discourage those you don't need.* You know that with your knowledge and skills in behavioral science you can adjust them as needed.

And last, when you meet your targets (because you know you will) you know to *pause and celebrate your achievements, because they did not occur by chance.* They occurred because you cared enough not to leave behavior to chance. You chose to apply the science of human behavior correctly, and it paid off.

Measurement

How to Develop Measures

I SUGGEST THAT you use three general steps to help develop good measures:

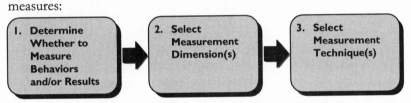

1. Determine Whether to Measure Behaviors and/or Results → 2. Select Measurement Dimension(s) → 3. Select Measurement Technique(s)

Step 1—Determine Whether to Measure Behaviors and/or Results

You measure *behaviors* by observing a person perform a task. You measure *results* by assessing the outcome, result, or product after the person is done. It sounds easy, but it may not be.

As I indicated in Chapter 2, a behavior is what a person actually says or does that can be verified using NORMS. Therefore, the performer obviously must be present when behavior measures are collected. Suppose you want to measure customer service behavior. You must observe the behaviors of a salesperson who is interacting with customers. Then you can rate the quality of his or her actions in satisfying customers and selling products.

Measuring results or outcome is different. A result is something left behind when a person finishes a task. The person does not have to be present when you measure the result. For example, profits are left behind after the sales rep and the customer complete their transaction.

A basic decision you need to make is whether to measure behavior and/or results when managing behavior change. As a general rule, try measuring results as your first option, because results usually are less expensive to measure and monitor.

Here are some tips for choosing whether to measure behavior, results, or both:

Measure Behaviors If . . .	Measure Results If . . .	Measure Both If . . .
The performer is learning a new skill and it's too early to know if results are improving	The performer already knows how to achieve results	Results and behaviors are important—it's important to be sure the right behaviors are leading to the results
The performer needs lots of feedback to get the right behaviors going	You are confident the performer is engaging in the right behaviors to achieve the results	You need examples of behavior to provide more meaningful feedback
You need to be sure that everyone is engaging in the right behavior to get the results	You only need a snapshot of how well people are performing	It appears that both the right results and the right behaviors are occurring

If you have the time and resources, the best approach is to measure both behavior and results. When you measure both, you can directly link behavior change with business-results change.

A simple example illustrates how measures work . . .

A product development group was having trouble hitting milestones that were critical to delivering products on time. They decided to meet weekly and review red flags submitted by project teams. Red flags indicated threats to the project schedule. Group leaders reviewed each flag carefully and identified immediate actions needed to overcome the threat. They measured the monthly milestones attained (results) and problem-solving steps that were followed (behaviors). Use of the

**problem-solving process was correlated with milestones at-
tained and on-time project completion.**

Measurement is not always so simple. I often work with leaders
whose direct reports are not even in the same country or time zone.
Often, these leaders can't observe the behaviors at all, and they see only
results. In such cases, it is tempting to simply ignore the behavior
measures and assume that everything is fine. Instead, I recommend a
more creative approach to be sure that desired behaviors are taking
place.

For example, one of my clients asked salespeople in the field to
submit customer-demand forecasts that would drive manufacturing
planning. The salespeople were in home offices across 25 states and
entered their information by laptop. They were never supervised directly. It would have been easy to accept their numbers without further
question.

So, I suggested one more level of measurement to find out
what behaviors were involved in collecting the forecast data. We asked
salespeople to describe how they obtained data, using four general cate-
gories: (1) interviewing customers, (2) estimating from past sales, (3)
projecting from market models, or (4) gut-level hunches. Using this
approach, managers measured the percentage of complete forecasts
submitted on time (result), and the dependability of the source (an indi-
rect measure of behavior). In this way, the actions involved in collecting the information could be changed if the forecasts were found to be
inaccurate or misleading.

Step 2—Select Measurement Dimension(s)

Once you decide whether to measure behavior or results, you can select
the type of data to collect. To stimulate your thinking, here are the
major types of data:

- *Quantity*—expressing a behavior or result by the number of
  occurrences
  - *Frequency*—the number of times something occurs (e.g., the
    number of sales calls made)

- *Rate*—how often something occurs per unit of time (e.g., the number of times feedback is given per month, or the number of products returned per week)
- *Percent*—the number of times a performance occurs divided by the number of attempts

- *Quality*—comparing behaviors or results to a standard
  - *Accuracy*—the degree to which some aspect of performance matches predefined criteria (e.g., the accuracy of information that was given or the number of errors in a letter to a customer)
  - *Novelty*—judgments (such as ratings) of a behavior or a result (e.g., development of a creative marketing strategy or creation of a new engineering design)

- *Cost*—financial value of a behavior or a result
  - *Labor*—the amount spent on wages, salaries, bonuses, and benefits
  - *Material*—the amount spent on items such as tools, machines, and energy
  - *Management*—the amount spent on the support necessary to produce desired results

- *Time*—expressing a behavior or result in terms of time
  - *Duration*—how long something lasts (e.g., the length of time spent repairing equipment or the length of time the computer network was operating)
  - *Timeliness*—comparing actual time to pre-targeted time
  - *Latency*—how long it takes to complete a task after it is available to the performer

When choosing a type of measurement, ask these questions:

- What do I need to know to judge the success of a behavior change or a results impact?
- Which measures can be collected most easily?

Step 3—Select Measurement Technique(s)

After you select types of measures, you need to define how you will collect the information. Four main measurement techniques are typically used to measure behavior and results: simple counting, behaviorally anchored rating scales (BARS), opinion rating scales, and opinion ranking. These are described below, from most objective to most subjective. Here is a quick look at each:

Counting (most objective)—Use this technique to count specific quantities of a behavior or result:

- Number of interruptions by a team member during a meeting
- Cost of an item relative to budget
- Length of a phone call with a customer
- Number of items reviewed in quality checks

Behaviorally Anchored Rating Scales (BARS)—Use this technique to behaviorally describe effective and ineffective performance.

Behavior: My leader identifies key behaviors that lead to achieving critical results.

1	2	3	4	5
• Does not discuss behaviors, only results.	• Has difficulty identifying specific behaviors that will lead to critical results. • Focuses mainly on result attainment, not the behaviors that lead to those results.	• Identifies behaviors that are critical to achieving a wide range of results. • Tells us which behaviors to do to be successful.	• Gets employees actively involved in identifying behaviors that lead to results. • Helps us see the correlation between our behaviors and results.	• Recognizes us for using data to analyze correlation between behaviors and results. • Has a process in place to identify key behaviors that lead to achieving critical results. • Benchmarks others to identify key behaviors that lead to critical results.

To create a BARS, follow these steps:

1. Identify the performance you wish to rate. This could be product knowledge, quality of feedback given, work habits, etc.

2. Identify the behaviors that would be included under a "5" rating. (Write each behavior on a Post-it® note.) Then, identify the behaviors that would be included under a "0" rating. Finally, fill in behaviors under "3." Try to maintain a correlation across the behaviors listed under each number.

3. Ask people who did not create the BARS to review it. This will help to ensure agreement with your ratings and behavioral descriptors.

4. Revise the behavioral descriptors if necessary.

It's a good idea to make sure you identify examples of objective behaviors and not personality characteristics. For example, a personality characteristic would be "is always motivated." Instead, use the behavior descriptor "Completes all assignments on time." Remember, behaviors are things that people say and do and can be described using the NORMS.

Opinion Rating Scales—Use this technique to tie general opinions to a scale, like this:

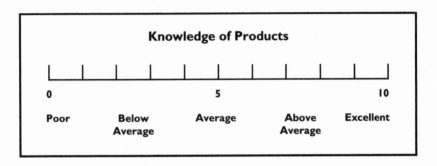

Questionnaires and surveys often use opinion rating scales. They are used to assess people's attitudes, viewpoints, opinions, and perceptions. They usually are a first pass at identifying areas of strength and areas for improvement.

Opinion Ranking (most subjective)—Use this technique to conduct a rank-order comparison of two or more items. For example, you might rank-order 20 suppliers, based on your perception of the quality of their services, with a rating of 1 assigned to the highest-quality supplier, and a rating of 20 assigned to the lowest-quality supplier. Although it might be possible to link these rankings to quantifiable data, an opinion ranking does not do so.

The ABC Analysis

Let's look deeper at the ABC Analysis. My goal is that you will make this your model for thinking about all actions—yours and others'—that are important to getting results. Here's a sample analysis, to refresh your memory:

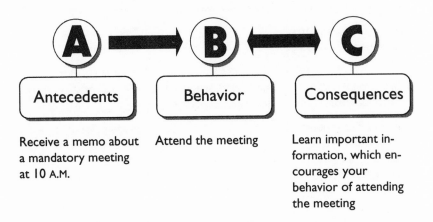

Antecedents	Behavior	Consequences
Receive a memo about a mandatory meeting at 10 A.M.	Attend the meeting	Learn important information, which encourages your behavior of attending the meeting

To illustrate the power of ABC Analysis, here is a story from a client we helped. Let's call them InvoicesForever, or IFCorp. The company was attempting to improve their vendor-management process as part of an overall cost-reduction initiative . . .

Working with IFCorp's purchasing department, we identified four key behaviors that were expected of Purchasing Agents. We carefully studied the antecedents and consequences for

each behavior. Of special interest was the behavior of "reviewing all invoices for errors," a task done by Purchasing Agents.

An ABC Analysis of "reviewing invoices" flagged a big surprise.

The desired behavior was simply to "review all invoices for errors" (the Behavior column below). The antecedents were all straightforward, as you can see in the first column. But what were the consequences to the people who actually performed the behavior? Look in the last column!

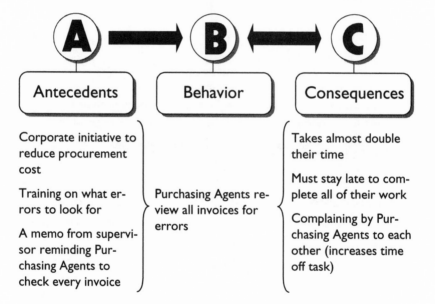

Antecedents	Behavior	Consequences
Corporate initiative to reduce procurement cost		Takes almost double their time
Training on what errors to look for	Purchasing Agents review all invoices for errors	Must stay late to complete all of their work
A memo from supervisor reminding Purchasing Agents to check every invoice		Complaining by Purchasing Agents to each other (increases time off task)

Whoa! The behavior is simple enough, and it's clearly the responsibility of the Purchasing Agents. The department has provided all of the right antecedents—a formal corporate initiative, training, and reminders. But the consequences reveal the problem. The individuals who must perform the task are experiencing numerous negative consequences.

These negative consequences decrease the likelihood that people will engage in the behavior that produces them. In this case, it means they decrease the likelihood that people will perform the desired new behavior. The Purchasing Agents won't review all invoices for errors. They will likely engage in other behaviors that they find more reinforcing.

And what are the consequences if they fail to review the invoices as instructed? Perhaps they might miss a few discrepancies in the math . . . but realistically, probably nothing. Or maybe just some more antecedents, like memos with stronger language urging them to review invoices for errors. (But remember, antecedents have only about 20 percent influence over behavior.)

What was the consequence history for those employees? They had routinely skipped the invoice check before, and this hadn't led to anything particularly good or bad—for years! Business continued as usual. And the employees continued to receive their salaries and good evaluations. So why bother checking invoices? (Remember, consequences have about 80 percent influence over behavior.)

Expenses had been continuously increasing and there was an "all hands on deck" directive to cut costs wherever possible and practical.

The executive who championed the vendor management initiative couldn't understand why IFCorp's Purchasing Agents didn't review every invoice. Furthermore, he couldn't understand why his memos were ineffective. After all, he had the power and authority to say what should be done. But what he didn't attend to, at least not initially, were the consequences that most closely affected the Purchasing Agents' behaviors.

This story has a happy ending. IFCorp changed the consequences by introducing a measurement system. Managers began delivering positive feedback to agents for catching errors on invoices. The measurement system showed the cost savings achieved through the vendor management program, and it demonstrated that errors detected from incorrect vendor invoices accounted for over 35 percent of the savings. The performance of the purchasing units was recognized (and positively reinforced) through personal letters of praise from the executive sponsor of this activity.

In fact, IFCorp's Purchasing Agents were singled out as major contributors to the company-wide cost reduction effort because, as it turned out, they uncovered several significant errors in their invoice reviews. Measurements of the behaviors linked to checking invoices were introduced, and several positive consequences began to compete with some of the negative ones. Overall, the positive consequences were sufficient to outweigh the negatives, so the desired behavior—checking invoices—was performed, recognized, and celebrated!

As a longer-term solution, IFCorp began passing on consequences to suppliers. Those who provided correct invoices and partnered in the cost containment effort benefited from a positive consequence: a continuing vendor relationship with IFCorp. To suppliers who provided invoices containing errors, IFCorp provided negative consequences: delays in payment because errors had to be corrected; high-level notices expressing displeasure with invoice errors; and deselection of vendors with use of invoice accuracy as a major criterion.

Let's take a closer look at the lessons from this story. Above all, this example demonstrates the relative power of consequences compared to antecedents. When IFCorp leaders pinpointed the key Purchasing Agent behavior of "reviewing all invoices for errors," they recognized their need to support Purchasing Agents in performing that behavior. So, they invested in a formal initiative, training, reminders, and so on. However, all of those investments were antecedents!

Purchasing Agents did not reliably perform the new behavior because, even though the antecedents changed, the consequences stayed the same. And the bulk of the consequences for the Purchasing Agents' behaviors of checking invoices were negative—reviewing each invoice was time-consuming, Purchasing Agents had to stay late to complete the task, and so on.

When IFCorp analyzed those consequences, they quickly saw the need to shift the balance so that the positive consequences for reviewing invoices would outweigh the negative ones. That's where the measurement system came in. Since the measurement system revealed that reviewing each invoice resulted in dollar savings, managers were able to provide regular feedback, praise, and recognition to the Purchasing Agents for their behavior and its impact on the bottom line.

This example reminds us that supplying antecedents alone (instructions, memos, authority, etc.) will not ensure that a change in behavior will occur. Analyzing the consequences is absolutely crucial. It allows you to discover what is currently reinforcing an undesired behavior and to create consequences that will reinforce a preferred behavior.

Let's now add a PIC/NIC analysis to our ABC Analysis, so that we can really examine the consequences that are operating.

PIC/NIC Analysis—Checking Invoices

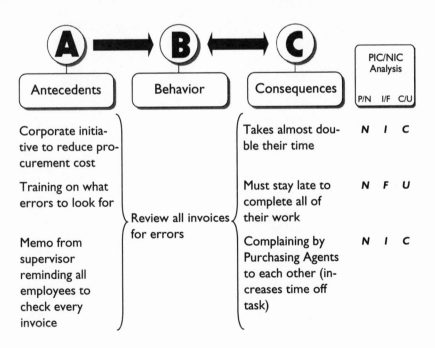

Antecedents	Behavior	Consequences	P/N	I/F	C/U
Corporate initiative to reduce procurement cost		Takes almost double their time	N	I	C
Training on what errors to look for	Review all invoices for errors	Must stay late to complete all of their work	N	F	U
Memo from supervisor reminding all employees to check every invoice		Complaining by Purchasing Agents to each other (increases time off task)	N	I	C

All three consequences are negative, and two of them are immediate and certain to happen. It's little wonder that no one wants to check those invoices!

But we can sharply improve this situation. If we use a PIC/NIC analysis to reveal patterns of consequences, we can work with the people involved to get their insights into how to redesign the consequences to be more favorable.

You can't always dispose of NICs, but you can create PICs. Both give us insight into what most heavily influences our pinpointed behavior. This insight allows us to identify the antecedents and consequences that are needed for the desired behavior to occur on a regular basis.

The following revised analysis of "Checking Invoices" includes new antecedents to prompt the behavior. New consequences are also added to sustain the behavior. The old consequences won't go away, but in the long run, the new and positive consequences are likely to overshadow the negative ones.

New PIC/NIC Plan—Checking Invoices

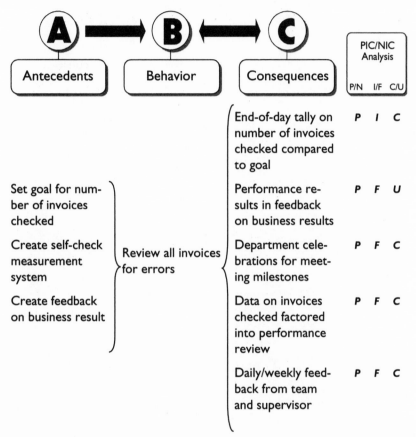

Antecedents	Behavior	Consequences	PIC/NIC Analysis P/N	I/F	C/U
		End-of-day tally on number of invoices checked compared to goal	P	I	C
Set goal for number of invoices checked	Review all invoices for errors	Performance results in feedback on business results	P	F	U
Create self-check measurement system		Department celebrations for meeting milestones	P	F	C
Create feedback on business result		Data on invoices checked factored into performance review	P	F	C
		Daily/weekly feedback from team and supervisor	P	F	C

All of a sudden, checking those invoices matters! It has become a visible part of the Purchasing Agent's job, with goals that the clerk tracks and with recognition for performance. When the business results roll in, each Purchasing Agent should feel proud for a behavior that once seemed like a waste of time.

Developing Your Feedback Skills

Hᴇʀᴇ ɪs a tip checklist to help you deliver effective feedback:

Tips for Coaching with Positive and Constructive Feedback	How to Do It
1. ❑ **Make sure you convey an intent to help, not harm, the other person**	• Be sure you are providing feedback to help the person be more successful rather than to make yourself look good or to vent • Explain how the behavior impacts the person's success
Example. "I made some observations during this afternoon's meeting. I'd like to share the feedback with you so that you understand the progress you're making in facilitating meetings."	
2. ❑ **Use the NORMS of objectivity to describe the behavior and its impact**	• Be objective about what the person did and what happened as a result of the behavior • Don't add your own interpretation or use loaded language to describe the behavior

Example. "I heard you suggest three possible solutions during the meeting this afternoon."

3. ❑ **Own your feedback by sharing your thoughts and feelings**	• Use "I" statements to describe your own thoughts and feelings about the behavior (e.g., "I thought . . .") • Describe the impact the behavior had on you

Example. "I think suggesting solutions was effective because I saw the group shift from blaming others to solving problems."

4. ❑ **Get the other person's point of view**	• Ask the person how he or she viewed the behavior and its impact • Ask the person if he or she agrees with your feedback

Example. "How do you feel your suggestions affected the group?"

5. ❑ **Share your personal struggles in changing the same behavior in yourself (if applicable)**	• Relate how you have seen the impact of your own behavior when you did something similar • Share one or two methods you used to change your behavior

Example. "When I began facilitating meetings, I felt it was my job to make decisions for the group. After a few meetings, the team members were disengaged and never offered ideas. I started letting the team make decisions while I facilitated the process for them."

6. ❑ **Help the person agree that the behavior is a problem**	• Ask the person if he or she feels the need to change the behavior • Ask the person to describe the impact he or she thinks the behavior has

Example. "Do you feel that you impact the team when you make group decisions? How so?"

<table>
<tr>
<td>

7. ❑ **Discuss alternative behaviors**
</td>
<td>

- Share some NORMS-based pinpoints of alternative behaviors that the person could do successfully
</td>
</tr>
</table>

Example. "Instead of making decisions for the group, you could ask the group to brainstorm solutions to a problem. You could also ask the group to select the best solution for the problem."

"What are some other ways you might be able to increase the involvement of team members?"

<table>
<tr>
<td>

8. ❑ **Discuss plans for providing support to the person**
</td>
<td>

- Ask the person to identify support he or she might need
- Identify resources for the person (training, feedback, books, etc.)
</td>
</tr>
</table>

Example. "How can I best help you? I suggest starting by observing each team meeting so I can gather data on your performance and track your progress."

<table>
<tr>
<td>

9. ❑ **Agree to follow-up plans**
</td>
<td>

- Make sure you have agreed on how to follow up with the person
</td>
</tr>
</table>

Example. "I'll provide feedback after each meeting. During our weekly coaching sessions, we can talk about your behavior and the impact it has on the team."

FAQs (Frequently Asked Questions) About Positive Feedback

Q. How can I ensure that my positive feedback is sincere?

A. Use these items to ensure sincere feedback:

- Be sure your intent is really to express appreciation for a job well done rather than to make yourself look good.

- Make and sustain eye contact with the person.

- Be sure to share specific, NORMS-based examples of the behavior you thought was particularly effective.

- Speak directly to the person when you deliver the feedback; don't talk about him or her to others in the room (e.g., "I really appreciated the way you kept the meeting on track").

- Tell the person how his or her behavior positively impacted you. Emphasize his or her role in the overall scheme of what the unit or organization is trying to make happen.

Q. How often should I give positive feedback?

A. During periods of high uncertainty and change, people need more feedback and recognition than usual.

People need confirmation that what they are doing is on target. As a general guideline, try to deliver four instances of positive feedback for every instance of constructive feedback. This is called the 4:1 rule. Target your feedback to a few specific desired behaviors that you would like to see from the person.

Q. How do I accept positive feedback?

A. It might be difficult for you to accept positive feedback right now because of all the changes that are happening.

Some people make light of the feedback they receive by saying, "It was nothing" or "I was just doing my job." But if you deflect positive feedback, the person who delivered the feedback is more likely to withdraw, and you will have a more difficult time keeping performance high. A better way to accept feedback is to assume that the giver genuinely wants to recognize something you did well. Ask questions if you'd like more specifics about what behaviors the giver found effective or about the impact of your behavior. Then, thank the person for giving you positive feedback.

Q. **What if others don't accept my positive feedback?**

A. **During periods of change and uncertainty, people tend to be skeptical about the sincerity of praise.**

Furthermore, some people, because of their personal histories or their relationship with you, may generally be uncomfortable receiving your positive feedback.

Q. **What if I like a behavior but there is still room for improvement?**

A. **Give positive feedback about the improvement so far.**

Say, "I've seen progress in the way you've been doing X. For example . . ." By all means, keep your feedback positive. If you say, "I've seen great progress in the way you've been doing X, but I think you could do even better," people will listen for the "but" every time you give positive feedback.

Q. **Should I provide positive feedback to people who provide me with positive feedback?**

A. **If you would like to thank the person for providing you with feedback, do so.**

However, if you want to provide positive feedback on an unrelated behavior, it's preferable to wait until another time. Otherwise the person might perceive you as being insincere—that you are searching for something nice to say.

Q. Is it possible to provide too much positive feedback?

A. If you only provide positive feedback over and over, you run the risk of being perceived as insincere.

I'm not suggesting you "look" for constructive feedback, but remember to keep the 4:1 rule in mind.

If you're trying to shape behavior, it's best to stay focused and reinforce the behavior you are targeting. Providing positive feedback on too many behaviors may confuse the performer. If other desirable behaviors are displayed, track them separately and discuss them with the performer at another time. This way, you keep your main feedback focused on the behavior you are shaping, while still allowing the opportunity to reinforce other positive behaviors.

FAQs About Constructive Feedback

Effective leaders recognize the importance of constructive feedback for continued growth and improvement. They are sensitive to how they deliver constructive feedback, especially in times of uncertainty or change. Leaders avoid using criticism, which is intended to stop behavior in a harmful way. Instead, they use constructive feedback. Constructive feedback helps decrease the likelihood that an undesired behavior will recur, and it replaces it with more effective behaviors.

Q. Why is it so hard to give constructive feedback?

A. Few of us have ever been trained in how to give constructive feedback, so we maybe unsure of our skills.

Further, during a time of high tension, it's difficult to provide constructive feedback because people are likely to react defensively. But it is important to remember that constructive feedback is necessary for improving business results. People will appreciate your constructive feedback if it helps them succeed.

Q. How can I use constructive feedback to help and not harm others?

A. Focus your constructive feedback on behaviors linked to business or personal success.

During periods of change, people need to focus on getting business results. Keep your feedback targeted on the behaviors that drive those results.

Ensure that your motive is to help the person succeed rather than to embarrass him or her or to make yourself appear more powerful. If your intent is to harm the person, wait until you are ready to take a more helpful approach.

Describe the behavior in NORMS-based terms so the person knows exactly what behavior was ineffective. Be sure to get the person involved early in the conversation. Talk about how the behavior made you feel and the impact it had on others and the business results. Be sure to discuss alternative behaviors that would be more effective. Find out what the person needs in order to change the behavior and help arrange for that support.

Q. What should I do if the receiver gets defensive?

A. Recognize that the receiver is probably under stress.

Stress often leads people to react more defensively than normal. It's important to stay calm and to not take his or her reaction personally. Listen to what the person is saying, not just how he or she is saying it. Respond to the person's concerns in a sensitive way and be sure to refocus the conversation on the issue at hand when appropriate.

Q. How can I be less defensive when receiving constructive feedback?

A. Recognize that you are probably under stress right now, and that stress is shaping the way you respond to feedback.

Try to understand your emotional reaction and then focus on what the person is trying to share with you. You can ask questions to objectively understand what the person is trying to say. Start with the assumption that the person giving you feedback wants to help you. If you can't do that, just sit back and listen. Remember that you have a choice about how you receive feedback. You can look at it as an opportunity to learn about yourself, or you can look at it as a threat. You also have a choice about what you do in response to the feedback. You can choose to change your behavior, or you can choose not to.

More Tips for Coaching Success

Part of successful coaching and delivering positive feedback is antici-pating how the receiver might react. You can use the following tips to handle the most common difficult reactions to feedback.

Receiver's Reaction	Suggested Response
Accepts: The receiver might gra-ciously accept the feedback by say-ing, "Thank you" or "I understand what I did wrong and I'm working to improve it."	It is tempting to end the conversa-tion when constructive feedback is well received. However, make sure you have a mutual, NORMS-based understanding of what happened and what needs to be done. Thank the person for being so open to feedback.
Deflects: The receiver might ac-knowledge the feedback but deflect it by saying, "I was only doing my job" or "It was nothing."	Personalize the feedback immedi-ately. Say that you wanted him or her to know that the performance was important to you. State how it positively affected you and how you felt about it. Then prompt the per-son to talk about what he or she did to warrant your feedback.
Questions Sincerity: The re-ceiver might question your sincerity by saying, "Why are you recognizing me now when you haven't done so in the past?" or "OK, now that you've told me what I did right, what have I done wrong?"	Acknowledge that you might not have been good at giving feedback in the past and that you are work-ing to create success in the unit by recognizing effective performance.

Receiver's Reaction	Suggested Response
Is Surprised: The receiver might indicate that he or she was unaware of the behavior. The person might get angry that no feedback was provided earlier.	Apologize if you did not provide feedback earlier. Use "I" statements to present the situation from your point of view. Ask the person to watch for further instances of the behavior and its consequences to see whether he or she agrees with your assessment. Set a follow-up time to talk or arrange a signal to provide feedback when the behavior occurs.
Confuses the Issue: The receiver might bring up unrelated issues.	Demonstrate that you heard the issue by paraphrasing it. Say you want to cover one issue at a time. Arrange another time to talk about it, even if the alternative time is at the end of your current meeting.
Questions Your Motives: The receiver might say that your motives are to get back at him or her, or to put him or her down.	Say that you are providing feedback because you care and that you believe members of strong teams should provide feedback directly to each other. Ask what you can do to develop a more trusting relationship.
Emotional Attack: The receiver might become very emotional and attack you by saying things like, "You're pretty lousy yourself" or "I remember when you . . ."	Reflect the person's emotions. Use a calm tone of voice while sticking to the main point. Set up another time to meet if the person continues to be emotional. Evaluate your own motives as to whether or not you provided the feedback to help or harm the person.

Receiver's Reaction	**Suggested Response**
Questions Your Assessment: The receiver might question the accuracy of your feedback.	Be open to the fact that your assessment might not be NORMS-based. Use "I" statements to verify that you are speaking from your own point of view. If others agree with your assessment, ask them to speak directly with the receiver.

The Author's Principles
for Successful Consulting

HERE IS MY personal credo for responsible, successful organizational consulting:

- *You must have a sincere desire to help and not harm.* Your clients must live in the organization long after you move on to your next project. You have an opportunity (often brief) to make a difference and influence how they approach issues, how team members work together, how problems get solved, etc. You also have the opportunity to affect the careers and lives of the folks with whom you are working. It is imperative that you approach this role with the highest of ethical standards and work to promote positive talk about people's accomplishments and efforts. Do not participate in negative gossip about individuals. Always provide objectivity and feedback directly to performers to change their behavior. *Establish yourself as a positive reinforcer of things that matter in their organization and their lives.*

- *You must focus on adding real, measurable value in ways that help the client.* How do you measure your added value? For example, if your graph goes up, signaling an increase in the number of widgets produced (your pinpoint), you did not necessarily add value—unless the client needed more widgets. If those widgets now sit in inventory, costing the client more money each day, you have done a disservice. *You add value by improving the client's performance and success—not by your standard of measurement, but by your client's.*

- ***You must begin where the client is—whether or not that fits your "model" of the ideal change effort.*** You are walking into an organization that has long preceded your arrival. The client may be more advanced or less advanced than what you thought—or than where your model would have them. One of the first tests of your analytical skills will be the ability of your "model" to adapt to the uniqueness of each client. *Start where they are and shape, shape, shape their behavior—and allow them to shape yours.*

- ***You must analyze and understand the context in which the client lives.*** Understand their industry, their past change efforts, their current strategy, and their consequence histories. You will add greater value if you truly understand what they are trying to do and why. You will never succeed in consulting unless you first do this. *Take the time and show them the respect of learning about their world and about the contingencies that operate within their world.*

- ***You must see their success as your success.*** Their success might mean not needing you anymore. Help them to become stronger, more self-reinforcing, etc. Help them celebrate their successes, no matter how small they might be. *Client self-sufficiency is a sure sign of your success!*

- ***You must be humble.*** You will never "know it all." You will bring important (behavioral) technology to the table, along with successes and lessons learned from other projects and clients. The client, too, will bring a lot to the table and should be respected for this. *It is your job to model collaboration, teamwork, and continuous learning.*

- ***You must practice what you preach.*** Behavioral scientists have the ability to make the world a better place if we use and apply what we know about behavior—consistently and ethically. Encourage negative gossipers to speak directly to the target of their discontent. Tell your peer or boss how much you appreciate all that he or she has done. Be objective. Use a 4:1

ratio of positive to constructive feedback. Analyze the contingencies that operate *(unintentionally) on behaviors within* the organization. Measure your effect. Reinforce. *Ensure that as a result of working with you, the client experiences consequences that match the antecedents you provided when you described all that you could do to help them.*

Index

About the Author

DR. LESLIE WILK BRAKSICK is a nationally known consultant who is noted for enabling dramatic business improvement in companies. Her unique blend of talents—skill in applying behavioral science to making organizations run better, entrepreneurship, energy, personality, and public speaking ability—make her the ideal author for *Unlock Behavior, Unleash Profits*. Dr. Braksick's strength as a consultant is her ability to analyze a company's complex organizational history and challenges and help them articulate business objectives and implementation strategies that really work. She designs interventions, organizes teams for change, and coaches executives toward successful implementation.

Dr. Braksick cofounded The Continuous Learning Group, Inc. (CLG) in 1993 and built the company into the world's largest behaviorally based consulting organization, with approximately 150 consultants working nationally and internationally. The company has fostered sustained organizational improvement for Aetna U.S. Healthcare, AT&T, Bell Atlantic, Chevron, Lucent Technologies, Mobil Oil, Sierra Pacific, Unum, UPS, and others. Dr. Braksick has built lasting relationships with executives of many companies, including Bell Atlantic, Chevron Chemical, GE, H.J. Heinz, Ingersoll-Rand, Lucent, and Mobil.

Her greatest recognition has come from her clients' return on their consulting investment and their ability to sustain and improve performance long after she has completed her work. She takes great pride in making her clients self-sufficient.

Dr. Braksick is a prolific speaker, often keynoting gatherings of executives, managers, and behavioral science professionals who are eager to understand her results-based people strategies.

In her personal life, Dr. Braksick practices what she preaches to business leaders. This is demonstrated by her commitment to balancing her strong family life, her consulting work with clients, and her energetic leadership as CLG's President and CEO.